Values

FUNDAMENTAL ISSUES IN PHILOSOPHY SERIES

WILLIAM L. REESE, EDITOR

Freedom: A Study Guide with Readings

Values: A Study Guide with Readings

Values

A Study Guide with Readings

edited by
William L. Reese

Humanity
Books

an imprint of Prometheus Books
59 John Glenn Drive, Amherst, New York 14228-2197

#44613064

Published 2000 by Humanity Books, an imprint of Prometheus Books

04 03 02 01 00   5 4 3 2 1

Library of Congress Cataloging-in-Publication Data

Values: a study guide with readings / edited by William L. Reese.
      p.   cm. — (Fundamental issues in philosophy series)
   Includes bibliographical references and index.
   ISBN 1–57392–870–4 (pbk.)
   1. Values. I. Reese, William L. II. Series.
BD232 .V264 2000
121'.8—dc21   00-057520
                                                               CIP

Contents

Preface

The volume at hand belongs to a series of eight volumes, making up a body of material capable of supporting both individual and course study in the beginning ranges of philosophy. Each volume features one of the eight unavoidable philosophical problems. The essential texts for interpreting the problems have been selected from thinkers, both classical and modern, Western and Eastern, allowing the student to experience the problem in something like its historical depth and complexity within a volume of modest size.

The eight unavoidable problems are:

(1) the nature and extent of one's personal *freedom*;
(2) one's value profile and its underlying theory of *value*;
(3) the nature of the *self*;
(4) one's relation to truth, and one's theory of *truth*;
(5) one's view of the nature and function of *beauty*;
(6) one's way of distinguishing between *right and wrong*, and its underlying theory;
(7) the principles making up one's *social philosophy*, and their defense;
(8) *God and immortality*—affirmation and denial producing contrasts in one's sensed relation to the universe.

Although in the above list only freedom is said to be personal, in fact all eight problems are personal in the Socratic sense of encouraging self-knowledge and the examined life. When the great philosophers are viewed as purveyors of final truth, that somehow closes them off from our experience. But when we think of them as engaged in working out their own personal philosophies, as must we, they become our associates and friends engaged in a common quest. Philosophers come to different conclusions, discovering different standing grounds. That is sometimes pointed to as a weakness in philosophy. I think it a strength. It means that their work offers us a set of important and well-reasoned alternatives, allowing us to philosophize from a state more informed than theirs, since we have their thought in addition to our own. What is at issue here is discovery of our personal truth about ourselves, the universe, and how the two relate. Final truth is at issue only indirectly. In the first place we do not expect to find it. In the second place, if we did find it and philosophers agreed in every way, life would be less interesting. To be sure we would like our personal truths to be flecked with final truth. The best hope of arriving at that position is finding our own standing ground, our own modicum of self-knowledge. In this sense philosophy is pandemic to the human condition; strictly speaking, it is inevitable and unavoidable. Its options are what William James (*q.v.* D4) called "forced, living, and momentous." It follows that philosophy is the most practical of all disciplines, for how can one live an ordered and rational life of self-knowledge without a standing ground?

The series has been ordered on the principle of increasing range. Although each volume is intelligible, standing alone, the volumes are mutually supporting. One can begin anywhere, with any problem. The independent reader, whose interest we heartily encourage, might select any volume of central interest, along with a *Dictionary* of philosophy.

Each of the eight volumes contains a Study Guide preceding the Readings, and on its special topic. The readings provide exposure to the arguments and explanations of philosophers in their own words, and are structured in terms of their role as alternative interpretations of the concept under investigation. The Study Guide shows how these sources may be utilized in thinking out one's position on this concept. The *Dictionary* of philosophy is intended to supplement the Study Guide and Readings, providing background information on philosophers, concepts, and movements. For those using the *Dictionary of Philosophy and Religion* exact paragraph locations are often specified. In each volume of the series the Study Guide, and the Readings are cross-referenced (as further explained in the Key). In the Study Guide alternatives proposed in the Readings are further clarified, and the relevance of various moves discussed; this is done in an open-structured manner leaving final decision to the student/reader.

Where the individual reader makes a personal selection, in formal instruction the selection is made by the instructor in order to achieve the objectives of the course. The principle of maximum flexibility allows the series to be relevant to many, if not all, philosophy courses in the beginning range. Introductory courses in philosophy are organized around problems, history, selected readings, or some combination of the three. When organized around problems or selected readings, this series is especially relevant. Given the customary limitation of philosophy courses to one semester, the total series contains more material than can ordinarily be used in a single course. The instructor might well, however, select one or more of the volumes, deemed to be most appropriate to the design of a given course, along with a *Dictionary* of philosophy to provide information on the other problems to be explored in the course. Appendix B provides the entry listings in the *Dictionary of Philosophy and Religion* for each of the eight problems of the series. These entries are available to all readers of the series on the Web page for Fundamental Issues in Philosophy, whose address is also in Appendix B. Should the instructor utilize a group approach, the entire series might be used. The class would be divided into subgroups working with some independence, each subgroup assigned, *e.g.*, two of the problems for intensive work during the semester, the groups taking turns in presenting their results to the rest of the class. For courses whose orientation is historical, the *Dictionary* can provide historical background for periods of philosophy not covered by the primary material (a text in the history of ancient, medieval, or modern philosophy, or philosophical classics within a period, such as, for ancient philosophy Plato's *Republic* or Aristotle's *Nicomachean Ethics*). Greater variety can be added to any course through the selection of one of the Readings volumes. For ethics courses the volumes on *Freedom, Value,* and *Right and Wrong* would be appropriate. For epistemology courses, the *Truth* volume; for aesthetics courses the nature and function of *Beauty*; for political philosophy the volumes on *Right and Wrong* and *Social Philosophy*; for philosophy of religion or metaphysics courses the volumes on *God and Immortality, Freedom,* or the *Self.* We invite your attention to the consideration of these possibilities.

How might the Study Guide be used? It might be used to strengthen the skills by whose means one gains an education. One educates oneself by listening, reading, writing, thinking, and talking. The stronger these skills the better one's education.

In the stereotypical course one listens to the instructor, reads the text, attempting to isolate possible examination questions, and then checks the appropriate box in multiple choice exams, or writes short answers. Listening, reading, and writing are involved, but hardly in their most intensive forms.

In courses stressing quizzes, sections of the Study Guide can be assigned, along with the related readings, and quizzes administered. There is at once, however, the possibility of class and group discussion, prior to any quiz, taking advantage of the reading and note taking which occurred in preparing the assignment. In discussion the fourth of the skills acquires a place, talking, representing oneself before others.

It is possible to make discussion more pointed if small group discussion with defined goals is added to class discussion, where both talking and listening are practiced.

Thinking in some form goes on most of the time. According to the philosopher John Dewey (q.v. D2) thinking, properly so-called, requires that one have a problem in mind, and is working toward its solution. Thinking can be encouraged, then, by directing the student's attention to the Study Guide as a problem to be solved in a rational manner. That can be done by the instructor taking the class through the steps of the Study Guide. It can be done by having the students keep journals in which they work for clarity, understanding, and personal response. The journals would then be submitted to the instructor, at stated times during the semester, for evaluation and feedback. The words directed to the independent student below on journal writing apply to the formal instruction-based journal as well. Finally, since each Study Guide has a problem-solving structure, requiring student decision at each step, it can become the basis of a problem-solving student paper on the topic of the volume under consideration.

In participative education each of the five skills will be promoted. Students will not only listen to their instructor in class, but to their fellow students in discussion groups. They will read the material, and think about its implications. They will participate in class discussion, as well as in discussion groups. They will write out their positions and think out the reasons which support them, either in the form of journals, or problem-solving papers. There will be times when they will present their positions in class, or in discussion groups, and defend them against the questions of their fellow students.

But where does this leave the independent student who has chosen one of the volumes and wishes to study it? One can envision several individuals with shared interests and perhaps circumstances working together on these problems. But whether one establishes an informal group or chooses to work in splendid isolation the Study Guide is now the sole instructor. By choosing to keep a journal of the responses which occur in working through the Study Guide and Readings, if not in preparation of a formal paper, the skills of reading, thinking, and writing are developed. As for the missing skills of listening and talking, one can talk with one's friends about newly occurrent ideas, and listen to their responses. One talks to oneself in any case while working out the articulation of one's ideas. One also listens to the voices of inner dialogue as one works to establish one's own standing ground. Plato believed this internal dialogue to be as significant as conversation with another person. Perhaps in the conflict of voices one may find one's own voice, a goal of which writers—especially novelists—often speak. In addition, all students are invited to communicate with the author and with each other on the Fundamental Issues in Philosophy web page mentioned above.

I wish to thank the students of my Introduction to Philosophy courses throughout my career, most recently those of my Introduction courses at the State University of New York at Albany, for their help through class participation in the analysis of these problems. My thanks to William L. Reese III for his contributions as Editorial and Research Assistant; many of the features of the series developed in the course of a continuous dialogue between us. I also wish to thank Keith Ashfield and Paul Kurtz for their support of this project.

William L. Reese
Slingerlands, New York
E-mail: wlr@albany.edu

Acknowledgments

Writer's Workshop.

Guatama Buddha, *The Dhammapada*, tr. P. Lal. By permission of P. Lal, Writers Workshop, 162/92 Lake Gardens, Calcutta 700045, India..

Bantam Books.

From *Tao Te Ching* by Lao Tzu, translated by Victor H. Mair, copyright © 1990 by Victor H. Mair. Used by permission of Bantam Books, a division of Random House, Inc.

From *Zen and the Art of Motorcycle Maintenance* by Robert M. Pirsig. Copyright © 1974 by Robert M. Pirsig. Reprinted by permission of HarperCollins Publishers, Inc.

From Robert M. Pirsig, *Lila* (New York: Bantam Books, 1991).

Penguin, UK.

From *The Analects* by Confucius, translated by D. C. Lau (Penguin Books, Ltd.: Harmondsworth, Middlesex, Eng., 1979), copyright © D. C. Lau, 1979. Reproduced by permission of Penguin Books Ltd.

Random House.

From *The Dialogues of Plato*, tr. B. Jowett, 2 vols.(Random House, 1937; original copyright © 1892).

Oxford at the Clarendon Press.

From *Thirteen Epistles of Plato*, tr. L. A. Post (England: Oxford at Clarendon Press, 1925).

Prometheus Books.

From *The Nicomachean Ethics*, tr. J. E. C. Welldon (Amherst, N.Y.: Prometheus Books, 1987).

From *The Essential Epicurus*, tr. and ed. E. O'Connor (Amherst, N.Y.: Prometheus Books, 1993).

Harvard University Press.

Reprinted by permission of the publisher and the Loeb Classical Library from Diogenes Laertius, *Lives of Eminent Philosophers*, vol. 2, tr. R. D. Hicks, Cambridge, Mass.: Harvard University Press, 1925.

Reprinted by permission of the publisher and the Loeb Classical Library from Epictetus, *The Discourses as Reported by Arian, the Manual, and Fragments*, translated by W. A. Oldfather, Cambridge, Mass.: Harvard University Press, 1925.

Reprinted by permission of the publisher and the Loeb Classical Library from Marcus Aurelius, *The Communings with Himself of Marcus Aurelius Antoninus, Emperor of Rome*, translated by C. R. Haines, Cambridge, Mass.: Harvard University Press, 1916.

Reprinted by permission of the publisher from "The Gospel of Wealth" by Andrew Carnegie in *The Gospel of Wealth and Other Timely Essays* edited by E. C. Kirkland, Cambridge, Mass.: The Belknap Press of Harvard University Press, Copyright © 1962 by the President and Fellows of Harvard College.

Polebridge Press.

From "The Saying Gospels Q," from *The Complete Gospels: Annotated Scholars Version*, 3d. ed., ed. Robert J. Miller (A Polebridge Press Book, HarperSanFrancisco, A Division of HarperCollins).

Dover.

From *The Chief Works of Spinoza*, vol. 2, tr. R. H. M. Elwes (New York: Dover Publications, Inc., 1951).

Thomas Y. Crowell.

From Thomas Hill Green, *Prolegomena to Ethics*, ed. A. C. Bradley (New York: Thomas Y. Crowell, 1969).

Russell & Russell.

From Friedrich Nietzsche, *The Dawn of Day*, tr. J. M. Kennedy (New York: Russell and Russell, 1964).

The Viking Press.

"The Antichrist" by Friedrich Nietzsche, "The Gay Science" by Walter Kaufmann, editor, "Thus Spoke Zarathustra" by Friedrich Nietzsche, "Twilight of the Idols" by Friedrich Nietzsche, from *The Portable Nietzsche*, edited by Walter Kaufmann, translated by Walter Kaufmann, copyright © 1954 by The Viking Press, renewed © 1982 by Viking Penguin Inc. Used by permission of Viking Penguin, a division of Penguin Putnam Inc.

Cambridge University Press.

From Friedrich Nietzsche, *Human, All Too Human*, tr. R. J. Hollingdale (New York: Cambridge University Press, 1986). Reprinted with the permission of Cambridge University Press.

Taylor & Francis Books, Ltd.

From *Existentialism and Humanism* by Jean-Paul Satre, tr. P. Mairet (London: Methuen and Co. Ltd). Copyright © 1948, Routledge (Methuen).

Villard Books.

From David Halberstam, *The Fifties* (New York: Villard Books, 1993).

Key

Q.v. ____ : (*quod vide*, "which see") Refer to ____
SG: "Study Guide"
R: "Readings"
D: *Dictionary* of philosophy
DPR: *Dictionary of Philosophy and Religion*

Examples of each of these from the text:

Aristotle (*q.v.* SG4b5): "Refer to Aristotle in section (4b5) of the Study Guide."

Andrew Carnegie (*q.v.* R10): "Refer to Andrew Carnegie, Reading 10."

Dewey (*q.v.* D2): Refer to Dewey in a *Dictionary* of philosophy. For those using DPR the reference is to numbered paragraph 2.

Many references, however, appear in compound form, *e.g.*:

Plato (*q.v.* SG4b4, R4): "Refer to Plato in section (4b4) of the Study Guide, and in Reading 4."

Nietzsche (*q.v.* D, SG4b12, R12): "Refer to Nietzsche in a *Dictionary* of philosophy, in section (4b12) of the Study Guide, and in Reading 12."

Most of the cross-references are between the Study Guide and Readings, although some also involve the *Dictionary*. The Index interrelates the Study Guide and Readings extensively.

The reader should note that the Study Guide (4b1–15) series of references is counterparted by the R1–15 series. The same individual is treated in (SG4b1) and in R1, namely, Buddha; in (SG4b15) and R15, Pirsig. The final number of each counterparting reference designates the same philosopher. This allows one to move freely between Study Guide and Readings, and one should do so, since the two accounts supplement each other.

The narrative comment preceding each Reading, and between some sections, supplied by us, is always in a larger typeface than the text of the Readings.

Our section numbers in the Readings are within parentheses. When the authors have also used section numbers they are visually subordinate to ours. The section headings, if in italics, were supplied by the editors; if not in italics, they came from the source; if in both italics and quotes, they were in the source and in italics.

All Endnotes are indicated by superscript numbers, even when the author used some other convention, *e.g.*, asterisks. The editor's notes appear in the "1 to n" sequence along with those of the authors; but ours are identifiable by "[Ed.]" following each such note. Sometimes, the author's work has already received editorial attention. These earlier editors, and in some cases the authors themselves, offer clarifying comments, as do we. In these cases their comments, when retained, also appear in the sequence with ours; once again, ours are set apart by "[Ed.]." The notes at the end of each Reading [in brackets] state the precise location of each segment used in the author's works.

Introduction

Let us grant a measure of truth to the claims made in these days about our values: that the contemporary Western world fails to give us value guidance; that we live in an age of value chaos; that we experience value vertigo; that the center fails to hold and, as Marx famously observed, there is no foundation all the way down the line; that social cohesion is on the wane; and that we have no sense of governing norms. Various claims are advanced to explain this situation: tradition has lost its binding power; the pace of social change has accelerated; many social forces play upon us, while there is no longer any preemptive social force capable of governing our lives. Suppose this, or a significant part of it, to be the case. What are we to do?

We are told that it is a personal matter; that no one can tell us what we value, or what we ought to value. If that is true, clearly the initiative lies with us. Jean-Paul Sartre (*q.v.* D and R13) claims that there is no guidance anywhere concerning what we ought to value, and that we must invent our values for ourselves. But can we not at least find by introspection the things we do value? Have not our decisions laid down a pattern of our value preferences; available to us simply by looking within our lives? Looking within is, admittedly, less clear than looking without. Looking without, we see some things with great clarity. Looking within, we see things rather dimly that we have been looking for, and have not seen without. But even so, reflecting on our lives through memory, we become aware of the choices we have made, and the patterns these choices have formed, and every pattern, perhaps every choice, is infused with value words. Given the pattern, a value springs to mind. Surely, we can be clear about this. Others, too, can (with slightly less clarity than ourselves) see that pattern, and know with somewhat less certainty what it is we value. But that doesn't help us concerning what we ought to value. Friedrich Nietzsche (*q.v.* D, SG4b12, R12) would hold our established values to represent a herd morality, based on unreflective choice, and requiring drastic transformation. Neither Sartre nor Nietzsche believes there is an Ought-to-be of value. Many others do, however, including Plato (4b4). Thinkers exist in both East and West, believing that contrasting value systems, embodied in contrasting lifestyles, can be compared and considered rationally. In the Readings we have brought together a number of the major options of these value types for consideration, with representatives of both East and West, classical and modern periods.

If the responsibility is ours, we had better begin measuring up to it, trying to find our values through introspection, among other strategies, and also considering whether there is an Ought-to-be of value. To address these issues, we shall take as our individual question: What are (and ought to be) my values?

SUMMARY OUTLINE

(1) Question: What are (and ought to be) my values?

(2) Definition of value (as distinguished from fact).

(3) Prospecting for the value words which belong to our value profiles, we shall begin with a list of value terms provided by past classes, altering and expanding the list through introspection and discussion.

(4) Ordering these value terms into our own value profiles.

   (a) We begin with consideration of a standard pyramidal form of ordering values, rising from instrumental values, and directed toward final values.

   (b) The value styles of the philosophers in the Readings are considered with respect to their relevance for our own value systems.

   (c) With this help we now order our values, articulating them in ordered ranks, using some version of the pyramidal form, and explaining how these chosen values interconnect for us.

(5) Step (5) asks you to return to the Readings, considering how the style of your value profile compares and contrasts with those of other philosophers.

(6) What status has value in your universe? More simply, what status have values in your philosophy? There are three possible answers:

   (a) they are objective (for example, *q.v.* Plato, SG4b4, R4, pp. 101–108)

(b) they are subjective (for example, *q.v.* Sartre, R13, pp. 231–37)

(c) they are in between objective and subjective (for example, *q.v.* Aristotle, SG4b5, R5, pp. 123–31).

(7) Evaluation of the three possibilities, giving your reasons for choosing one of them.

(8) Conclusion.

Brief comments on the Summary Outline:

In (1) above, the phrase "and ought to be" is in parentheses. You may find an "Ought-to-be" of value, or decide with Sartre that there is no such thing. In considering the Readings you will have an opportunity to resolve the issue one way or the other.

In (2) we ask you to consider the definition of value in relation to fact, since the contrast between them suggests the properties belonging to each.

In (3) we initially "brainstorm" the list of values. Typical discussion of the standard list (adumbrated in a to p) of the detailed outline (SG3) provides student reaction to the list, adding additional terms, removing others. Since the list is considered in relation to the Final Value entry (*D* or *DPR*), philosophers are discussed who have held these values, or denied them. The point of (3) is to provide a rich mix of values which will be adequate to the variegated dimensions of your life. At times we have called this a dumpster of values since the values are not yet ordered, or connected. Although we speak in (3) and (4) of "our value profiles" each value profile is unique and individual.

The goal of (4) is to order and interconnect your values. We give a number of strategies for accomplishing this in the detailed outline (SG4); but all of them involve the pyramidal form, rising from instrumental values, moving toward final values. This may not be the natural way of representing your values. You will see in (4b) however, that many philosophers use this structure or some modification of it. If it does not work for you, try a different approach. Appendix A contains a discussion of several alternative designs. The pyramid, however, used by so many, is worth considering. (4b) is the most important reference of the volume, taking one to each of the fifteen intellectual options concerning value.

(4c) returns us to the Study Guide to discuss the connections and relations in your value profile.

(5) asks you to compare your value scheme with those of the philosophers and religious leaders treated in both (SG4b) and R1–15.

(6–8) take you through a problem-solving exercise. In (6) the question is asked: what status has value in your universe? Three answers are suggested.

In (7) the three answers are examined, reasons given, and evaluated. In (8) the strongest answer is accepted as one's conclusion.

We turn now to the Study Guide for Value. The divisions of the Study Guide are at the same time steps of the Detailed Outline.

Study Guide for Values

Detailed Outline Providing the Opportunity to Work Out One's Value Profile

(1) Question: what are (and ought to be) my values?

The question cannot be answered by anyone else. If you can answer it for yourself that would be momentous. You would have reduced the value chaos of the world by 1 over the number of humans now living. You probably have a responsibility to do this; that is, it is right for you to gain clarity about your values. But do note that we are not now considering the basis of right and wrong (although the terms "morality" and "ethics" are used in some of the readings). W. D. Ross (*q.v.* D) distinguished between the good and the right. When working with our values, we are considering the question of what is the good for us (so far as we can determine it, and only incidentally the right, as part of the good). Food is good, and something we value, but it would be odd to call it "right." Notice that the list of value terms in (3) below includes "beauty," "health," "humor," "pleasure." Clearly, the good (for us) extends beyond the right.

(2) Definition of value. To begin, we need an adequate definition of value. We are not likely to find this in the often circular definitions of ordinary dictionaries. An adequate definition will bring together the qualities which belong to the term "value" while rejecting the qualities which do not belong. A convenient means of sorting out the needed qualities is available by contrasting "value" with "fact."

(2a) Facts call for recognition, values for selection, a value is the object of a preference; a fact becomes a value (without ceasing to be a fact) when we desire it.

(2b) What we now desire may turn out to be undesirable with added experience, or "in the long run" as one also says. Does this give us a class of apparent values?

(2c) We sometimes value states of being which we do not have (*e.g.,* health when we are sick). We also value states of being which we do have, and do not wish to lose (*e.g.,* health when we are healthy).

(2d) Very likely there are values—not only facts and things but ideals, purposes, goals, states of being—of which we have not even thought, but which would turn out to be desirable for us, and which we would desire, if we knew about them. If this is so for you, then you are recognizing an "ought to be" of values; and the parenthesis in our controlling, initial question should be removed when you put the question.

Taking account of these and other points, set down your definition of value along with whatever discussion appears to you to be relevant.

(3) Arranging one's value profile. Let us begin with the following list of words:

Accomplishment	Humor	Peace of mind
Beauty	Individuality	Pleasure
Compassion/mercy	Justice	Possessions
Courage	Kindness	Relaxation
Creativity	Knowledge	Self-respect
Equality	Love	Security
Family	Loyalty	Spirituality
Freedom	Meaningful sex	Strength
Friendship	Meaningless sex	Survival
Happiness	Moderation	Tolerance
Health	Modesty/Purity	Trustworthiness
Honesty	Patience	Truth
		Understanding

These are value words often listed by my students, when I ask them for their values. Although alphabetized for easier reference, this is just raw value material for you, a dumpster of values. Our first concern is to ask: which values on the list are yours, and what values should be added? The dumpster list obviously does not and could not contain all your values. A subset of the list would represent you still less than the full list. Further, there are probably values here to which you do not subscribe, but I should think that virtually all of these value terms are part of your scheme. While it would be scarcely possible to set down every value term your life supports, the goal is for you to put together a representative list, including all the values of special importance to you.

You might begin by highlighting the terms on the list you recognize as belonging to your set of values, and adding others which are important to you, but not on the list. If using a computer, put these terms on the computer, and tailor the list so that it represents you. Consider the values you share with your family, and those which belong to you in a special way. Consider the values you share with your peer group, and values you hold which your peer group does not hold. Add these. What other values in these relationships would you wish to add? The dumpster list is to be considered in relation to all the other value terms which should, perhaps, be added.

Let us discuss the list as it now stands, plus additional suggestions from the other philosophers.

(3a) On occasion, the terms "family," "religion," "church," "God," or "faith" would be offered for the list. Since we were trying, along the way, to define fact and value, I would ask how the fact that there are families, religions, churches, instances of faith, and presumably a God or gods, relates to the values one discovers in these facts. That would turn the class to naming the values for which these facts stand. The effort probably accounts for "spirituality" as a value on the list, and perhaps some others. It may be that those offering the terms gave way too easily on the point. It is possible that they meant to value specifically "this" family, religion, church, and faith, in addition to the value terms which might be excavated from them. After all, William Temple (*q.v.* D) held "God" to be the final value of human life. These, then, might be facts which we turn into values by desiring them, and in which we also find a cluster of more abstract values. Should such a fact term be truly prized by you, that should be added to the list, for later consideration. Note that "family" is already on the list.

(3b) Invariably, and early in the discussion, the term "love" would be offered. Often, this term would be countered by a "tough-minded" realist, always male, offering the term "sex" as a value. Frequently, a third person would qualify plain "sex" with the adjective "meaningful." The tough-minded realist, or one like-minded, would counter again, urging that if "meaningful sex" is to be on the list so should be "meaningless sex." I would take this as an effort to nudge the whole list in the direction of hedonism (*q.v.* D). As a dutiful scribe, I would add all three terms on the ground that support for any value term indicates a value (real or apparent). That bit of dialogue might be taken as a support for the presence of "pleasure" on the list.

(3c) In any case, you may wish to specify several varieties of love, going beyond sex. One type of love is present in "friendship," on the list and discussed at length by Aristotle in his *Nicomachean Ethics* (bks. VIII and IX); and as a second type, love within families. "Patriotism" is not on the list. No student has ever volunteered the term. When I ask about it, and discussion leads to its definition as "love of country," some students recognize it as a value, and take it as an obligation to serve one's country if the cause is just; some, under whatever circumstances. The form of love central to Christianity is *agápe* (*q.v.* D), or altruism, or selfless love. It is also stressed in Mahayana Buddhism (*q.v.* D1), as compassion, and may be one of the values you find in religious faith. Specification of types of love may hold importance for you.

(3d) At the point where meaningful sex, possessions, and pleasure have made the list, it typically occurs to me to point out that hundreds of thousands of novitiates, entering Western religious orders, have taken vows of "chastity, poverty, and obedience." There are similar vows in the religious orders of many Eastern religions. When I ask about these values I am usually met with silence. Finally, someone offers that the appearance of AIDS calls for a kind of care approaching chastity. Perhaps the list's value of self-respect calls for that kind of care in one's commitments, (modesty/purity of the original list). As for "possessions," sometimes offered as "wealth" or "riches," both Spinoza (*q.v.* D10; and R9, sec. 1) and the Stoics (*q.v.* Stoicism D; and R7a, secs. 9–13) argue for simplicity in one's life, reducing one's dependence on things. It is a bit more difficult to argue for obedience. In monasticism the vow was obedience to the rule of the order, and obedience to God. That may lack resonance for you. "Children, obey your parents." But why not obedience to a higher call? That, or something like it, is surely what obedience to God must have meant, must still mean.

(3e) The list contains "knowledge," "honesty," "understanding," and "truth." Some students list "education" among their values with "knowledge" as its product. Knowledge, honesty, and understanding all have some relation to truth: knowing it, telling it, understanding it. The list doesn't contain "wisdom," but both Plato (*q.v.* D5c; and R4, sec. 2), and Spinoza (*q.v.* D10; and R9, sec. 1) recommend it, Plato defining it as "knowledge of the whole," and Spinoza as "knowledge of the union existing between the human mind and the whole of nature." In common parlance truth involves applying knowledge to situations in an understanding way, that is, with sensitivity and finesse. Spinoza held wisdom to be the chief value of any list, and the primary source of enduring happiness. By contrast, the values of fame, riches, and pleasures of sense (which he thought most people seek) are false values (identical to "apparent values" in 2, above).

(3f) "Survival" is on the list, which Telesio (*q.v.* D4) called "self-preservation." Students sometimes claim this to be the final value. Socrates (*q.v.*

D1) argued against the claim, saying that not life (just the fact of existing), but a good life is chiefly to be valued. He also held that the unexamined life is not worth living. It may be that one holds on to life from the sheer instinct of survival, even though the life worth living requires additional values, including self-knowledge. The Zen Buddhist (*q.v.* D3, Suzuki, D5; and *Freedom* R2c6, secs. 14–20) value of "seeing into one's own nature" is an Eastern equivalent of self-knowledge. (*Qv.* [3n] below.)

(3g) Having added "wisdom," and having "courage," and "justice" on the list we need one more value to reproduce the four Greek cardinal virtues (*q.v.* D1 and Plato 5c): wisdom, courage, temperance, justice. "Temperance" is perhaps not as common in usage as "moderation," which is on the list, and which Aristotle (*q.v.* D11; and R5, secs. 6–7) stressed in his advice to seek the mean between extremes.

(3h) Add "faith" and "hope" (the value at the bottom of Pandora's box of troubles) to "love" (already on the list but understood in this context as *agápe*, or selfless love) and we have the theological virtues (*q.v.* Aquinas D8) which constituted the analysis of virtue (*q.v.* D8) throughout the Middle Ages, providing a total of seven cardinal virtues.

(3i) Josiah Royce (*q.v.* D1a) suggested that "loyalty," also not on the initial list, is one of the more important values, leading to the maxim: "Be loyal to loyalty."

(3j) Albert Schweitzer (*q.v.* D4) found that "reverence for life" played a key role in his analysis of both the good and the right. In addition to its other applications, the value implies an ecological commitment in the present age.

(3k) "Authenticity" is singled out by Ortega y Gasset (*q.v.* D3), Karl Jaspers (*q.v.* D1–2), and Jean-Paul Sartre (*q.v.* D3–4; and R13, sec. 6) as having capital importance.

(3l) Confucius (*q.v.* D2–5) stressed the values of propriety (*li*) and humanity (*jen*), or humanheartedness (something like Marx's, *q.v.* D, suggestion that we should develop our "species being"). Ch'eng Hao (*q.v.* D3) added the value of "sincerity."

(3m) Chuang Tzu (*q.v.* D3) added the value of *wu wei* (acting through inaction), centered in the concept of the *tao*, and requiring flexibility and adaptability. Are these values which one should stress?

(3n) Just recently a student insisted that *satori* (*q.v.* D; and *Freedom* R2c6, sec. 3, pp. 186–187) should be placed on the list. *Satori* is the final value of Zen Buddhism (*q.v.* D) with implications of absolute enlightenment, and "seeing into one's own nature." It somewhat parallels the Hindu term *moksha* (*q.v.* D). It is similar to the Western term, self-realization, implicit in Aristotle (*q.v.* D11), and made central by T. H. Green (*q.v.* D2, 3; and R11, secs. 1, 2, 9). One or more of these terms may belong in your set of values. To go back to the discussion in (3a) above of the values present in religion, church, God, or faith, one important value to be registered from all of this is "salvation." In the West that is similar to *satori* and *moksha.*

(3o) "Equality" is on the list. Discussion of this term leads at times to Emerson's (*q.v.* D) "principle of compensation" as well as to "equal opportunity" and "equality before the law," directing us to the area of social philosophy.

(3p) The point is to provide a significant, and fairly complete list of the values of your life.

(4) Given your now expanded list, the question is: How do you think your values should be ordered, to show how they hang together, and how they interrelate?

(4a) You can begin to introduce order into the multiplicity of your value terms by compiling a deck of value cards. This can be accomplished manually by typing or writing one value term on each of a sufficient number of, *e.g.*, 1" by 2" cards, to accommodate your list.

(4a1) If you have registered your values on a computer screen, the cards can be produced by your computer. Increase the font size. Copy your list of values to a file; separate the values enough that each value can appear on a separate card. Print the file, and scissor the list into separate items. These can now be arranged experimentally on your desk as you work on the structure of your values.

(4a2) Needing to weight your values in terms of their importance to you, go through the deck penciling on numbers "1" through "5," letting "1" stand for "most important," "5" for "least important." Arrange the value cards in rank by number. Does the result match the sense you have about your values? If not, rearrange them.

(4a3) The classical value pattern is pyramidal, with one or a few values at the top, grading down to many values at the bottom. The values at the top are called "final values"; those at the bottom, "instrumental values."

Both Plato and Aristotle wrote of the difference between end values and means values. Plato (*q.v.* D14) suggested that some of one's values are instrumental, others are final, and in between the two are still others—in one sense instrumental, in another sense, final. Instrumental values serve to get us to other values; they are means values, leading to other values desired more for themselves alone. Instrumental values are sometimes called "extrinsic values," final values are sometimes called "intrinsic values." The values in between are sometimes called "intrinsic-extrinsic." Plato held money to be the "instrument of instruments." One wants it not for itself, but for what it brings one. "Possessions," then, would be the instruments of life, the instrumental values. Following out the suggestion one would put at the bottom of one's value scheme the concrete instrumental values which support one's more abstract values. Aristotle (*q.v.* R5, sec. 4) is in agreement, essentially, on all these points.

At the other extreme, the implication is that one's final values are wanted for themselves alone. Plato's suggestion, seconded by Aristotle, is that we regard them as having intrinsic value, as being valuable in themselves, although Glaucon's somewhat different version (*Republic*, bk. II, pars. 357–58) is never challenged. When you question yourself about values and come to those you want not for the sake of another value, but for themselves alone, you have come upon final values. Question yourself about your values, and see which ones gain the place of final value. Ask yourself, "why do I want this?" When you answer, "I want it because I want it," you have come upon a final value.

Just as your instrumental values would be at the bottom of your value scheme (following Plato), your final values would be at its top.

The values which seem to you partly instrumental, and partly final would go in between.

If this procedure suits you, then your scheme will have a pyramidal shape, rising from a broad base. If you follow Aristotle the pyramid will culminate in a single, final value at its peak. If you follow Plato you will have a blunted pyramid with several final values—in his case, beauty, truth, and the good (*q.v.* R4, secs. 3–6)—of equal importance.

It would be helpful to go through your value scheme with a partner, questioning the placement of your values. [On the other hand if the pyramid does not lend itself to your value scheme, see Appendix A for other suggestions.]

(4b) We now ask you to consider the value Readings. There are several reasons for this. First, you will be able to compare your judgments about value with those of other philosophers. Since some of these thinkers are from the East, their value judgments may differ markedly from yours; this may stimulate you to enrich your scheme with their ideas. Second, the differences among philosophers with respect to final values may help you to a clearer appreciation of the final value(s) appropriate to your value profile. Third, we especially want you to consider how they have put their values together. In most cases we have drawn from the Readings their basic value terms, and have put them down in a kind of diagram, similar to the weighting we ask of you. This may help you to compare the styles of alternative value profiles. Eventually, you will be asked to discuss your value profile, and to compare it with those of the other philosophers.

(4b1) For Buddha (*q.v.* D; and R1), enlightenment, or one could also say Nirvana, is the final value of human life. His procedure was an experiential therapy designed to come to terms with the pain and suffering of life. One has to overcome desire in the process leading to enlightenment. While the state of Nirvana (*q.v.* D) is the ultimate goal, Buddha will not allow us to speculate about its nature. Also, he insists that there is no "self" or "soul," and our physical and psychic life consists of a complex of aggregates. We are to follow a middle way. The values seem to be:

enlightenment
freedom from desire

right views	right profession
right intentions	(or livelihood)
(or aspirations)	right effort
right speech	right watchfulness
right action	(or mindfulness)
(or conduct)	right concentration
	(or contemplation)

This eight-fold path is filled in by other values one finds in the reading: serenity, freedom, material loss, thrift, solitude, performance of good.

(4b2) We have put Lao Tzu between Buddha and Confucius, although chronological details here are extremely difficult to fix. His concept of the *Tao*, or Way, is itself a final value. It is a pattern of living which is self-justifying. The values making up the Way, according to the *Tao-Te Ching* (*q.v.* D and Final Value 4; also R2) are adaptability, inaction (*wu wei*), and emptiness. They are sometimes associated with the feminine values of the *yin* (*q.v.* D and *Yin Yang* Philosophy). Notice that the *Tao* is a universal force, or pattern, at work in the world. Compare emptiness with Sartre's non-being (*q.v.* 4b13 below).

The *Tao*
(the Way or pattern)

adaptation	inaction	emptiness
	(or *wu wei*)	
modesty	gentleness	truth
good order	effectiveness	timeliness
	quietness	

(4b3) We place Confucius after Lao Tzu, since Confucius is in accord with the *Tao-Te Ching* in recommending the Way. But Confucius (*q.v.* D; and R3) was interested in the good society, both in political and in personal terms, and taught his students how to work in government administration to achieve it. His final value might be the *Tao*, as with Lao Tzu, but it was to be achieved through the development of tradition into personal excellence. Politically, the scheme rises from Chinese culture:

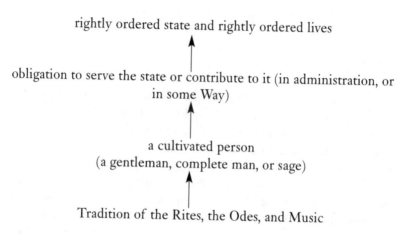

rightly ordered state and rightly ordered lives

⬆

obligation to serve the state or contribute to it (in administration, or in some Way)

⬆

a cultivated person
(a gentleman, complete man, or sage)

⬆

Tradition of the Rites, the Odes, and Music

Translated into personal terms it might have the following aspect

The *Tao*

propriety ("*li*")		Benevolence or human-heartedness ("*jen*")
	virtue: following	
aesthetic	the mean	doing one's best
appreciation	justice	generosity
wisdom	trustworthiness	self-correction
reverence	filial obligation	sense of shame

These values are taken from the reading in somewhat random fashion. Notice that Confucius has a sense of destiny in his view, "the decree of heaven," which applies both to emperors and ordinary individuals.

(4b4) Plato (*q.v.* D1; and R4) nominates truth, beauty, and the good as the final values. As final values, these are absolutes; we rise toward them, experience them in part, never wholly reach them. The good, in his sense, is a principle of harmony working to attract humans to each other, and provide order in the entire universe. His values may have the following structure:

The Good

Beauty   Truth

Reason

wisdom   courage   temperance   justice

the best (*aristos*), or excellence

honor (*timos*)

wealth

freedom

The pattern reflects many of the values important to Plato. Good is the top value; but Beauty, Truth, and Good form a triad and every other value has some measure of each of these top values. We move from a base of more or less beautiful, true, and good things to the overlapping pyramids, whose overlapping ways of relating to the world exhibit a complex unity. Reason is to be our guide. Wisdom, courage, temperance, justice are the four cardinal virtues, important in both personal and political terms. The first three virtues are specific to the classes of the state: Wisdom/rulers, Courage/guardians, and Temperance (an ordered life)/artisans, Justice applying to all three classes. He defines justice as having and doing what is one's own and not interfering with what belongs to another.

Meanwhile, the best or excellence, honor, wealth, and freedom define four of the five political forms: aristocracy, timocracy, oligarchy, and democracy. The wealth of oligarchy is low on the list, wealth being the chief instrumental value, properly under the control of higher values. Freedom is rated even below wealth, because of the lawlessness associated with it. The fifth political form, tyranny, is characterized by disvalues, not values, hence is not on the list. Our personal quest is to increase in all three of the final values: beauty, truth, and goodness.

(4b5) Aristotle (*q.v.* D11; and R5) names happiness (*eudaimonia*) as final value, and claims this to be the value which all humans seek, but in different ways. His view requires rational self-development and the Mean between extremes, often referred to as the Golden Mean.

Happiness (*eudaimonia*)
Rationality   Moderation   Self-Realization

Mean between Extremes

deficiency—   —excess
Courage
cowardice—   —foolhardiness
Temperance
insensibility—   —licentiousness
Friendship
obsequiousness—   —contentiousness
Justice
being trampled   —trampling on
on by others—   others

The goal of happiness is the product of Rationality, Moderation, and Self-realization: Rationality because Reason is in Aristotle's view the defining characteristic of human beings; self-realization because all living things have a drive to actualize their potential. It is their final cause. Moderation because that approach to life allows the fullest range of value-actualization while requiring that one find the mean between extremes in passions and actions (*q.v.* R5, sec. 6). Some actions and passions (*e.g.,* murder, *q.v.* R5, sec. 7, p. 125) have no mean state. They are always wicked actions, and the emotions giving rise to them are wicked emotions. Each of the three values under happiness concerns actualization: of one's reason, of one's potential as a person, of one's values. Since each mean-between-extremes value has a deficiency and an excess, and these are not values but disvalues, they are on the chart only to show how the virtue, or the value state, rises above its deficiency and excess, and stands between them. For this reason we have shown the value in a higher position than its deficiency or its excess, and presented the latter in lower case and smaller type. The mean-between-extremes approach goes on to other values. We present a sample list, taken from his discussion. (Consider whether the values on your list have a deficiency and an excess, not themselves values, but disvalues.)

Aristotle's discussion of this mean-between-extremes approach is in (R5), sec. 7, pp. 124–30. The discussion of justice, both distributive and corrective, is in secs. 8–11, pp. 130–33.

(4b6) Epicurus (*q.v.* D10 and R6) follows Aristippus (*q.v.* D) and Democritus (*q.v.* D11) in holding pleasure to be the chief value of human life and that our bodies are so constituted that we necessarily seek pleasure and try to avoid pain. Aristotle, in the above reference, holds that pleasure is not the final value, but just a feeling which accompanies successful functioning. On the Epicurean account the goal of life is to experience the greatest sum of pleasures, and the smallest sum of pains. For Aristippus one would seek out the most intense pleasures, and prefer physical to intellectual pleasures. For Epicurus pleasure (*ataraxia*) is a state free from mental or physical disturbance. "Prudence" becomes a chief value, involving "sober reasoning" over the grounds of every choice and avoidance, as well as honor and justice. It seems to me virtually certain that Epicurus would interpret Aristotle's "happiness" as the achievement of a significant balance of pleasure over pain in one's life, and one's sense of gratification (generalized pleasure) that this is the case. A start on his value structure would feature:

pleasure

prudence, honor, justice

Any other value would be considered for its propensity to produce pleasure without disturbance in one's life.

(4b7) The Stoic philosophers, *e.g.*, Epictetus (*q.v.* D1–2; and R7a), Marcus Aurelius (*q.v.* D1; and R7b), look down on happiness and pleasure, as self-indulgent. What one should try for is peace of mind, or serenity. (The Greek word is *apathia*, which has gotten a different, and negative, meaning in English.)

Serenity or Peace of Mind

wisdom	responsibility	independence
rationality	obligation	integrity
appreciation of	destiny	simplicity
nature		

limiting possessions to those necessary for meeting
one's obligations

Notice the presence in the Stoic readings of a universal reason controlling the universe, to which one's own reason can relate.

(4b8) Jesus (*q.v.* D1–5; and R8) like Lao Tzu, taught a way which men should follow. Using the earliest passages, Jesus' way was more like that of Confucius than that of Lao Tzu. But where Confucius is held to have believed that it was impossible to achieve the *Tao*, Jesus believed it was possible with the help of the Father (his name for God) to achieve the

Kingdom. The details remain unclear; the goal, however, was the Kingdom. In a way, achieving that order of things was the final value. But perhaps, too, the final value is social justice. That would be a translation of human brotherhood. But the fatherhood of God is also important, and that translates into religious faith in a God of love.

the Kingdom

absolute love (*agápe*)	absolute happiness or joy	absolute compassion
absolute sensitivity	absolute integrity	absolute forgiveness
absolute faith	limited importance of possessions repentance	absolute humility human possibilities boundless

(4b9) Spinoza (*q.v.* D5c, 10; and R9) argued for wisdom as the chief value of human life, and against fame, riches, and pleasures of sense. The preeminence of wisdom lay in its certitude. One can continue all one's life to acquire wisdom. Compared to that fame, riches, and pleasures of sense reveal their transitory nature. Here the chief value, and the final value, differ. Final values have to be enduring values. A metaphysical point is that since God and the eternal aspects of the world are identical, a life of final value is "living under the aspect of eternity."

enduring happiness (which may be identical to serenity)
wisdom (as chief means to the final value)
(plus the Stoic values)
fame, riches, pleasures of sense singled out as false values

This is what he tells us in the Reading (R9). On the final page of the Reading he mentioned knowing a thing through its essence. If we suppose this to be the kind of knowledge characteristic of the *Ethics*, the values become part of a more complex structure, where the purpose of human life is to rise from limited to enduring thoughts and feelings, from the first to the third stage:

3rd stage—*scientia intuitiva*
seeing things through their essence
"living under the aspect of eternity"
enduring happiness
wisdom

↑

2nd stage—*ratio*
scientific knowledge
concepts

↑

lst stage—images
pleasure—pain
fame, riches, pleasures of sense

One begins with images and false or apparent values, rises to concepts and scientific knowledge. Finally, in the third stage one's widened perspective sees things in their essence, rising to enduring values which participate in the divine (*q.v.* Spinoza D5).

(4b10) In his *Gospel of Wealth* Andrew Carnegie (*q.v.* R10) opposes both Spinoza and Plato, arguing for riches as a highly laudable final value. Wealth acquired through one's own efforts, and philanthropy, including its proper distribution in one's own lifetime, are the twin final values men should seek.

We began this section with a classical pyramidal scheme, leading from instrumental to final values. The instrumental value dropped out in our later examples, yet some manner of exercising control over possessions is present in almost all of these examples. Plato urged that instrumental values not be put in the final place. When money does become one's final value, the meanings of Plato's formerly final values, now subordinate to money, change in meaning. It could be argued that the truth values (including knowledge and wisdom) turn into cunning to help in one's competitive questing; beauty turns into narcissistic self-satisfaction in possessing the latest, most admired, and powerful instruments; the good turns into various forms of self-interest, friendship for example becoming temporary alliances for the doing of mutual favors. Status values appear, surrounding money. Carnegie dealt with this problem by a double final value.

riches	philanthropy
instrumental	love of
values	man
competition	service
struggle for	to
survival	others

We are to direct ourselves to riches in the first part of our lives; when we have achieved this goal, we must turn to a second final value and begin to administer our wealth for the good of others, better than government could do it, or than the people could do it for themselves. Again we have two pyramids, the first headed by what is called the false value of riches in (4b9) above. The second, headed by philanthropy, supports the quite different values of (4b8). The pyramids have a temporal separation. Notice that the values of the first list are those of Social Darwinism (*q.v.* D2, 3).

(4b11) There are still other possibilities. Take, for example, the value "accomplishment" in the dumpster list (3, above). One might ask, "Why do I want accomplishment?" Whatever your answer, the final value involved might be "self-realization." T. H. Green (*q.v.* D2–3; and R11) held this to be the final value of one's individual life. Could that be part of your scheme? Green says, quite uncommonly, that the value goal of society is "human perfection." That introduces other connections. Aristotle (*q.v.* D10) believed that all living things in their development were seeking perfection, each in its own way, and that God was absolutely perfect. Each thing, then, is seeking to be God in its own way. Human beings are seeking to actualize their potentialities. He supports the goal of self-realization (as a component of happiness). The sense of perfection as the goal of life is present also in Jesus' teachings (*q.v.* Christ, D2), and explains why the appropriate form of love is *agápe* (3h above). When William Temple (*q.v.* D) held God to be the final value, the attribute of "perfection" was part of what he intended. Green, too, linked the values of self-realization and perfection to the presence of the divine, working through our lives.

the *summum bonum*
human perfection
self-realization
rationality   self-consciousness
development of the sciences and the arts

The metaphysical framework supposes a principle of the divine, working in human life.

(4b12) Nietzsche (*q.v.* D3; and R12) held that we are motivated by a will-to-power, and this will, transferred into diverse forms of excellence, produces the appropriate final values. When Pirsig in *Zen and the Art of Motorcycle Maintenance* held "quality" to be the final value he was making a similar judgment about value (*q.v.* 4b15 below, and R, secs. 1–5, pp. 211–17).

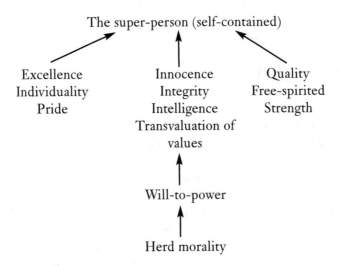

The super-person (self-contained)

Excellence	Innocence	Quality
Individuality	Integrity	Free-spirited
Pride	Intelligence	Strength

Transvaluation of values

Will-to-power

Herd morality

The initial will-to-power in one's nature interacts with the watered-down "herd morality" values around one, transforming the inferior values of one's environment into personal excellence.

(4b13) Sartre is among those presenting "Authenticity" as the chief value of human life (Ortega D3; Jaspers D2; Sartre D3–4, and R13, sec. 6, pp. 234–36), and the means whereby all values receive their appropriate form. For Sartre the structure would seem to be:

freedom   authenticity
the disvalues of bad faith
(to be overcome)
subjectivity of all values

Sartre's underlying metaphysics requires "nonbeing" in supporting human freedom. Compare to Lao Tzu's "emptiness" (*q.v.* 4b2 above and R, secs. 4, 21, pp. 59, 66).

(4b14) Dan Enright (*q.v.* R14), a television producer, stands against Plato and Spinoza in claiming the values of appearance to be his final goals; success, accompanied by greed for authority, power, prestige, respect.

success
authority, power, prestige, respect
(greed for)

(4b15) Robert M. Pirsig (R15, secs. 1–5, pp. 240–47) urges the recognition of quality as final value, relating established goods to its static form, and creativity to its dynamic form.

	dynamic quality	
art	workmanship (care)	creativity

	static quality	
science	order morality	ritual
	obligation (duty)	

(4c) We have arrived at the culminating stage of step (4). Your values, we may assume, are now ordered. You have a patterned value structure. If the pyramidal form of ordering did not fit your scheme, you have referred to Appendix A, seeking other possible ordering patterns. Whatever the form of your structure, it is now time to discuss what you have achieved, centering on the interrelations of your values. Notice, for example, that wisdom is possible only if you also value knowledge as well as a sensitive understanding of when and how to apply it. Knowledge and understanding lead to wisdom on a higher level. See if you can chart such relations in your scheme of values, describing how they require and lead in to each other.

(5) The fifth step is to compare your value profile to those of the other philosophers. With which philosophers do you agree? Which of these lifestyles do you oppose? Discuss similarities and differences.

(6–8) Steps six to eight take one through a problem-solving exercise. In (6) the question is raised: What status do you give values in your philosophy? Are they objective, subjective, or in between?

(a) If they are objective, then they can be discovered, and are not just made up. Plato (*q.v.* R4, sec. 6, p. 108 *et seq.*) is the most extreme on this point. Values are essences, or forms, which can be grasped by the understanding. They provide a vision of what human life ought to be. The more of these values we incorporate into our lives the more closely we fit the definition of what it is to be human.

(b) If they are subjective then they are the result of our invention. Sartre (*q.v.* R13) is the most extreme here. Existence precedes essence. We were thrown into the world willy nilly, and must now produce our own essence. We must invent the person we want to be, and be it with all our hearts. Still, Sartre appears to hold one value to be somehow objective. It is authenticity. We must be authentic in our decisions and avoid bad faith.

(c) What could be meant by the third alternative, that values are neither objective nor subjective, but in between? Aristotle denied Plato's view that values were among the essences or forms, after which the world is patterned. In Aristotle's view then they aren't objective and the result of discovery in any direct sense. At the same time, they aren't just invented since they represent our human interests. This may be called an interest theory of value. He believed that everyone has happiness as final value, but happiness is different for different people, depending upon their interests. One doesn't have value until people are acting out their interests. As soon as this happens there are values; and there is also a mean between extremes, called the Golden Mean (*q.v.* D), which is objectively better than any other way of satisfying that interest. It is, he says (R5, sec. 7, p. 125 *et seq.*), a "mean relative to us" as "determined by a rational principle." So satisfying a value is comparable to an archer aiming at the bull's-eye of a target. It requires making the appropriate response in the right way to the right person to the right degree at the right time (*q.v.* Aristotle D11). Dewey (*q.v.* D5–6), relating value to "prizing," also held an interest theory of value.

In (7) the three positions are examined. Reasons for and against each are adduced, and weighed. Before going all the way with Sartre, consider whether you want to say that Hitler's values are as good as those of Jesus, that murder is as good as preserving life. If the latter alternatives are objectively better than the former you are on the way to Plato's objective view of value. If Sartre's values of freedom and authenticity are subjective, how does it happen that there are no alternatives to them? If "bad faith" is condemned, then "good faith" seems indispensable. Should that not also be considered an objective value leading to authenticity? As for Aristotle's in-between theory, you may find that to your liking as itself a mean between extremes. Notice that for Aristotle (*q.v.* R5, sec. 7) there are specific actions and emotions which are always wicked. But if malice and murder are always wicked (to cite two of his examples), aren't benevolence and preserving life always good?

In (8) the strongest of the answers is accepted as one's conclusion. If you have worked through the steps of the outline with care, it is almost certain that you have achieved a rational position. This will be your standing ground with respect to value, a hard-won position which you will be able to defend, and which you will *continue* to test against whatever questions, challenges, or objections may yet arise.

Readings

1

Gautama Buddha

563–483 B.C.E.

The Dhammapada

Value discussion in the East predated such discussions in the West. Following chronology, we begin with Eastern alternatives. Buddha will enter the Readings on more than one topic. Here we are interested in his values. We are also interested in the material which can be attributed to Buddha, rather than to his disciples. The search for authenticity is important with respect to all religious leaders. Teachings and sayings tend to be earlier and more authentic than doctrinal statements (*q.v.* Jesus, 4b8). The material presented here is from the *Sutta Pitaka* ("basket of discourse"). This is the Second Basket of the Pali Canon, of which the *Dhammapada* ("the way of truth") is a part. The contents of the *Sutta Pitaka* are usually attributed to Buddha himself. Although the Pali Canon was completed only in the first century B.C.E., prior to that date Buddhist Councils concerned with establishing and/or preserving the authenticity of the teachings, among other matters, had been held as early as 483, shortly after Buddha's death. The Council of 240 dealt specifically with determining the canon of teachings of the Buddhist oral tradition. It can be presumed that the selections which follow, while not literally in the voice of Gautama Buddha, do reflect his basic ideas, and sometimes his exact words. The proper names entering the selections are followers of Gautama Buddha. Ananda was Buddha's personal attendant, cousin, and favorite disciple. Some of the other names can be identified; some are identified as lords and kings. Most are monks, members of the order. Part of the material, as in the *Dhammapada* (sec. 2 below), was cast in verse form, presumably at a later time, to facilitate memorization.

Also see Study Guide (4b1), p. 30.

(1) SAYINGS

The Dhamma

"I will teach you Dhamma. Here is Dhamma: if *this* is, *that* also is; if *this* is reborn, *that* is reborn; if *this* is not, *that* also is not; when *this* stops, *that* stops too."

❧   ❧   ❧

"No matter whose the teachings, my friend, if you are sure of this— These doctrines conduce to passion, not serenity; bondage, not freedom; increase, not loss, of material gain; greed, not thrift; restlessness, not calm; noisy company, not solitude; sloth, not energy; delight in evil, not performance of good—well, rest assured that is not the Dhamma, that is not the Discipline, that is not the Master's Way.

"But if there are teachings, no matter whose, you are sure will conduce to serenity, not passion; freedom, not bondage; loss, not increase, of material gain; thrift, not greed; calm, not restlessness; solitude, not noisy company; energy, not sloth; performance of good, not delight in evil—that is the Dhamma, that is the Discipline, that is the Master's Way."

"The ocean has only one taste, the taste of salt. Dhamma has only one taste, the taste of Nirvana."

❧   ❧   ❧

Questions which edify and those which do not

"Consider, Malunkyaputta, this story of a man wounded by a poisoned arrow. His friends, relatives, and well-wishers gather around him and a surgeon is called. But the wounded man says, 'Before he takes out this arrow, I want to know if the man who shot me was a Kshatriya, a Brahmin, a merchant, or an untouchable.'[1]

"Or he says, 'I won't let this arrow be removed until I know the name and tribe of the man who shot me.'

"Or: 'Was he tall, short, or of medium height?'"

"Or: 'Was he black, brown, or yellow-skinned?'

"What do you think would happen to such a man, Malunkyaputta? Let me tell you. He will die.

"And that is what happens when a man comes to me and says, 'I will not follow the Dhamma until the Buddha tells me whether the world is eternal or not eternal, whether the world is finite or infinite, whether the soul and the body are the same or different, whether the liberated person exists or does not exist after death, or both exists and does not exist after death, whether he neither exists nor does not exist after death.' He will die, Malunkyaputta, before I get a chance to make everything clear to him.

"Being religious and following Dhamma has nothing to do with the dogma that the world is eternal; and it has nothing to do with the other dogma that the world is not eternal. For whether the world is eternal or otherwise, birth, old age, death, sorrow, pain, misery, grief, and despair exist. I am concerned with the extinction of these.

"Therefore, consider carefully, Malunkyaputta, the things that I have taught and the things that I have not taught. What are the things I have not taught?

"I have not taught that the world is eternal. I have not taught that the world is not eternal. I have not taught that the world is finite. I have not taught that the world is infinite. I have not taught that the soul and the body are the same. I have not taught that the soul and the body are different. I have not taught that the liberated person exists after death. I have not taught that he does not exist after death. I have not taught that he both exists and does not exist after death; that he neither exists nor does not exist after death.

"Why, Malunkyaputta, have I not taught all this? Because all this is useless, it has nothing to do with real Dhamma, it does not lead to cessation of passion, to peace, to supreme wisdom, and the holy life, to Nirvana. That is why I have not taught all this.

"And what have I taught, Malunkyaputta? I have taught that suffering exists, that suffering has an origin, that suffering can be ended, that there is a way to end suffering.

"Why, Malunkyaputta, have I taught this? Because this is useful, it has to do with real Dhamma, it leads to the cessation of passion, it brings peace, supreme wisdom, the holy life, and Nirvana. That is why I have taught all this.

"Therefore, Malunkyaputta, consider carefully what I have taught and what I have not taught."

❧   ❧   ❧

"Tell me, O Enlightened One, is there a Self?"

The Buddha kept silent.

"Is there, then, no Self?"

He did not reply.

Vacchagotta rose and left. The noble Ananda asked the Buddha, "Why, lord, did you not answer Vacchagotta's questions?"

"Supposing, Ananda, I had replied that there is a Self; that would have meant siding with those ascetics and Brahmins who describe themselves as Eternalists. If I had replied there is no Self, that, Ananda, would have meant siding with those ascetics and Brahmins who class themselves as Annihilationists. I have constantly held that all things are not-Self—would it have been right on my part then to have told Vacchagotta that there *is* a Self? And if I had replied that there is not a Self, wouldn't this have confused him even more? He would have gone away saying to himself, 'I believed in a Self. What is there left for me now?'"

❧   ❧   ❧

The fire of desire

"All things, O monks, are on fire. And what are these things which are on fire?

"The eye is on fire. Things seen are on fire. Eye vision is on fire. Impressions received by the eye are on fire. Whatever sensation, pleasant or unpleasant, is connected with the eye, is on fire.

"With what are these on fire?

"With the fire of desire, with the fire of hate and delusion; with birth, old age, death, sorrow, lamentation, misery, grief, and despair.

"All things are burning.

"The ear is on fire; sounds are on fire . . . The nose is on fire; odors are on fire. . . The tongue is on fire; tastes are on fire . . . The body is on fire; things touched are on fire . . . The mind is on fire; ideas are on fire . . . Mind-awareness is on fire; impressions received by the mind are on fire . . . whatever sensation, pleasant or unpleasant, is connected with the mind is also on fire . . .

"With what are these on fire?

"With the fire of desire, with the fire of hate and delusion; with birth, old age, death, sorrow, lamentation, misery, grief, and despair.

"All things are burning.

"Cultivate aversion, O monks; and be free of the fire of desire . . . . "

❧   ❧   ❧

The Middle Path

"Avoid these two extremes, monks. Which two? On the one hand, low, vulgar, ignoble, and useless indulgence in passion and luxury; on the other, painful, ignoble, and useless practice of self-torture and mortification. Take the Middle Path advised by the Buddha, for it leads to insight and peace, wisdom and enlightenment, and to Nirvana.

"What, you will ask me, is the Middle Path? It is the Eightfold Way. Right views, right intentions, right speech, right action, right profession, right effort, right watchfulness, right concentration. This is the Middle Path, which leads to insight, peace, wisdom, enlightenment, and Nirvana.

"For there is suffering, and this is the noble truth of suffering—birth is painful, old age is painful, sickness is painful, death is painful; lamentation, dejection, and despair are painful. Contact with the unpleasant is painful, not getting what you want is painful.

"Suffering has an origin, and this is the noble truth of the origin of suffering—desire creates sorrow, desire mixed with pleasure and lust, quick pleasure, desire for life, and desire even for nonlife.

"Suffering has an end, and this is the noble truth of the end of suffering—nothing remains of desire, Nirvana is attained, all is given up, renounced, detached, and abandoned.

"And this is the noble truth that leads to Nirvana—it is the Eightfold Way or right views, right intentions, right speech, right action, right profession, right watchfulness, and right concentration.

"This is the noble truth of suffering. This must be understood."

❧   ❧   ❧

"I do not quarrel with the world, monks; it Is the world that quarrels with me. How can a true disciple of Dhamma quarrel with the world? If the learned are agreed that a thing is, I agree with the learned that it is. If the learned are agreed that it is not, I agree with the learned that it is not.

"What are the learned agreed upon as 'It is not'? The material world is permanent, stable, eternal, unchanging—they are agreed that this is not so. I agree with them that this is not so. And the same applies to feeling, perception, consciousness, and thought structure.

"What are the learned agreed upon as 'It is'? The material world is impermanent, unstable, changing, and full of suffering—they are agreed that this is so. I agree with them that this is so. And the same applies to feeling, perception, consciousness, and thought structure . . .

"Just as a blue, red, or white lotus grows in stagnant water, but rises clear and unpolluted out of it, a truth-finder grows up in the world but overcomes it, and is not soiled by it."

⚭   ⚭   ⚭

Parable-type stories

"Look, Assalayana, Brahmin women have periods, conceive, give birth, and breast feed their children. And yet these Brahmins, born as all other children are born, say that they are better than children from the other castes . . .

"What do you think, Assalayana? Is only a Brahmin capable of having a heart of gold, can only a Brahmin show love, gentleness, and goodness? Can't a warrior, a merchant, a worker? . . . Can only a Brahmin go to the river with a string of bath balls and powder and wash himself clean of dirt? Can't a warrior, a merchant, a worker? Is the fire produced by a Brahmin rubbing two *sal* sticks together any brighter than the fire produced by a trapper, bamboo weaver, or scavenger who picks up two sticks from a pigsty or dog trough?"

⚭   ⚭   ⚭

A village chief came to the Buddha and asked:
"Is the Buddha compassionate to all living creatures, big and small?"
"Yes," he replied.
"Then why does the Buddha teach Dhamma in full to some and not to others ?"
"A good question. Tell me, village chief, supposing a farmer had three fields, one fertile, one average, and one rocky—when the time came to sow seed, which would he sow first?"
"First the fertile, then the average, then perhaps the rocky one, because that would not even give him cattle fodder."
The Buddha said, "For the same reason, I teach Dhamma in full, in beginning, middle, and end, in spirit and in letter, to the monks and nuns first . . . Then I teach it to the lay followers . . . Then the others."

❧　　❧　　❧

"Take a physician skilled in his science, a learned and humane person. He has many sons—let us say ten, or twenty, or, if you like, a hundred. He is called to some important business in a foreign land; in his absence his sons take some harmful drugs, which send them rolling on the ground in fever and frenzy. He returns just in time, and what does he find? Some are beyond cure; others are still in their senses. These welcome him and kneeling before him say, 'How good for us that you have returned in time! We were fools. We didn't know the drugs were so poisonous. Please make us well again.'

"The father is moved by their suffering and selects some fine plants and herbs, delicately flavored and colored. He pounds, sifts, and mixes them in the right proportions and gives the medicine to them, saying, 'This is good medicine. Take it: it is delicately flavored and colored. It will cure you of your suffering.'

"The sensible ones see quickly the truth of his words, take the medicine, and are cured.

"The others are happy too that their father is back and ask him to heal their illness, but when the medicine is offered, they refuse it. Why? Because the drugs they have taken have confused their power of judgment, and they are not sure if this excellent medicine is really as excellent as claimed.

"So the father thinks to himself: 'What a pity they cannot see straight. They are glad to see me back but are unwilling to take the medicine I give them. Let me see what can be done.'

"He tells them, 'I am an old man, I haven't long to live. I must make preparations to leave this world. I leave behind this medicine. Keep it with you. It won't lose its power to heal.' So he goes away to a foreign land and sends a messenger to them with this news: 'Your father is dead.'

"The news shocks them. 'Our father is dead,' they whisper among themselves. 'If he were living, he would give us the right medicine. He would cure us. But he has died in a foreign land.'

"They are grief-stricken, and their grief soon opens their eyes. Now they see the value of the delicately flavored and colored medicine their father gave them before he left. They quickly take it and are cured. When the news reaches their father that they are cured, he returns.

"Tell me, my friends, what do *you* think? Who is there among you who will condemn the good physician for telling a lie?"

❧　　❧　　❧

They called her Kisha Gautami, the "Frail" Gautami, because she was delicate and tired easily. She had sung the song heard by the young would-be Buddha as he entered the palace; she had received the necklace he had sent her, and thought he was in love with her. Then she had died, quickly and suddenly. She was reborn as Kisha Gautami in the house of poor people in the city of Savatthi. They married her off early because her husband's people were well-off.

But because she came of poor parents, her in-laws neglected her; they would even mock her. When she gave birth to a son, they stopped neglecting and mocking her. For the first time she knew what it was to be respected.

The boy grew up and reached the age when he could play and run about with friends. Then, quietly and suddenly, he died. Kisha felt a deep pain inside her. "They respected me because I gave birth to him. What will they do to me now? What will they do to him? They will throw his body away."

She placed her dead son on her left hip and went from house to house, saying, "Give my son medicine. Bring my son back to me."

They laughed. *Medicine for the dead?* They clapped their hands and made fun of her. *What do you mean? You must be mad.*

A wise man saw her and said to himself, "If there is any medicine to be had for a person in such a condition, it will be found with the Buddha."

So he said to her, "Good woman, go to the Tathagatha, the one who has reached what has to be reached. There is none greater than him in the world of men and the world of gods. Go to the monastery where he meditates. Ask him for medicine." With her son on her left hip, she went and stood on the outside of the crowd that had gathered around the Buddha.

"O holy one," she said loudly, "give me medicine for my son!"

He looked at her.

"You did well, Kisha Gautami," he replied, "in coming here for medicine. Listen to me carefully. Go back to the city, begin at the beginning, and bring me a fistful of mustard seed from the first house in which no one has ever died."

"I will do so, holy one," she said gratefully.

Joyfully she entered the first house and said, "The holy one wants me to bring him a fistful of mustard seed as medicine for my son. Can you give me mustard seed?"

They brought out and gave her mustard seed.

"Has anyone died in this house?" she asked.

"They have never stopped dying," they replied. "So many deaths . . . "

"Take back the seed," Kisha Gautami said. "The holy one told me not to bring mustard seed from a house in which a death had taken place."

"Poor Gautami," they said, "the dead are everywhere."

She went to a second house—to a third—and a fourth. There must be *one* without a death in it! The Buddha could not have been so cruel. He would have had some pity on her.

She could not find a single house to bring mustard seed from.

She took her son to the cremation ground, holding him in front of her in her arms.

"O my son, my little son, my dear son," she said, "I thought when you died, only you died. But death is everywhere. It is a universal law—all must die. Village law, market law, house law are passing; only this law is eternal." She placed her child on the cremation ground and went back to the Buddha.

"Kisha Gautami," he asked, "did you get the mustard seed?"

"Holy one," she replied, "enough of this business of the mustard seed! Only give me refuge."

*　　*　　*

"Monks, listen to the parable of the raft. A man going on a journey sees ahead of him a vast stretch of water. There is no boat within sight, and no bridge. To escape from the dangers of this side of the bank, he builds a raft for himself out of grass, sticks, and branches. When he crosses over, he realizes how useful the raft has been to him and wonders if he should not lift it on his shoulders and take it away with him. If he did this, would he be doing what he should do?"

"No."

"Or, when he has crossed over to safety, should he keep it back for someone else to use, and leave it, therefore, on dry and high ground? This is the way I have taught Dhamma, for crossing, not for keeping. Cast aside even right states of mind, monks, let alone wrong ones, and remember to leave the raft behind."

*　　*　　*

"Take the case of the raja of Savatthi. He ordered a man to assemble all the blind subjects of the kingdom and bring an elephant in front of them.

"This was done. The man said to the assembled group: 'This is an elephant.' He let one feel the elephant's head, another its ear, still another its tusk; and so on until the trunk, foot, back, tail and tail tuft were covered. To each who felt, he said, 'This is an elephant.'

"The raja turned to his blind subjects and asked them, one by one, what they thought an elephant was. The head feeler thought an elephant was a pot. The ear feeler was convinced it was a winnowing basket. The tusk became a plowshare, the trunk a plow, the foot a pillar, the tail a whip, and the tuft a floor duster.

"And they quarreled, shouting, 'I know what an elephant is!' 'No, I do!' 'You're wrong!' 'It's like this!' They came to blows. The raja was pleased, for he had made his point.

"So you see, monks, how the sects quarrel over Dhamma, each thinking it has the full truth. They are blind, they do not know, they do not see the goal."

≈   ≈   ≈

"The noble Eightfold Way arises by living with what is lovely. If already risen, it grows to perfection by constant friendship with what is lovely."

≈   ≈   ≈

He picked up a flower and showed it to the assembled people.

"They did not understand. Only Mahakashyapa smiled.

" 'I have in my hand,' he said, 'the doctrine of the right Dhamma, birthless, deathless, formless, inscrutable. It is beyond sacred texts; it does not need words to explain it. I give it to Mahakashyapa.' "

"This must be your motto, monks: No shrinking back, no giving up the struggle, only the going forward. Always have this thought in your mind: 'Let me be reduced to skin and bone, and let my flesh and blood dry up; so long as I have a glimmer of energy I will not give up the search for truth.' This must be the way you train yourselves."

≈   ≈   ≈

"I am now eighty years old, Ananda. The end of my journey has come. I drag my body along like a worn-out bullock cart, with great hardship.

"It is only when my thoughts are completely concentrated on the inner vision that has no bodily object that my body is at peace.

"Therefore, Ananda, be a lamp to yourself. Be an island. Learn to look after yourself; do not wait for outside help.

"Hold fast to the truth as a lamp. Be an island. Only truth can save you. Do not look for any help besides yourself.

"How is this to be done, Ananda? How is one to be a lamp to oneself and not wait for outside help, hold fast to the truth, and seek Nirvana in the truth? How is one to be an island?

"Let a man, though living in the body, so treat his body that, with right effort, right watchfulness, and right concentration, he will overcome the sorrow that is produced by the sensations that arise in the body . . .

"Whoever, now or after I die, shall be a lamp to himself, an island to himself, and shall not look outside of himself for refuge—he alone, Ananda, shall attain what is important to be attained. But he must make the effort himself . . .

"No, Ananda, no weeping. How often have I told you that it is in the very nature of life that what we love most must be taken from us? How can it be otherwise? What is born is doomed at the moment of its birth to die. There is no other way.

"Some of you will say, 'The Teacher is no more, we have no one left to lead us.' But is not the Dhamma with you, and the Sangha?[2] Have I not left these behind? Let them be your Teachers.

"One last word, bhikkus.[3] Whatever consists of component parts will die. Work out your Nirvana with diligence."

(2) *Select verses from* The Dhammapada

Punishment

All fear punishment, all fear death.
Therefore, do not kill, or cause to kill.
Do as you would want done to you.

All fear punishment, all love life.
Therefore, do not kill, or cause to kill.
Do as you would want done.

A man seeks his happiness and strikes with a stick
others who seek happiness just like himself.
He will not find happiness after his death.

Another seeks his happiness and does not strike others
who seek happiness just like himself.
He will find happiness after his death.

Speak gently, and they will respond.
Angry words hurt, and rebound on the speaker.

Nirvana:
When the agitated mind is as still as
a broken gong.

Like a cowherd with his staff pushing cattle into new pasture,
old age with death pushes the world's creatures into new lives.

Your Self

Value your self, look after your self.
Be watchful throughout your life.

Learn what is right; test it and see;
then teach others—is the way of the pandit.

You are your own refuge;
there is no other refuge.
This refuge is hard to achieve.

One's self is the lord of oneself;
there is no other lord.
This lord is difficult to conquer.

Diamond breaks diamond,
evil crushes the evildoer.

As the creeper strangles the *sal* tree,
evil overpowers the evildoer.
His enemy could not be more delighted.

Easy to do an evil deed,
easy to harm oneself.
Difficult to do a good deed,
very difficult indeed.

NOTES

1. Members of the warrior, priestly, and Vaishya castes, respectively. The untouchables were those without a caste, that is the "outcastes." [Ed.]

2. The community of monks.

3. Monks.

[Gautama Buddha. *The Dhammapada*, tr. P. Lal (N.Y.: Farrar, Straus and Giroux, 1967). (1) pp. 18–34. (2) pp. 93–94.]

Lao Tzu

Sometime after 500 B.C.E.

Tao-Te Ching

Although the *Analects* of Confucius record a meeting between Confucius and Lao Tzu, there is no reliable evidence that an individual with Lao Tzu as his proper name ever existed. The name simply means "old master," and all great Chinese philosophers were called "master" (*Tzu*) including, of course, Confucius. Mair has it that these sayings came together in the fourth century B.C.E., and were written down in the third. Still, some one, or group, supplied these comments about the Way. Since Confucius referred to the *Tao* as an established idea, we allow the "old master" material to precede Confucius.

Also see Study Guide (4b2), p. 30.

Te (integrity)

(1) The person of superior integrity
          does not insist upon his integrity;
     For this reason, he has integrity.
     The person of inferior integrity
          never loses sight of his integrity;
     For this reason, he lacks integrity.

     The person of superior integrity takes no action,
          nor has he a purpose for acting.
     The person of superior humaneness takes action,
          but has no purpose for acting.
     The person of superior righteousness takes action,
          and has a purpose for acting.

The person of superior etiquette takes action,
    but others do not respond to him;
Whereupon he rolls up his sleeves
    and coerces them.

Therefore,
    When the Way is lost,
        afterward comes integrity.
    When integrity is lost,
        afterward comes humaneness.
    When humaneness is lost,
        afterward comes righteousness.
    When righteousness is lost,
        afterward comes etiquette.

Now,
    Etiquette is the attenuation of trustworthiness,
        and the source of disorder.
    Foreknowledge is but the blossomy ornament of the Way,
        and the source of ignorance.

For this reason,
    The great man resides in substance,
        not in attenuation.
    He resides in fruitful reality,
        not in blossomy ornament.
Therefore,
    He rejects the one and adopts the other.

(2)   In olden times, these attained unity:
    Heaven attained unity,
        and thereby became pure.
    Earth attained unity,
        and thereby became tranquil.
    The spirits attained unity,
        and thereby became divine.
    The valley attained unity,
        and thereby became full.
    Feudal lords and kings attained unity,
        and thereby all was put right.

Yet, pushed to the extreme,
It implies that,
    If heaven were ever pure,
        it would be likely to rend.
It implies that,
    If earth were ever tranquil,
        it would be likely to quake.
It implies that,
    If the spirits were ever divine,
        they would be likely to dissipate.
It implies that,
    If the valley were ever full,
        it would be likely to run dry.
It implies that,
    If feudal lords and kings were ever noble
        and thereby exalted,
    they would be likely to fall.

Therefore,
    It is necessary to be noble,
        and yet take humility as a basis.
    It is necessary to be exalted,
        and yet take modesty as a foundation.

Now, for this reason,
    Feudal lords and kings style themselves
        "orphaned," "destitute," and "hapless."
    Is this not because they take humility as their basis?

Therefore,
    Striving for an excess of praise,
        one ends up without praise.
Consequently,
    Desire not to be jingling as jade
        nor stolid as stone.

(3)   When the superior man hears the Way,
        he is scarcely able to put it into practice.
    When the middling man hears the Way,
        he appears now to preserve it, now to lose it.

When the inferior man hears the Way,
    he laughs at it loudly.
If he did not laugh,
    it would not be fit to be the Way.

           ⟿   ⟿   ⟿

(4)   Reversal is the movement of the Way;
    Weakness is the usage of the Way.

    All creatures under heaven are born from being;
    Being is born from nonbeing.

(5)   The softest thing under heaven
       gallops triumphantly over
    The hardest thing under heaven.

Nonbeing penetrates nonspace.
Hence,
    I know the advantages of nonaction.

The doctrine without words,
The advantage of nonaction—
    few under heaven can realize these!

(6)   Great perfection appears defective,
       but its usefulness is not diminished.
    Great fullness appears empty,
       but its usefulness is not impaired.

    Great straightness seems crooked,
    Great cleverness seems clumsy,
    Great triumph seems awkward.

    Bustling about vanquishes cold,
    Standing still vanquishes heat.

    Pure and still,
       one can put things right everywhere under heaven.

(7)   When the Way prevails under heaven,
            swift horses are relegated to fertilizing fields.
      When the Way does not prevail under heaven,
            warhorses breed in the suburbs.

      No guilt is greater than giving in to desire,
      No disaster is greater than discontent,
      No crime is more grievous than the desire for gain.

Therefore,
      Contentment that derives from knowing
            when to be content
      is eternal contentment.

(8)   Without going out-of-doors,
            one may know all under heaven;
      Without peering through windows,
            one may know the Way of heaven.

      The farther one goes,
      The less one knows.

For this reason,
      The sage knows without journeying,
            understands without looking,
            accomplishes without acting.

(9)   The pursuit of learning results in daily increase,
      Hearing the Way leads to daily decrease.
      Decrease and again decrease,
            until you reach nonaction.
      Through nonaction,
            no action is left undone.

      Should one desire to gain all under heaven,
      One should remain ever free of involvements.

For,
      Just as surely as one becomes involved,
      One is unfit for gaining all under heaven.

(10) The sage never has a mind of his own;
>He considers the minds of the common people
>>to be his mind.

>Treat well those who are good,
>Also treat well those who are not good;
>>thus is goodness attained.

>Be sincere to those who are sincere,
>Also be sincere to those who are insincere;
>>thus is sincerity attained.

>The sage
>>is self-effacing in his dealings with all under heaven,
>>and bemuddles his mind for the sake of all under heaven.

>The common people all rivet their eyes and ears upon him,
>And the sage makes them all chuckle like children.

(11) Rule the state with uprightness,
>Deploy your troops with craft,
>Gain all under heaven with noninterference.

>How do I know this is actually so?

Now,
>The more taboos under heaven,
>>the poorer the people;
>The more clever devices people have,
>>the more confused the state and ruling house;
>The more knowledge people have,
>>the more strange things spring up;
>The more legal affairs are given prominence,
>>the more numerous bandits and thieves.

For this reason,
The sage has a saying:
>"I take no action,
>>yet the people transform themselves;
>I am fond of stillness,

yet the people correct themselves;
I do not interfere in affairs,
    yet the people enrich themselves;
I desire not to desire,
    yet the people of themselves become
        simple as unhewn logs."

(12) A large state is like a low-lying estuary,
    the female of all under heaven.
In the congress of all under heaven,
    the female always conquers the male
        through her stillness.
Because she is still,
    it is fitting for her to lie low.
By lying beneath a small state,
    a large state can take over a small state.
By lying beneath a large state,
    a small state can be taken over by a large state.

Therefore,
    One may either take over or be taken over by lying low.

Therefore,
    The large state wishes only to annex and nurture others;
    The small state wants only to join with and serve others.

Now,
    Since both get what they want,
    It is fitting for the large state to lie low.

(13) Act through nonaction,
    Handle affairs through noninterference,
    Taste what has no taste,
    Regard the small as great, the few as many,
    Repay resentment with integrity.

    Undertake difficult tasks
        by approaching what is easy in them;
    Do great deeds
        by focusing on their minute aspects.

All difficulties under heaven arise from what is easy,
All great things under heaven arise from what is minute.

For this reason,
> The sage never strives to do what is great.

Therefore,
> He can achieve greatness.

> One who lightly assents
> > will seldom be believed;
> One who thinks everything is easy
> > will encounter much difficulty.

For this reason,
> Even the sage considers things difficult.
Therefore,
> In the end he is without difficulty.

(14) Sincere words are not beautiful,
Beautiful words are not sincere.
He who knows is not learned,
He who is learned does not know.
He who is good does not have much,
He who has much is not good.

> The sage does not hoard.
> The more he does for others,
> > the more he has himself;
> The more he gives to others,
> > the more his own bounty increases.

Therefore,
> The Way of heaven benefits but does not harm,
> The Way of man acts but does not contend.

(15) To realize that you do not understand is a virtue;
Not to realize that you do not understand is a defect.

The reason why
    The sage has no defects,
    Is because he treats defects as defects.

Thus,
    He has no defects.

(16) Human beings are
        soft and supple when alive,
        stiff and straight when dead.

    The myriad creatures, the grasses and trees are
        soft and fragile when alive,
        dry and withered when dead.

Therefore, it is said:
    The rigid person is a disciple of death;
    The soft, supple, and delicate are lovers of life.

    An army that is inflexible will not conquer;
    A tree that is inflexible will snap.

    The unyielding and mighty shall be brought low;
    The soft, supple, and delicate will be set above.

(17) The Way of heaven is like the bending of a bow—
        the upper part is pressed down,
        the lower part is raised up,
        the part that has too much is reduced,
        the part that has too little is increased.
Therefore,
    The Way of heaven
        reduces surplus to make up for scarcity;
    The Way of man
        reduces scarcity and pays tribute to surplus.
    Who is there that can have a surplus
        and take from it to pay tribute to heaven?
    Surely only one who has the Way!

For this reason,
>   The sage
>>   acts but does not possess,
>>   completes his work but does not dwell on it.
>   In this fashion,
>>   he has no desire to display his worth.

Tao (the Way)

(18) The ways that can be walked are not the eternal Way;
>   The names that can be named are not the eternal name.
>   The nameless is the origin of the myriad creatures;
>   The named is the mother of the myriad creatures.

Therefore,
>   Always be without desire
>>   in order to observe its wondrous subtleties;
>   Always have desire
>>   so that you may observe its manifestations.

>   Both of these derive from the same source;
>   They have different names but the same designation.

>   Mystery of mysteries,
>   The gate of all wonders!

(19) The Way is empty,
>>   yet never refills with use;
>   Bottomless it is,
>>   like the forefather of the myriad creatures.
>   It files away sharp points,
>>   unravels tangles,
>>   diffuses light,
>>   mingles with the dust.
>   Submerged it lies,
>>   seeming barely to subsist.
>   I know not whose child it is,
>>   only that it resembles the predecessor of God.

(20) The highest good is like water;
      Water is good at benefiting the myriad creatures
          but also struggles
    to occupy the place loathed by the masses.
Therefore,
    It is near to the Way.

    The quality of an abode is in its location,
    The quality of the heart is in its depths,
    The quality of giving lies in trust,
    The quality of correct governance lies in orderly rule,
    The quality of an enterprise depends on ability,
    The quality of movement depends on timing.

Now,
    It is precisely because one does not compete
      that there is no blame.

(21) Thirty spokes converge on a single hub,
      but it is in the space where there is nothing
        that the usefulness of the cart lies.
    Clay is molded to make a pot,
      but it is in the space where there is nothing
        that the usefulness of the clay pot lies.
    Cut out doors and windows to make a room,
      but it is in the spaces where there is nothing
        that the usefulness of the room lies.
Therefore,
    Benefit may be derived from something,
      but it is in nothing that we find usefulness.

(22) "Being favored is so disgraceful that it startles,
    Being honored is an affliction as great as one's body."

What is the meaning of
    "Being favored is so disgraceful that it startles"?

    Favor is debasing;
    To find it is startling,
    To lose it is startling.

This is the meaning of
    "Being favored is so disgraceful that it startles."

What is the meaning of
    "Being honored is an affliction as great as one's body"?
    The reason I suffer great afflictions is because I have a body;
    If I had no body, what affliction could I suffer?

Therefore,
    When a man puts more emphasis on caring for his body
        than on caring for all under heaven,
        then all under heaven can be entrusted to him.
    When a man is sparing of his body in caring
        for all under heaven,
        then all under heaven can be delivered to him.

(23) We look for it but do not see it;
        we name it "subtle."
    We listen for it but do not hear it; we name it "rare."
    We grope for it but do not grasp it;
        we name it "serene."

These three cannot be fully fathomed,
Therefore,
    They are bound together to make unity.

Of unity,
        its top is not distant,
        its bottom is not blurred.
Infinitely extended
    and unnameable,
It returns to nonentity.
This is called
    "the form of the formless,
    the image of nonentity."
This is called "the amorphous."

Following behind it,
    you cannot see its back;

Approaching it from the front,
    you cannot see its head.

Hold to the Way of today
    to manage the actualities of today,
    thereby understanding the primeval beginning.
This is called "the thread of the Way."

(24) Those of old who were adept in the Way
    were subtly profound and mysteriously perceptive,
So deep
    they could not be recognized.

Now,
    Because they could not be recognized,
    One can describe their appearance only with effort:
        hesitant,
            as though crossing a stream in winter;
        cautious,
            as though fearful of their neighbors all around;
        solemn,
            as though guests in someone else's house;
        shrinking,
            as ice when it melts;
        plain,
            as an unhewn log;
        muddled,
            as turbid waters;
        expansive,
            as a broad valley.

If turbid waters are stilled,
    they will gradually become clear;
If something inert is set in motion,
    it will gradually come to life.

Those who preserved this Way did not wish to be full.
Now,
    Simply because they did not wish to be full,
        they could be threadbare and incomplete.

(25) Attain utmost emptiness,
　　　Maintain utter stillness.

　　　The myriad creatures arise side by side,
　　　　　thus I observe their renewal.
　　　Heaven's creatures abound,
　　　　　but each returns to its roots,
　　　　　which is called "stillness."
　　　This is termed "renewal of fate."
　　　Renewal of fate is perpetual—
　　　To know the perpetual is to be enlightened;
　　　Not to know the perpetual is to be reckless—
　　　　　recklessness breeds evil.
　　　To know the perpetual is to be tolerant—
　　　　　tolerance leads to ducal impartiality,
　　　　　ducal impartiality to kingliness,
　　　　　kingliness to heaven,
　　　　　heaven to the Way,
　　　　　the Way to permanence.

　　　To the end of his days,
　　　　　he will not be imperiled.

(26) If it
　　　　　is bent,
　　　　　　　it will be preserved intact;
　　　　　is crooked,
　　　　　　　it will be straightened;
　　　　　is sunken,
　　　　　　　it will be filled;
　　　　　is worn-out,
　　　　　　　it will be renewed;
　　　　　has little,
　　　　　　　it will gain;
　　　　　has much,
　　　　　　　it will be confused.

　　　For these reasons,
　　　　　The sage holds on to unity
　　　　　　　and serves as the shepherd of all under heaven.

He is not self-absorbed,
  therefore he shines forth;
He is not self-revealing,
  therefore he is distinguished;
He is not self-assertive,
  therefore he has merit;
He does not praise himself,
  therefore he is long-lasting.

Now,
  Simply because he does not compete,
  No one can compete with him.

  The old saying about the bent being preserved intact
    is indeed close to the mark!

  Truly, he shall be returned intact.

(27) To be sparing of speech is natural.

  A whirlwind does not last the whole morning,
  A downpour does not last the whole day.
  Who causes them?
  If even heaven and earth cannot cause them to persist,
    how much less can human beings?

Therefore,
  In pursuing his affairs,
    a man of the Way identifies with the Way,
    a man of integrity identifies with integrity,
    a man who fails identifies with failure.

  To him who identifies with integrity,
    the Way awards integrity;

  To him who identifies with failure,
    the Way awards failure.

(28) There was something featureless yet complete,
    born before heaven and earth;

Silent—amorphous—
　　it stood alone and unchanging.

We may regard it as the mother of heaven and earth.
Not knowing its name,
　　I style it the "Way."
If forced to give it a name,
　　I would call it "great."
Being great implies flowing ever onward,
Flowing ever onward implies far-reaching,
Far-reaching implies reversal.

The Way is great,
Heaven is great,
Earth is great,
The king, too, is great.

Within the realm there are four greats,
　　and the king is one among them.

Man
　　patterns himself on earth,
Earth
　　patterns itself on heaven,
Heaven
　　patterns itself on the Way,
The Way
　　patterns itself on nature.

[Lao Tzu, *Tao-Te Ching*, tr. Victor H. Mair (from the Ma-Wang-Tui Silk Manuscripts) (N.Y.: Bantam Books, 1990). (1) [1],* pp. 3–4 (2) [2], pp. 5–6. (3) [3], p. 7. (4) [4], p. 8. (5) [6], p. 11. (6) [8], p. 13. (7) [9], p. 14. (8) [10], p. 15. (9) [11], p. 16. (10) [12], p. 17. (11) [20], p. 26. (12) [24], p. 31. (13) [26], p. 33. (14) [31], p. 40. (15) [36], p. 46. (16) [41], p. 52. (17) [42], p. 53. (18) [45], p. 59. (19) [48], p. 60. (20) [52], p. 67. (21) [55], p. 70. (22) [57], p. 73. (23) [58], pp. 74–75. (24) [59], pp. 76–77. (25) [60], p. 78. (26) [67], pp. 87–88. (27) [68], p. 89. (28) [69], p. 90.]

* The numbers in brackets are Mair's section numbers.

3

Confucius

551–479 B.C.E.

The Analects

Concentrating his attention on the values of human life, it was unusual for Confucius to comment on anything beyond. An observation on time is present in bk. IX, 17 (p. 98).

17. While standing by a river, the Master said, "What passes away is, perhaps, like this. Day and night it never lets up."

But when one of his students asked about religious matters (his students and disciples frequently enter the *Analects* with a question or comment), Confucius (bk. XI, 12, p. 98) refused to answer:

12. Chi-lu asked how the spirits of the dead and the gods should be served. The Master said, "You are not able even to serve man. How can you serve the spirits?"
"May I ask about death?"
"You do not understand even life. How can you understand death?"

He believed there was a way in which individual and society should behave. He was interested in calling them both back to that way. That way is *the* way, the *Tao* (*q.v.* D and *Tao-Te Ching*). At times the way is beyond reach. At those times one is still obligated to take one's stand upon it. His interest was in describing the components of the way in individual and social life. Rectification goes both ways, national to individual, and individual to national. The emperor has a special obligation to find the way, and reflect it into society. Each of us has a similar obligation.

In the *Dictionary* the values of Confucius (*q.v.* D2–5 and Value, 3) are said to be *li* ("propriety"), *jen* ("human-heartedness"), and *t'ien* ("ethical providence"). In the Readings which follow, these are among the many values which are discussed, and which must be honored if the individual and society are to achieve their appropriate forms. He relates these values to the gentleman (*chün tzu*, literally, "son of a great prince," but by Confucius' time also, and especially, a man of perfected virtue, or of outstanding talent along with virtue). *Jen* is here translated as "benevolence," and the types of man Confucius discusses—the sage (*shang jen*), the good man (*shan jen*), the complete man (*ch'eng jen*), and the small man (*hsiao jen*)—differ, first to last, in the decreasing amount of benevolence characterizing their lives. That also includes differences in wisdom and knowledge. *Li* is translated here as "rites," including both traditional ceremonies, and traditional rules of conduct (hence, "propriety"). Such rules may be modified, however, to fit changing conditions.

Also see Study Guide (4b3), p. 31.

The Way

Although we shall begin with statements from Confucius about the Way, Confucius also speaks here about the gentleman, the sage, the small man, benevolence, virtue, and courage.

(1) 6. The Master said, "I set my heart on the Way, base myself on virtue, lean upon benevolence for support, and take my recreation in the arts."

(2) 8. The Master said, "He has not lived in vain who dies the day he is told about the Way."

9. The Master said, "There is no point in seeking the views of a Gentleman who, though he sets his heart on the Way, is ashamed of poor food and poor clothes."

(3) 14. The Master said, "The gentleman seeks neither a full belly nor a comfortable home. He is quick in action but cautious in speech. He goes to men possessed of the Way to be put right. Such a man can be described as eager to learn."

(4) 2. Yu Tzu said, "It is rare for a man whose character is such that he is good as a son and obedient as a young man to have the inclination to

transgress against his superiors; it is unheard of for one who has no such inclination to be inclined to start a rebellion. The gentleman devotes his efforts to the roots, for once the roots are established, the Way will grow therefrom. Being good as a son and obedient as a young man is, perhaps, the root of a man's character."

(5) 29. The Master said, "It is Man who is capable of broadening the Way. It is not the Way that is capable of broadening Man."

There are passages relating the Way to the state:

(6) 3. The Master said, "When the Way prevails in the state, speak and act with perilous high-mindedness; when the Way does not prevail, act with perilous high-mindedness but speak with self-effacing diffidence."

(7) 2. Confucius said, "When the Way prevails in the Empire, the rites and music and punitive expeditions are initiated by the Emperor. When the Way does not prevail in the Empire, they are initiated by the feudal lords. When they are initiated by the feudal lords, it is surprising if power does not pass from the Emperor within ten generations. When they are initiated by the Counsellors, it is surprising if power does not pass from the feudal lords within five generations. When the prerogative to command in a state is in the hands of officials of the Counsellors it is surprising if power does not pass from the Counsellors within three generations. When the Way prevails in the Empire, policy does not rest with the Counsellors. When the Way prevails in the Empire, the Commoners do not express critical views."

(8) 13. The Master said, "Have the firm faith to devote yourself to learning, and abide to the death in the good way. Enter not a state that is in peril; stay not in a state that is in danger. Show yourself when the Way prevails in the Empire, but hide yourself when it does not. It is a shameful matter to be poor and humble when the Way prevails in the state. Equally, it is a shameful matter to be rich and noble when the Way falls into disuse in the state."

(9) 36. Kung-po Liao spoke ill of Tzu-lu to Chi-Sun. Tzu-fu Ching-po reported this, saying, "My master shows definite signs of being swayed by Kung-po Liao, but I still have enough influence to have his carcass exposed in the marketplace."

The Master said, "It is Destiny if the Way prevails; it is equally Destiny if the Way falls into disuse. What can Kung-po Liao do in defiance of Destiny?"

There are passages relating the Way to the life of the gentleman:

(10) 25. The Master said, "The gentleman is easy to serve but difficult to please. He will not be pleased unless you try to please him by following the Way, but when it comes to employing the services of others, he does so within the limits of their capacity. The small man is difficult to serve but easy to please. He will be pleased even though you try to please him by not following the Way, but when it comes to employing the services of others, he demands all-round perfection."

(11) 38. Tzu-lu put up for the night at the Stone Gate. The gatekeeper said, "Where have you come from?" Tzu-lu said, "From the K'ung[1] family." "Is that the K'ung who keeps working towards a goal the realization of which he knows to be hopeless?"

Finally, there are statements about the Way, related to Confucius and other individuals where the term is not capitalized, but seems to refer to an individual adaptation to the Way.

(12) 12. Jan Ch'iu said, "It is not that I am not pleased with your way, but rather that my strength gives out." The Master said, "A man whose strength gives out collapses along the course. In your case you set the limits beforehand."

(13) 15. The Master said, "Ts'an! There is one single thread binding my way together."

Tseng Tzu assented.

After the Master had gone out, the disciples asked, "What did he mean?"

Tseng Tzu said, "The way of the Master consists in doing one's best and in using oneself as a measure to gauge others. That is all."

(14) 16. The Master said of Tzu-ch'an that he had the way of the gentleman on four counts: he was respectful in the manner he conducted himself; he was reverent in the service of his lord; in caring for the common people, he was generous and, in employing their services, he was just.

(15) 5. The Master said, "Wealth and high station are what men desire but unless I got them in the right way I would not remain in them. Poverty and low station are what men dislike, but even if I did not get them in the right way I would not try to escape from them.

"If the gentleman forsakes benevolence, in what way can he make a name for himself? The gentleman never deserts benevolence, not even for as long as it takes to eat a meal. If he hurries and stumbles one may be sure that it is in benevolence that he does so."

And sometimes it is not clear that it is the same idea.

(16) 19. Duke Ting asked, "What is the way the ruler should employ the services of his subjects? What is the way a subject should serve his ruler?"

Confucius answered, "The ruler should employ the services of his subjects in accordance with the rites. A subject should serve his ruler by doing his best."

(17) 30. The Master said, "Not to mend one's ways when one has erred is to err indeed."

The Confucian alternative arises from a respect for tradition. The Way is founded in the rites (ceremonies and dress, related to court behavior and decorum), the *Odes* (classics of Chinese poetry), and music (to which Confucius was especially sensitive), leading to the rectification of names and rising into virtue.

The ideal types of the gentleman, the complete man, and the sage are also implicit in this material, as is the "Decree from Heaven," the pattern of providence applied initially to the emperor, but, in Confucius' teaching, to every individual life.

(18) 8. The Master said, "Be stimulated by the *Odes*, take your stand on the rites and be perfected by music."

(19) 13. Ch'en Kang asked Po-yü,[2] "Have you not been taught anything out of the ordinary?"

"No, I have not. Once my father was standing by himself. As I crossed the courtyard with quickened steps,[3] he said, 'Have you studied the *Odes*?' I answered, 'No.' 'Unless you study the *Odes* you will be ill-equipped to speak.' I retired and studied the *Odes*.

"Another day, my father was again standing by himself. As I crossed the courtyard with quickened steps, he said, 'Have you studied the rites?' I answered, 'No.' 'Unless you study the rites you will be ill-equipped to take your stand.' I retired and studied the rites. I have been taught these two things."

Ch'en Kang retired delighted and said, "I asked one question and got three answers. I learned about the *Odes*, I learned about the rites, and I learned that a gentleman keeps aloof from his son."

(20) 2. The Master said, "Unless a man has the spirit of the rites, in being respectful he will wear himself out, in being careful he will become timid, in having courage he will become unruly, and in being forthright he will become intolerant.

"When the gentleman feels profound affection for his parents, the common people will be stirred to benevolence. When he does not forget friends of long standing, the common people will not shirk their obligations to other people."

(21) 9. The Master said, "Why is it none of you, my young friends, study the *Odes*? An apt quotation from the *Odes* may serve to stimulate the imagination, to show one's breeding, to smooth over difficulties in a group and to give expression to complaints.

"Inside the family there is the serving of one's father; outside, there is the serving of one's lord; there is also the acquiring of a side knowledge of the names of birds and beasts, plants and trees."[4]

10. The Master said to Po-yü, "Have you studied the *Chou nan* and *Shao nan*?[5] To be a man and not to study them is, I would say, like standing with one's face directly towards the wall."

(22) 2. The Master said, "The *Odes* are three hundred in number.
They can be summed up in one phrase,
 Swerving not from the right path."[6]

3. The Master said, "Guide them by edicts, keep them in line with punishments, and the common people will stay out of trouble but will have no sense of shame. Guide them by virtue, keep them in line with the rites, and they will, besides having a sense of shame, reform themselves."

4. The Master said, "At fifteen I set my heart on learning; at thirty I took my stand; at forty I came to be free from doubts; at fifty I understood the Decree of Heaven; at sixty my ear was attuned; at seventy I followed my heart's desire without overstepping the line."

5. Meng Yi Tzu asked about being filial. The Master answered, "Never fail to comply."

Fan Ch'ih was driving. The Master told him about the interview, saying, "Meng-sun asked me about being filial. I answered, 'Never fail to comply.'"

Fan Ch'ih asked, "What does that mean?"

The Master said, "When your parents are alive, comply with the rites in serving them; when they die, comply with the rites in burying them; comply with the rites in sacrificing to them."

(23) 3. Tzu-lu said, "If the Lord of Wei left the administration (*cheng*) of his state to you, what would you put first?"

The Master said, "If something has to be put first, it is, perhaps, the rectification (*cheng*)[7] of names."

Tzu-lu said, "Is that so? What a roundabout way you take! Why bring rectification in at all?"

The Master said, "Yu, how boorish you are. Where a gentleman is ignorant, one would expect him not to offer any opinion. When names are not correct, what is said will not sound reasonable; when what is said does not sound reasonable, affairs will not culminate in success; when affairs do not culminate in success, rites and music will not flourish; when rites and music do not flourish, punishments will not fit the crimes; when punishments do not fit the crimes, the common people will not know where to put hand and foot. Thus when the gentleman names something, the name is sure to be usable in speech, and when he says something this is sure to be practicable. The thing about the gentleman is that he is anything but casual, where speech is concerned."

Rectification also involves personal transformation.

(24) 24. The Master said, "One cannot but give assent to exemplary words, but what is important is that one should rectify oneself. One cannot but be pleased with tactful words, but what is important is that one should reform oneself. I can do nothing with the man who gives assent but does not rectify himself or the man who is pleased but does not reform himself."

Benevolence is also involved.

(25) 1. Yen Yüan asked about benevolence. The Master said, "To return to the observance of the rites through overcoming the self constitutes benevolence. If for a single day a man could return to the observance of the rites through overcoming himself, then the whole Empire would consider benevolence to be his. However, the practice of benevolence depends on oneself alone, and not on others."

Yen Yüan said, "I should like you to list the items." The Master said, "Do not look unless it is in accordance with the rites; do not listen unless it is in accordance with the rites; do not speak unless it is in accordance with the rites; do not move unless it is in accordance with the rites."

Yen Yüan said, "Though I am not quick, I shall direct my efforts towards what you have said."

(26) 3. Confucius said, "A man has no way of becoming a gentleman unless he understands Destiny; he has no way of taking his stand unless he understands the rites; he has no way of judging men unless he understands words."

(27) 18. The Master said, "The gentleman has morality as his basic stuff and by observing the rites puts it into practice, by being modest gives it expression, and by being trustworthy in word brings it to completion. Such is a gentleman indeed!"

An ethic of reciprocity emerges from this background, including a sense of reverence for one's parents.

(28) 6. Meng Wu Po asked about being filial. The Master said, "Give your father and mother no other cause for anxiety than illness."

7. Tzu-yu asked about being filial. The Master said, "Nowadays for a man to be filial means no more than that he is able to provide his parents with food. Even hounds and horses are, in some way, provided with food. If a man shows no reverence, where is the difference?"

(29) 6. Tzu-chang asked about going forward without obstruction. The Master said, "If in word you are conscientious and trustworthy and in deed singleminded and reverent, then even in the lands of the barbarians you will go forward without obstruction. But if you fail to be conscientious and trustworthy in word or to be singleminded and reverent in deed, then can you be sure of going forward without obstruction even in your own neighborhood? When you stand you should have this ideal there in front of you, and when you are in your carriage you should see it leaning against the handle-bar. Only then are you sure to go forward without obstruction."

Tzu-chang wrote this down on his sash.

(30) 22. The Master said, "I do not see how a man can be acceptable who is untrustworthy in word? When a pin is missing in the yoke-bar of a large cart or in the collar-bar of a small cart, how can the cart be expected to go?"

(31) 13. Yu Tzu said, "To be trustworthy in word is close to being moral in that it enables one's words to be repeated. To be respectful is close

to being observant of the rites in that it enables one to stay clear of disgrace and insult. If, in promoting good relationship with relatives by marriage, a man manages not to lose the good will of his own kinsmen, he is worthy of being looked up to as the head of the clan."

(32) 13. The Master said, "I suppose I should give up hope. I have yet to meet the man who is as fond of virtue as he is of beauty in women."

Virtue

(33) 29. The Master said, "Supreme indeed is the Mean as a moral virtue. It has been rare among the common people for quite a long time."

(34) 1. The Master said, "The rule of virtue can be compared to the Pole Star which commands the homage of the multitude of stars without leaving its place."

(35) 21. Fan Ch'ih was in attendance during an outing to the Rain Altar. He said, "May I ask about the exaltation of virtue, the reformation of the depraved, and the recognition of misguided judgment?" The Master said, "What a splendid question! To put service before the reward you get for it, is that not exaltation of virtue?[9] To attack evil as evil and not as evil of a particular man, is that not the way to reform the depraved? To let a sudden fit of anger make you forget the safety of your own person or even that of your parents, is that not misguided judgment?"

(36) 24. Tzu-kung asked, "Is there a single word which can be a guide to conduct throughout one's life?" The Master said, "It is perhaps the word '*shu*.'[10] Do not impose on others what you yourself do not desire."

(37) 34. Someone said,
            " 'Repay an injury with a good turn.'
What do you think of this saying?"
The Master said, "What, then, do you repay a good turn with? You repay an injury with straightness, but you repay a good turn with a good turn."

(38) 25. The Master said, "Make it your guiding principle to do your best for others and to be trustworthy in what you say. Do not accept as friend anyone who is not as good as you. When you make a mistake do not be afraid of mending your ways."
(39) 17. The Master said, "When you meet someone better than your-

self, turn your thoughts to becoming his equal. When you meet someone not as good as you are, look within and examine your own self."

(40) 23. Tzu-kung asked about how friends should be treated. The Master said, "Advise them to the best of your ability and guide them properly, but stop when there is no hope of success. Do not ask to be snubbed."

(41) 8. The Master said, "To fail to speak to a man who is capable of benefiting is to let a man go to waste. To speak to a man who is incapable of benefiting is to let one's words go to waste. A wise man lets neither men nor words go to waste."

(42) 11. The Master said, "How true is the saying that after a state has been ruled for a hundred years by good men it is possible to get the better of cruelty and to do away with killing."

(43) 23. The Master said, "Heaven is author of the virtue that is in me. What can Huan T'ui do to me?"

The gentleman

The paradigm case of virtue is the gentleman whose central value is benevolence, and whose life is compared to that of the "small man." He discusses other types as well: the sage, the good man, the complete man. A contemporary Chinese philosopher agreed with me that the male emphasis in all of this required revision, and he thought that possible.

(44) 10. Confucius said, "There are nine things the gentleman turns his thought to: to seeing clearly when he uses his eyes, to hearing acutely when he uses his ears, to looking cordial when it comes to his countenance, to appearing respectful when it comes to his demeanor, to being conscientious when he speaks, to being reverent when he performs his duties, to seeking advice when he is in doubt, to the consequences when he is enraged, and to what is right at the sight of gain."

(45) 28. The Master said, "There are three things constantly on the lips of the gentleman none of which I have succeeded in following: 'A man of benevolence never worries, a man of wisdom is never in two minds, a man of courage is never afraid.'" Tzu-kung said, "What the Master has just quoted is a description of himself."

(46) 18. The Master said, "When there is a preponderance of native substance over acquired refinement, the result will be churlishness. When there is a preponderance of acquired refinement over native substance, the result will be pedantry. Only a well-balanced admixture of these two will result in gentlemanliness."

(47) 7. Confucius said, "There are three things the gentleman should guard against. In youth when the blood and *ch'i*[12] are still unsettled, he should guard against the attraction of feminine beauty. In the prime of life when the blood and *ch'i* have become unyielding, he should guard against bellicosity. In old age when the blood and *ch'i* have declined, he should guard against acquisitiveness."

(48) 28. Tzu-lu asked, "What must a man be like before he deserves to be called a Gentleman?" The Master said, "One who is, on the one hand, earnest and keen and, on the other, genial deserves to be called a Gentleman—earnest and keen amongst friends and genial amongst brothers."

(49) 9. Tzu-hsia said, "In the three following situations the gentleman gives a different impression. From a distance he appears formal; when approached, he appears cordial; in speech he appears stern."

(50) 19. The Master said, "The gentleman is troubled by his own lack of ability, not by the failure of others to appreciate him."

(51) 27. The Master said, "The gentleman is ashamed of his word outstripping his deed."

(52) 24. The Master said, "The gentleman desires to be halting in speech but quick in action."

(53) 20. The Master said, "The gentleman hates not leaving behind a name when he is gone."

(54) 2. The Master said, "A Gentleman who is attached to a settled home is not worthy of being a Gentleman."

(55) 24. Tzu-kung said, "Does even the gentleman have dislikes?" The Master said, "Yes. The gentleman has his dislikes. He dislikes those who proclaim the evil in others. He dislikes those who, being in inferior posi-

tions, slander their superiors. He dislikes those who, while possessing courage, lack the spirit of the rites. He dislikes those whose resoluteness is not tempered by understanding."

(56) 10. The Master said, "In his dealings with the world the gentleman is not invariably for or against anything. He is on the side of what is moral."

(57) 37. The Master said, "The gentleman is devoted to principle but not inflexible in small matters."

(58) 23. The Master said, "The gentleman does not recommend a man on account of what he says, neither does he dismiss what is said on account of the speaker."

(59) 9. The Master said, "For Gentlemen of purpose and men of benevolence while it is inconceivable that they should seek to stay alive at the expense of benevolence, it may happen that they have to accept death in order to have benevolence accomplished."

(60) 20. Tzu-kung asked, "What must a man be like before he can be said truly to be a Gentleman?" The Master said, "A man who has a sense of shame in the way he conducts himself and, when sent abroad, does not disgrace the commission of his lord can be said to be a Gentleman."

～   ～   ～

"What about men who are in public life in the present day?"

The Master said, "Oh, they are of such limited capacity that they hardly count."

The gentleman compared to the small man

(61) 8. Confucius said, "The gentleman stands in awe of three things. He is in awe of the Decree of Heaven. He is in awe of great men. He is in awe of the words of the sages. The small man, being ignorant of the Decree of Heaven, does not stand in awe of it. He treats great men with insolence and the words of the sages with derision."

(62) 23. The Master said, "The gentleman gets through to what is up above; the small man gets through to what is down below."

(63) 37. The Master said, "The gentleman is easy of mind, while the small man is always full of anxiety."

(64) 21. The Master said, "What the gentleman seeks, he seeks within himself; what the small man seeks, he seeks in others."

(65) 23. The Master said, "The gentleman agrees with others without being an echo. The small man echoes without being in agreement."

(66) 16. The Master said, "The gentleman understands what is moral. The small man understands what is profitable."

(67) 12. The Master said, "If one is guided by profit in one's actions, one will incur much ill will."

(68) 16. The Master said, "The gentleman helps others to realize what is good in them; he does not help them to realize what is bad in them. The small man does the opposite."

(69) 14. The Master said, "The gentleman enters into associations but not cliques; the small man enters into cliques but not associations."

(70) 22. The Master said, "The gentleman is conscious of his own superiority without being contentious, and comes together with other gentlemen without forming cliques."

(71) 34. The Master said, "The gentleman cannot be appreciated in small things but is acceptable in great matters. A small man is not acceptable in great matters but can be appreciated in small things."

(72) 11. The Master said, "While the gentleman cherishes benign rule, the small man cherishes his native land. While the gentleman cherishes a respect for the law, the small man cherishes generous treatment."

(73) 23. Tzu-lu said, "Does the gentleman consider courage a supreme quality?" The Master said, "For the gentleman it is morality that is supreme. Possessed of courage but devoid of morality, a gentleman will make trouble while a small man will be a brigand."

(74) 33. The Master said, "In unstinted effort I can compare with others, but in being a practising gentleman I have had, as yet, no success."

Benevolence

(75) 6. Tzu-chang asked Confucius about benevolence. Confucius said, "There are five things and whoever is capable of putting them into practice in the Empire is certainly 'benevolent.'"

"May I ask what they are?"

"They are respectfulness, tolerance, trustworthiness in word, quickness, and generosity. If a man is respectful he will not be treated with insolence. If he is tolerant he will win the multitude. If he is trustworthy in word his fellow men will entrust him with responsibility. If he is quick he will achieve results. If he is generous he will be good enough to be put in a position over his fellow men."

(76) 2. Chung-kung asked about benevolence. The Master said, "When abroad behave as though you were receiving an important guest. When employing the services of the common people behave as though you were officiating at an important sacrifice. Do not impose on others what you yourself do not desire. In this way you will be free from ill will whether in a state or in a noble family."

Chung-kung said, "Though I am not quick, I shall direct my efforts towards what you have said."

3. Ssu-ma Niu asked about benevolence. The Master said, "The mark of the benevolent man is that he is loath to speak."

"In that case, can a man be said to be benevolent simply because he is loath to speak?"

The Master said, "When to act is difficult, is it any wonder that one is loath to speak?"[13]

(77) 19. Fan Ch'ih asked about benevolence. The Master said, "While at home hold yourself in a respectful attitude; when serving in an official capacity be reverent; when dealing with others do your best. These are qualities that cannot be put aside, even if you go and live among the barbarians."

(78) 30. The Master said, "Is benevolence really far away? No sooner do I desire it than it is here."

(79) 3. The Master said, "It is only the benevolent man who is capable of liking or disliking other men."

4. The Master said, "If a man sets his heart on benevolence, he will be free from evil."

(80) 17. The Master said, "It is rare, indeed, for a man with cunning words and an ingratiating face to be benevolent."

(81) 35. The Master said, "Benevolence is more vital to the common people than even fire and water. In the case of fire and water, I have seen men die by stepping on them, but I have never seen any man die by stepping on benevolence."

36. The Master said, "When faced with the opportunity to practise benevolence do not give precedence even to your teacher."

Benevolence and wisdom

(82) 22. Fan Ch'ih asked about wisdom. The Master said, "To work for the things the common people have a right to and to keep one's distance from the gods and spirits while showing them reverence can be called wisdom."

Fan Ch'ih asked about benevolence. The Master said, "The benevolent man reaps the benefit only after overcoming difficulties. That can be called benevolence."[14]

(83) 22. Fan Ch'ih asked about benevolence. The Master said, "Love your fellow men."

He asked about wisdom. The Master said, "Know your fellow men." Fan Ch'ih failed to grasp his meaning. The Master said, "Raise the straight and set them over the crooked. This can make the crooked straight."

Fan Ch'ih withdrew and went to see Tzu-hsia, saying, "Just now, I went to see the Master and asked about wisdom. The Master said, 'Raise the straight and set them over the crooked. This can make the crooked straight.' What did he mean?"

Tzu-hsia said, "Rich, indeed, is the meaning of these words. When Shun possessed the Empire, he raised Kao Yao from the multitude and by so doing put those who were not benevolent at a great distance. When T'ang possessed the Empire, he raised Yi Yin from the multitude and by so doing put those who were not benevolent at a great distance."

(84) 29. The Master said, "The man of wisdom is never in two minds, the man of benevolence never worries; the man of courage is never afraid.

Benevolence and the sage

(85) 30. Tzu-kung said, "If there were a man who gave extensively to the common people and brought help to the multitude, what would you think of him? Could he be called benevolent?"

The Master said, "It is no longer a matter of benevolence with such a man. If you must describe him, 'sage' is, perhaps, the right word. Even Yao and Shun would have found it difficult to accomplish as much. Now, on the other hand, a benevolent man helps others to take their stand insofar as he himself wishes to take his stand,[15] and gets others there insofar as he himself wishes to get there. The ability to take as analogy what is near at hand[16] can be called the method of benevolence."

(86) 26. The Master said, "I have no hopes of meeting a sage. I would be content if I met someone who is a gentleman."

The Master said, "I have no hopes of meeting a good man. I would be content if I met someone who has constancy. It is hard for a man to have constancy who claims to have when he is wanting, to be full when he is empty, and to be comfortable when he is in straitened circumstances."

(87) 34. The Master said, "How dare I claim to be a sage or a benevolent man? Perhaps it might be said of me that I learn without flagging and teach without growing weary." Kung-hsi Hua said, "This is precisely where we disciples are unable to learn from your example."

(88) 17. The Master said, "Yu, shall I tell you what it is to know. To say you know when you know, and to say you do not when you do not, that is knowledge."

(89) 9. Confucius said, "Those who are born with knowledge are the highest. Next come those who attain knowledge through study. Next again come those who turn to study after having been vexed by difficulties. The common people, in so far as they make no effort to study even after having been vexed by difficulties, are the lowest."

(90) 28. The Master said, "There are presumably men who innovate without possessing knowledge, but that is not a fault I have. I use my ears widely and follow what is good in what I have heard; I use my eyes widely and retain what I have seen in my mind. This constitutes a lower level of knowledge."

(91) 8. The Master said, "Yu, have you heard about the six qualities and the six attendant faults?"

"No."

"Be seated and I shall tell you. To love benevolence without loving learning is liable to lead to foolishness. To love cleverness without loving learning is liable to lead to deviation from the right path. To love trustworthiness in word without loving learning is liable to lead to harmful behavior. To love forthrightness without loving learning is liable to lead to intolerance. To love courage without loving learning is liable to lead to insubordination. To love unbending strength without loving learning is liable to lead to indiscipline."

The complete man

(92) 12. Tzu-lu asked about the complete man. The Master said, "A man as wise as Tsang Wu-chung, as free from desires as Meng Kung-ch'uo, as courageous as Chuang-tzu of Pien and as accomplished as Jan Ch'iu, who is further refined by the rites and music, may be considered a complete man." Then he added, "But to be a complete man nowadays one need not be all these things. If a man remembers what is right at the sight of profit, is ready to lay down his life in the face of danger, and does not forget sentiments he has repeated all his life even when he has been in straitened circumstances for a long time, he may be said to be a complete man."

NOTES

1. That is, Confucius. As elsewhere here a student of Confucius enters the sayings. In XVII, 7, p. 151, Tzu-lu comments on the Way: "The gentleman takes office in order to do his duty. As for putting the Way into practice, he knows all along that it is hopeless."

2. Confucius' son.

3. As a sign of respect.

4. To these activities the study of the *Odes* must, presumably, be relevant, but the point is not explicitly made. This is very likely due to some corruption in the text.

5. These are the opening sections of the *Book of Odes*.

6. This line is from Ode 297 where it describes a team of horses going straight ahead without swerving to left or right.

7. For a discussion about the two words pronounced *cheng* see note to XII.17. [The passage is as follows:]

Chi K'ang Tzu asked Confucius about government. Confucius answered, "To govern (*cheng*) is to correct (*cheng*).[8] If you set an example by being correct, who would dare to remain incorrect?" [Footnote 8 States:]

8. Besides being homophones, the two words in Chinese are cognate, thus showing that the concept of "governing" was felt to be related to that of "correcting."

9. The two words *te* (to get) and *te* (virtue) seem to be cognate. Virtue is what one makes one's own by the pursuit of the *tao* (Way). (For a discussion of this point in a Taoist context, see the *Tao-Te Ching*, p. 42).

10. *I.e.*, using oneself as a measure in gauging the wishes of others.

11. According to tradition, this was said on the occasion when Huan T'ui, the Minister of War in Sung, attempted to kill him.

12. *Ch'i* is the basic constituent of the universe. The refined *ch'i* fills the human body and, among other things, circulates with the blood. (It is the "native substance" of the preceding passage. [Ed.])

13. For fear that one may be unable to live up to one's words. Cf. IV.22, IV.24.

14. This saying is quoted in *Mencius*, III.A.2.

15. It is on the rites that one takes one's stand. *Cf.* "Take your stand on the rites" (VIII.8) and "unless you study the rites you will not be able to take your stand" (XVI.13).

16. *Viz.*, oneself.

[Confucius. All passages from *The Analects*, tr. and intro., D. C. Lau (Penguin Books, Ltd.: Harmondsworth, Middlesex, Eng., 1979). (1) Bk. VII, p. 86 [6]. (2) Bk IV, p. 73 [8 and 9]. (3) Bk. I, p. 61 [14]. (4) Bk. I, p. 59 [2]. (5) Bk. IV, p. 136 [29]. (6) Bk. XIV, p. 124 [3]. (7) Bk. XVI, p. 139 [2]. (8) Bk. VIII, p. 94 [13]. (9) Bk. XIV, p. 130 [36]. (10) Bk. XIII, pp. 122–23 [25]. (11) Bk. XIV, p. 130 [38], and fn. from bk XVII, p. 151 [7]. (12) Bk. XI, pp. 182–83 [12]. (13) Bk. IV, p. 75 [15]. (14) Bk. V, p. 78 [16]. (15) Bk. IV, p. 72 [5]. (16) Bk. III, p. 70 [19]. (17) Bk. XV, p. 136 [30]. (18) Bk. VIII, p. 93 [8]. (19) Bk. XVI, p. 148 [13]. (20) Bk. VIII, p. 92 [2]. (21) Bk. XVII, p. 145 [9, 10]. (22) Bk. II, p. 63 [2–5]. (23) Bk. XIII, p. 119 [3] and fn. bk. XII, p. 115 [17]. (24) Bk. IX, p. 99 [24]. (25) Bk. XII, p. 112 [1]. (26) Bk. XX, p. 160 [3]. (27) Bk. XV, p. 134 [18]. (28) Bk. II, p. 64 [6, 7]. (29) Bk. XV, pp. 132–33 [6]. (30) Bk. II, p. 66 [22]. (31) Bk. I, p. 61 [13]. (32) Bk. XV, p. 134 [13]. (33) Bk. VI, p. 85 [29]. (34) Bk. II, p. 63 [1]. (35) Bk. XII, p. 116 [21]. (36) Bk. XV, p. 135 [24]. (37) Bk. XIV, p. 129 [34]. (38) Bk. IX, p. 99 [25]. (39) Bk. IV, p. 74 [17]. (40) Bk. XII, p. 117 [23]. (41) Bk. XV, p. 133 [8]. (42) Bk. XIII, p. 120 [11]. (43) Bk. VII, p. 89 [23]. (44) Bk. XVI, pp. 140–41 [10]. (45) Bk. XIV, p. 128 [28]. (46) Bk. VI, p. 83 [18]. (47) Bk. XVI, p. 140 [7]. (48) Bk. XIII, p. 123 [28]. (49) Bk. XIX, p. 154 [9]. (50) Bk. XV, p. 134 [19]. (51) Bk. XIV, p. 128

[27]. (52) Bk. IV, p. 75 [24]. (53) Bk. XV, p. 135 [20]. (54) Bk. XIV, p. 124 [2]. (55) Bk. XVII, p. 148 [24]. (56) Bk. IV, p. 73 [10]. (57) Bk. XV, p. 137 [37]. (58) Bk. XV, p. 135 [23]. (59) Bk. XV, p. 133 [9]. (60) Bk. XIII, pp. 121–22 [20]. (61) Bk. XVI, p. 140 [8]. (62) Bk. XIV, p. 128 [23]. (63) Bk XII, p. 91 [37]. (64) Bk. XV, p. 135 [21]. (65) Bk. XIII, p. 122 [23]. (66) Bk. IV, p. 74 [16]. (67) Bk. IV, p. 73 [12]. (68) Bk. VII, p. 115 [16]. (69) Bk. II, p. 65 [14]. (70) Bk. XV, p. 135 [22]. (71) Bk. XV, p. 136 [34]. (72) Bk. IV, p. 73 [11]. (73) Bk. XVII, pp. 147–48 [23]. (74) Bk. VII, p. 90 [33]. (75) Bk. XVII, p. 144 [6]. (76) Bk. XII, p. 112 [2, 3]. (77) Bk. XIII, p. 121 [19]. (78) Bk. VII, p. 90 [30]. (79) Bk. IV, p. 72 [3, 4]. (80) Bk. XVII, p. 146 [17]. (81) Bk. XV, pp. 136–37 [35, 36]. (82) Bk. VI, p. 84 [22]. (83) Bk. XII, pp. 116–17 [22]. (84) Bk. IX, p. 100 [29]. (85) Bk. VI, p. 85 [30]. (86) Bk. VII, p. 89 [26]. (87) Bk. VII, pp. 90–91 [34]. (88) Bk. II, p. 65 [17]. (89) Bk. XVI, p. 140 [9]. (90) Bk. VII, p. 81 [28]. (91) Bk. XVII, pp. 144–45 [8]. (92) Bk. XIV, pp. 125–26 [12].

4

Plato

428–348 B.C.E.

The Philebus, Symposium, Republic,
and *Epistle VII*

ON VALUES AS ABSOLUTE

Plato argued that each basic value term represented an idea or form perfect in its own way. The good or valuable life requires us to heighten our appreciation to the point where these kinds of perfection inform our lives. This heightened appreciation is superior to the disorder of the uninformed life.

Also see Study Guide (4b4), pp. 31–32.

The Greek philosophers in general spent a considerable amount of time discussing whether pleasure is the final good. In the *Philebus* Socrates (here and elsewhere the central figure in Plato's early dialogues) decides not only that it is not in first place, it is in fifth place. Socrates discusses the question with Protarchus, who is standing in for his teacher, Philebus.

On pleasure and wisdom

(1) *Soc.* I remember to have heard long ago certain discussions about pleasure and wisdom, whether awake or in a dream I cannot tell; they were to the effect that neither the one nor the other of them was the good, but some third thing, which was different from them, and better than either. If this be clearly established, then pleasure will lose the victory, for the good will cease to be identified with her:—Am I not right?

Pro. Yes.

Soc. And there will cease to be any need of distinguishing the kinds of pleasures, as I am inclined to think, but this will appear more clearly as we proceed.

Pro. Capital, Socrates; pray go on as you propose.

Soc. But, let us first agree on some little points.

Pro. What are they?

Soc. Is the good perfect or imperfect?

Pro. The most perfect, Socrates, of all things.

Soc. And is the good sufficient?

Pro. Yes, certainly, and in a degree surpassing all other things.

Soc. And no one can deny that all percipient beings desire and hunt after good, and are eager to catch and have the good about them, and care not for the attainment of anything which is not accompanied by good.

Pro. That is undeniable.

Soc. Now let us part off the life of pleasure from the life of wisdom, and pass them in review.

Pro. How do you mean?

Soc. Let there be no wisdom in the life of pleasure, nor any pleasure in the life of wisdom, for if either of them is the chief good, it cannot be supposed to want anything, but if either is shown to want anything, then it cannot really be the chief good.

Pro. Impossible.

Soc. And will you help us to test these two lives?

Pro. Certainly.

Soc. Then answer.

Pro. Ask.

Soc. Would you choose, Protarchus, to live all your life long in the enjoyment of the greatest pleasures?

Pro. Certainly I should.

Soc. Would you consider that there was still anything wanting to you if you had perfect pleasure?

Pro. Certainly not.

Soc. Reflect; would you not want wisdom and intelligence and forethought, and similar qualities? would you not at any rate want sight?

Pro. Why should I? Having pleasure I should have all things.

Soc. Living thus, you would always throughout your life enjoy the greatest pleasures?

Pro. I should.

Soc. But if you had neither mind, nor memory, nor knowledge, nor true opinion, you would in the first place be utterly ignorant of whether you were pleased or not, because you would be entirely devoid of intelligence.

Pro. Certainly.

Soc. And similarly, if you had no memory you would not recollect that you had ever been pleased, nor would the slightest recollection of the pleasure which you feel at any moment remain with you; and if you had no true opinion you would not think that you were pleased when you were; and if you had no power of calculation you would not be able to calculate on future pleasure, and your life would be the life, not of a man, but of an oyster or "pulmo marinus." Could this be otherwise?

Pro. No.

Soc. But is such a life eligible?

Pro. I cannot answer you, Socrates; the argument has taken away from me the power of speech.

Soc. We must keep up our spirits;—let us now take the life of mind and examine it in turn.

Pro. And what is this life of mind?

Soc. I want to know whether any one of us would consent to live, having wisdom and mind and knowledge and memory of all things, but having no sense of pleasure or pain, and wholly unaffected by these and the like feelings?

Pro. Neither life, Socrates, appears eligible to me, or is likely, as I should imagine, to be chosen by any one else.

Soc. What would you say, Protarchus, to both of these in one, or to one that was made out of the union of the two?

Pro. Out of the union, that is, of pleasure with mind and wisdom?

Soc. Yes, that is the life which I mean.

Pro. There can be no difference of opinion; not some but all would surely choose this third rather than either of the other two, and in addition to them.

Soc. But do you see the consequence?

Pro. To be sure I do. The consequence is, that two out of the three lives which have been proposed are neither sufficient nor eligible for man or for animal.

Soc. Then now there can be no doubt that neither of them has the good, for the one which had would certainly have been sufficient and perfect and eligible for every living creature or thing that was able to live such a life; and if any of us had chosen any other, he would have chosen contrary to the nature of the truly eligible, and not of his own free will, but either through ignorance or from some unhappy necessity.

Pro. Certainly that seems to be true.

Soc. And now have I not sufficiently shown that Philebus' goddess is not to be regarded as identical with the good?

Phi. Neither is your "mind" the good, Socrates, for that will be open to the same objections.

Soc. Perhaps, Philebus, you may be right in saying so of my "mind"; but of the true, which is also the divine mind, far otherwise. However, I will not at present claim the first place for mind as against the mixed life; but we must come to some understanding about the second place. For you might affirm pleasure and I mind to be the cause of the mixed life; and in that case although neither of them would be the good, one of them might be imagined to be the cause of the good. And I might proceed further to argue in opposition to Philebus, that the element which makes this mixed life eligible and good, is more akin and more similar to mind than to pleasure. And if this is true, pleasure cannot be truly said to share either in the first or second place, and does not, if I may trust my own mind, attain even to the third.

Pro. Truly, Socrates, pleasure appears to me to have had a fall; in fighting for the palm, she has been smitten by the argument, and is laid low. I must say that mind would have fallen too, and may therefore be thought to show discretion in not putting forward a similar claim. And if pleasure were deprived not only of the first but of the second place, she would be terribly damaged in the eyes of her admirers, for not even to them would she still appear as fair as before.

Soc. Well, but had we not better leave her now, and not pain her by applying the crucial test, and finally detecting her?

Pro. Nonsense, Socrates.

Soc. Why? because I said that we had better not pain pleasure, which is an impossibility?

Pro. Yes, and more than that, because you do not seem to be aware that none of us will let you go home until you have finished the argument.

(2) *Soc.* Well then, by Zeus, let us proceed, and I will make what I believe to be a fair summary of the argument.

Pro. Let me hear.

Soc. Philebus says that pleasure is the true end of all living beings, at which all ought to aim, and moreover that it is the chief good of all, and that the two names "good" and "pleasant" are correctly given to one thing and one nature; Socrates, on the other hand, begins by denying this, and further says, that in nature as in name they are two, and that wisdom partakes more than pleasure, of the good. Is not and was not this what we were saying, Protarchus?

Pro. Certainly.

Soc. And is there not and was there not a further point which was conceded between us?

Pro. What was it?

Soc. That the good differs from all other things.

Pro. In what respect?

Soc. In that the being who possesses good always everywhere and in all things has the most perfect sufficiency, and is never in need of anything else.

Pro. Exactly.

Soc. And did we not endeavor to make an imaginary separation, of wisdom and pleasure, assigning to each a distinct life, so that pleasure was wholly excluded from wisdom, and wisdom in like manner had no part whatever in pleasure?

Pro. We did.

Soc. And did we think that either of them alone would be sufficient?

Pro. Certainly not.

Soc. And if we erred in any point, then let any one who will, take up the enquiry again and set us right; and assuming memory and wisdom and knowledge and true opinion to belong to the same class, let him consider whether he would desire to possess or acquire—I will not say pleasure, however abundant or intense, if he has no real perception that he is pleased, nor any consciousness of what he feels, nor any recollection, however momentary, of the feeling,—but would he desire to have anything at all, if these faculties were wanting to him? And about wisdom I ask the same question; can you conceive that any one would choose to have all wisdom absolutely devoid of pleasure, rather than with a certain degree of pleasure, or all pleasure devoid of wisdom, rather than with a certain degree of wisdom?

Pro. Certainly not, Socrates; but why repeat such questions any more?

Soc. Then the perfect and universally eligible and entirely good cannot possibly be either of them?

Pro. Impossible.

Soc. Then now we must ascertain the nature of the good more or less accurately, in order, as we were saying, that the second place may be duly assigned?

Pro. Right.

Soc. Have we not found a road which leads towards the good?

Pro. What road?

Soc. Supposing that a man had to be found, and you could discover in what house he lived, would not that be a great step towards the discovery of the man himself?

Pro. Certainly.

Soc. And now reason intimates to us, as at our first beginning, that we should seek the good, not in the unmixed life but in the mixed.

Pro. True.

Soc. There is greater hope of finding that which we are seeking in the life which is well mixed than in that which is not?

Pro. Far greater.

Soc. Then now let us mingle, Protarchus, at the same time offering up a prayer to Dionysus or Hephaestus, or whoever is the god who presides over the ceremony of mingling.

Pro. By all means.

Soc. Are not we the cup-bearers? and here are two fountains which are flowing at our side: one, which is pleasure, may be likened to a fountain of honey; the other, wisdom, a sober draught in which no wine mingles, is of water unpleasant but healthful; out of these we must seek to make the fairest of all possible mixtures.

Pro. Certainly.

Soc. Tell me first;—should we be most likely to succeed if we mingled every sort of pleasure with every sort of wisdom?

Pro. Perhaps we might.

Soc. But I should be afraid of the risk, and I think that I can show a safer plan.

Pro. What is it?

Soc. One pleasure was supposed by us to be truer than another, and one art to be more exact than another.

Pro. Certainly.

Soc. There was also supposed to be a difference in sciences; some of them regarding only the transient and perishing, and others the permanent and imperishable and everlasting and immutable; and when judged by the standard of truth, the latter, as we thought, were truer than the former.

Pro. Very good and right.

Soc. If, then, we were to begin by mingling the sections of each class which have the most of truth, will not the union suffice to give us the loveliest of lives, or shall we still want some elements of another kind?

Pro. I think that we ought to do what you suggest.

Soc. Let us suppose a man who understands justice, and has reason as well as understanding about the true nature of this and of all other things.

Pro. We will suppose such a man.

Soc. Will he have enough of knowledge if he is acquainted only with the divine circle and sphere, and knows nothing of our human spheres and circles, but uses only divine circles and measures in the building of a house?

Pro. The knowledge which is only superhuman, Socrates, is ridiculous in man.

Soc. What do you mean? Do you mean that you are to throw into the cup and mingle the impure and uncertain art which uses the false measure and the false circle?

Pro. Yes, we must, if any of us is ever to find his way home.

Soc. And am I to include music, which, as I was saying just now, is full of guesswork and imitation, and is wanting in purity?

Pro. Yes, I think that you must, if human life is to be a life at all.

Soc. Well, then, suppose that I give way, and, like a doorkeeper who is pushed and overborne by the mob, I open the door wide, and let knowledge of every sort stream in, and the pure mingle with the impure?

Pro. I do not know, Socrates, that any great harm would come of having them all, if only you have the first sort.

Soc. Well, then, shall I let them all flow into what Homer poetically terms "a meeting of the waters"?

Pro. By all means.

Soc. There—I have let him in, and now I must return to the fountain of pleasure. For we were not permitted to begin by mingling in a single stream the true portions of both according to our original intention; but the love of all knowledge constrained us to let all the sciences flow in together before the pleasures.

Pro. Quite true.

Soc. And now the time has come for us to consider about the pleasures also, whether we shall in like manner let them go all at once, or at first only the true ones.

Pro. It will be by far the safer course to let flow the true ones first.

Soc. Let them flow, then; and now, if there are any necessary pleasures, as there were arts and sciences necessary, must we not mingle them?

Pro. Yes; the necessary pleasures should certainly be allowed to mingle.

Soc. The knowledge of the arts has been admitted to be innocent and useful always; and if we say of pleasures in like manner that all of them are good and innocent for all of us at all times, we must let them all mingle?

Pro. What shall we say about them, and what course shall we take?

Soc. Do not ask me, Protarchus; but ask the daughters of pleasure and wisdom to answer for themselves.

Pro. How?

Soc. Tell us, O beloved—shall we call you pleasures or by some other name?—would you rather live with or without wisdom? I am of opinion that they would certainly answer as follows:

Pro. How?

Soc. They would answer, as we said before, that for any single class to be left by itself pure and isolated is not good, nor altogether possible; and that if we are to make comparisons of one class with another and choose, there is no better companion than knowledge of things in general, and likewise the perfect knowledge, if that may be, of ourselves in every respect.

Pro. And our answer will be:—In that ye have spoken well.

Soc. Very true. And now let us go back and interrogate wisdom and mind: Would you like to have any pleasures in the mixture?

And they will reply: "What pleasures do you mean?"

Pro. Likely enough.

Soc. And we shall take up our parable and say: Do you wish to have the greatest and most vehement pleasures for your companions in addition to the true ones? "Why, Socrates," they will say, "how can we? seeing that they are the source of ten thousand hindrances to us; they trouble the souls of men, which are our habitation with their madness; they prevent us from coming to the birth, and are commonly the ruin of the children which are born to us, causing them to be forgotten and unheeded; but the true and pure pleasures, of which you spoke, know to be of our family, and also those pleasures which accompany health and temperance, and which every Virtue, like a goddess has in her train to follow her about wherever she goes,—mingle these and not the others; there would be great want of sense in any one who desires to see a fair and perfect mixture, and to find in it what is the highest good in man and in the universe, and to divine what is the true form of good—there would be great want of sense in his allowing the pleasures, which are always in the company of folly and vice, to mingle with mind in the cup."—Is not this a very rational and suitable reply, which mind has made, both on her own behalf, as well as on the behalf of memory and true opinion?

Pro. Most certainly.

Soc. And still there must be something more added, which is a necessary ingredient in every mixture.

Pro. What is that?

Soc. Unless truth enter into the composition, nothing can truly be created or subsist.

Pro. Impossible.

Soc. Quite impossible; and now you and Philebus must tell me whether anything is still wanting in the mixture, for to my way of thinking the argument is now completed, and may be compared to an incorporeal law, which is going to hold fair rule over a living body.

Pro. I agree with you, Socrates.

Soc. And may we not say with reason that we are now at the vestibule of the habitation of the good?

Pro. I think that we are.

Soc. What, then, is there in the mixture which is most precious, and which is the principal cause why such a state is universally beloved by all? When we have discovered it, we will proceed to ask whether this omnipresent nature is more akin to pleasure or to mind.

Pro. Quite right; in that way we shall be better able to judge.

Soc. And there is no difficulty in seeing the cause which renders any mixture either of the highest value or of none at all.

Pro. What do you mean?

Soc. Every man knows it.

Pro. What?

Soc. He knows that any want of measure and symmetry in any mixture whatever must always of necessity be fatal, both to the elements and to the mixture, which is then not a mixture, but only a confused medley which brings confusion on the possessor of it.

Pro. Most true.

Soc. And now the power of the good has retired into the region of the beautiful; for measure and symmetry are beauty and virtue all the world over.

Pro. True.

Soc. Also we said that truth was to form an element in the mixture.

Pro. Certainly.

Soc. Then, if we are not able to hunt the good with one idea only, with three we may catch our prey; Beauty, Symmetry, Truth are the three, and these taken together we may regard as the single cause of the mixture, and the mixture as being good by reason of the infusion of them.

Pro. Quite right.

Soc. And now, Protarchus, any man could decide well enough whether pleasure or wisdom is more akin to the highest good, and more honorable among gods and men.

Pro. Clearly, and yet perhaps the argument had better be pursued to the end.

Soc. We must take each of them separately in their relation to pleasure and mind, and pronounce upon them; for we ought to see to which of the two they are severally most akin.

Pro. You are speaking of beauty, truth, and measure?

Soc. Yes, Protarchus, take truth first, and, after passing in review mind, truth, pleasure, pause awhile and make answer to yourself, —as to whether pleasure or mind is more akin to truth.

Pro. There is no need to pause, for the difference between them is palpable; pleasure is the veriest impostor in the world; and it is said that in the pleasures of love, which appear to be the greatest, perjury is excused by the gods; for pleasures, like children, have not the least particle of reason in them; whereas mind is either the same as truth, or the most like truth, and the truest.

Soc. Shall we next consider measure, in like manner, and ask whether pleasure has more of this than wisdom, or wisdom than pleasure?

Pro. Here is another question which may be easily answered; for I imagine that nothing can ever be more immoderate than the transports of pleasure, or more in conformity with measure than mind and knowledge.

Soc. Very good; but there still remains the third test: Has mind a greater share of beauty than pleasure, and is mind or pleasure the fairer of the two?

Pro. No one, Socrates, either awake or dreaming, ever saw or imagined mind or wisdom to be in aught unseemly, at any time, past, present, or future.

Soc. Right.

Pro. But when we see some one indulging in pleasures, perhaps in the greatest of pleasures, the ridiculous or disgraceful nature of the action makes us ashamed; and so we put them out of sight, and consign them to darkness, under the idea that they ought not to meet the eye of day.

Soc. Then, Protarchus, you will proclaim everywhere, by word of mouth to this company, and by messengers bearing the tidings far and wide, that pleasure is not the first of possessions, nor yet the second, but that in measure, and the mean, and the suitable, and the like, the eternal nature has been found.

Pro. Yes, that seems to be the result of what has been now said.

Soc. In the second class is contained the symmetrical and beautiful and perfect or sufficient, and all which are of that family.

Pro. True.

Soc. And if you reckon in the third class mind and wisdom, you will not be far wrong, if I divine aright.

Pro. I dare say.

Soc. And would you not put in the fourth class the goods which we were affirming to appertain specially to the soul—sciences and arts and true opinions as we called them? These come after the third class, and form the fourth, as they are certainly more akin to good than pleasure is.

Pro. Surely.

Soc. The fifth class are the pleasures which were defined by us as painless, being the pure pleasures of the soul herself, as we termed them, which accompany, some the sciences, and some the senses.

Pro. Perhaps.

Soc. And now, as Orpheus says,

"With the sixth generation cease the glory of my song."

Here, at the sixth award, let us make an end; all that remains is to set the crown on our discourse.

Pro. True.

Soc. Then let us sum up and reassert what has been said, thus offering the third libation to the savior Zeus.

Pro. How?

Soc. Philebus affirmed that pleasure was always and absolutely the good.

Pro. I understand; this third libation, Socrates, of which you spoke, meant a recapitulation.

Soc. Yes, but listen to the sequel; convinced of what I have just been saying, and feeling indignant at the doctrine, which is maintained, not by Philebus only, but by thousands of others, I affirmed that mind was far better and far more excellent, as an element of human life, than pleasure.

Pro. True.

Soc. But, suspecting that there were other things which were also better, I went on to say that if there was anything better than either, then I would claim the second place for mind over pleasure, and pleasure would lose the second place as well as the first.

Pro. You did.

Soc. Nothing could be more satisfactorily shown than the unsatisfactory nature of both of them.

Pro. Very true.

Soc. The claims both of pleasure and mind to be the absolute good have been entirely disproven in this argument, because they are both wanting in self-sufficiency and also in adequacy and perfection.

Pro. Most true.

Soc. But, though they must both resign in favor of another, mind is ten thousand times nearer and more akin to the nature of the conqueror than pleasure.

Pro. Certainly.

Soc. And, according to the judgment which has now been given, pleasure will rank fifth.

Pro. True.

Soc. But not first; no, not even if all the oxen and horses and animals in the world by their pursuit of enjoyment proclaim her to be so;—although the many trusting in them, as diviners trust in birds, determine that pleasures make up the good of life, and deem the lusts of animals to be better witnesses than the inspirations of divine philosophy.

Pro. And now, Socrates, we tell you that the truth of what you have been saying is approved by the judgment of all of us.

Soc. And will you let me go?

Pro. There is a little which yet remains, and I will remind you of it, for I am sure that you will not be the first to go away from an argument.

Having finally put pleasure in its place, Plato next considers what values are absolute. In what follows, in the *Symposium* and the *Republic* beauty, truth, and the good share in having the topmost place, and interpenetrating with each other. The conversation concerning beauty which Socrates recounts in the *Symposium* is allegedly with Diotima, a priestess of Montinea in Arcadia, and possibly an invention of Socrates. We enter with Diotima asking a question about the good and Socrates answering.

On beauty, truth, and the good

(3) "... there is nothing which men love but the good. Is there anything?" "Certainly, I should say, that there is nothing." "Then," she said, "the simple truth is, that men love the good." "Yes," I said. "To which must be added that they love the possession of the good?" "Yes, that must be added." "And not only the possession, but the everlasting possession of the good?" "That must be added too." "Then love," she said, "may be described generally as the love of the everlasting possession of the good?" "That is most true."

"Then if this be the nature of love, can you tell me further," she said, "what is the manner of the pursuit? what are they doing who show all this eagerness and heat which is called love? and what is the object which they have in view? Answer me." "Nay, Diotima," I replied, "if I had known, I should not have wondered at your wisdom, neither should I have come to learn from you about this very matter." "Well," she said, "I will teach you:—The object which they have in view is birth in beauty, whether of body or soul." "I do not understand you," I said; "the oracle requires an explanation." "I will make my meaning clearer," she replied. "I mean to say, that all men are bringing to the birth in their bodies and in their souls. There is a certain age at which human nature is desirous of procreation—procreation which must be in beauty and not in deformity; and this procreation is the union of man and woman, and is a divine thing; for conception and generation are an immortal principle in the mortal creature, and in the inharmonious they can never be. But the deformed is always inharmonious with the divine, and the beautiful harmonious. Beauty, then, is the destiny or goddess of parturition who presides at birth, and therefore, when approaching beauty, the conceiving power is propitious, and diffusive, and benign, and begets and bears fruit: at the sight of ugliness she frowns and contracts and has a sense of pain, and turns away, and shrivels up, and not without a pang refrains from conception. And this is the reason why, when the hour of conception arrives, and the teeming nature is full, there is such a flutter and ecstasy about beauty whose approach is the alleviation of the pain of travail. For love, Socrates, is not, as you imagine, the love of the beautiful only." "What then?" "The love of generation and of birth in beauty." "Yes," I said. "Yes, indeed," she replied. "But why of generation?" "Because to the mortal creature, generation is a sort of eternity and immortality," she replied; "and if, as has been already admitted, love is of the everlasting possession of the good, all men will necessarily desire immortality together with good: Wherefore love is of immortality."

(4) "These are the lesser mysteries of love, into which even you, Socrates, may enter; to the greater and more hidden ones which are the crown of these, and to which, if you pursue them in a right spirit, they will lead, I know not whether you will be able to attain. But I will do my utmost to inform you, and do you follow if you can. For he who would proceed aright in this matter should begin in youth to visit beautiful forms; and first, if he be guided by his instructor aright, to love one such form only— out of that he should create fair thoughts; and soon he will of himself perceive that the beauty of one form is akin to the beauty of another; and then if beauty of form in general is his pursuit, how foolish would he be not to recognize that the beauty in every form is one and the same! And when he perceives this he will abate his violent love of the one, which he will despise and deem a small thing, and will become a lover of all beautiful forms; in the next stage he will consider that the beauty of the mind is more honorable than the beauty of the outward form. So that if a virtuous soul have but a little comeliness, he will be content to love and tend him, and will search out and bring to the birth thoughts which may improve the young, until he is compelled to contemplate and see the beauty of institutions and laws, and to understand that the beauty of them all is of one family, and that personal beauty is a trifle; and after laws and institutions he will go on to the sciences, that he may see their beauty, being not like a servant in love with the beauty of one youth or man or institution, himself a slave mean and narrow-minded, but drawing towards and contemplating the vast sea of beauty, he will create many fair and noble thoughts and notions in boundless love of wisdom; until on that shore he grows and waxes strong, and at last the vision is revealed to him of a single science,

which is the science of beauty everywhere. To this I will proceed; please to give me your very best attention:

"He who has been instructed thus far in the things of love, and who has learned to see the beautiful in due order and succession, when he comes toward the end will suddenly perceive a nature of wondrous beauty (and this, Socrates, is the final cause of all our former toils)—a nature which in the first place is everlasting, not growing and decaying, or waxing and waning; secondly, not fair in one point of view and foul in another, or at one time or in one relation or at one place fair, at another time or in another relation or at another place foul, as if fair to some and foul to others, or in the likeness of a face or hands or any other part of the bodily frame, or in any form of speech or knowledge, or existing in any other being, as for example, in an animal, or in heaven, or in earth, or in any other place; but beauty absolute, separate, simple, and everlasting, which without diminution and without increase, or any change, is imparted to the ever-growing and perishing beauties of all other things. He who from these ascending under the influence of true love, begins to perceive that beauty, is not far from the end. And the true order of going, or being led by another, to the things of love, is to begin from the beauties of earth and mount upwards for the sake of that other beauty, using these as steps only, and from one going on to two, and from two to all fair forms, and from fair forms to fair practices, and from fair practices to fair notions, until from fair notions he arrives at the notion of absolute beauty, and at last knows what the essence of beauty is. This, my dear Socrates," said the stranger of Mantineia, "is that life above all others which man should live, in the contemplation of beauty absolute; a beauty which if you once beheld, you would see not to be after the measure of gold, and garments, and fair boys and youths, whose presence now entrances you; and you and many a one would be content to live seeing them only and conversing with them without meat or drink, if that were possible—you only want to look at them and to be with them. But what if man had eyes to see the true beauty—the divine beauty, I mean, pure and clear and unalloyed, not clogged with the pollutions of mortality and all the colors and vanities of human life—thither looking, and holding converse with the true beauty simple and divine? Remember how in that communion only, beholding beauty with the eye of the mind, he will be enabled to bring forth, not images of beauty, but realities (for he has hold not of an image but of a reality), and bringing forth and nourishing true virtue to become the friend of God and be immortal, if mortal man may. Would that be an ignoble life?"

Such, Phaedrus—and I speak not only to you, but to all of you—

were the words of Diotima; and I am persuaded of their truth. And being persuaded of them, I try to persuade others, that in the attainment of this end human nature will not easily find a helper better than love. And therefore, also, I say that every man ought to honor him as I myself honor him, and walk in his ways, and exhort others to do the same, and praise the power and spirit of love according to the measure of my ability now and ever.

(5)...I must first come to an understanding with you, and remind you of what I have mentioned in the course of this discussion, and at many other times.

What?

The old story, that there is a many beautiful and a many good, and so of other things which we describe and define; to all of them "many" is applied.

True, he said.

And there is an absolute beauty and an absolute good and of other things to which the term "many" is applied there is an absolute; for they may be brought under a single idea, which is called the essence of each.

Very true.

The many, as we say, are seen but not known, and the ideas are known but not seen.

Exactly.

And what is the organ with which we see the visible things?

The sight, he said.

And with the hearing, I said, we hear, and with the other senses perceive the other objects of sense?

True.

But have you remarked that sight is by far the most costly and complex piece of workmanship which the artificer of the senses ever contrived?

No, I never have, he said.

Then reflect: has the ear or voice need of any third or additional nature in order that the one may be able to hear and the other to be heard?

Nothing of the sort.

No, indeed, I replied; and the same is true of most, if not all, the other senses—you would not say that any of them requires such an addition?

Certainly not.

But you see that without the addition of some other nature there is no seeing or being seen?

How do you mean?

Sight being, as I conceive, in the eyes, and he who has eyes wanting to see; color being also present in them, still unless there be a third nature specially adapted to the purpose, the owner of the eyes will see nothing and the colors will be invisible.

Of what nature are you speaking?

Of that which you term light, I replied.

True, he said.

Noble, then, is the bond which links together sight and visibility, and great beyond other bonds by no small difference of nature; for light is their bond, and light is no ignoble thing?

Nay, he said, the reverse of ignoble.

And which, I said, of the gods in heaven would you say was the lord of this element? Whose is that light which makes the eye to see perfectly and the visible to appear?

You mean the sun, as you and all mankind say.

May not the relation of sight to this deity be described as follows?

How?

Neither sight nor the eye in which sight resides is the sun?

No.

Yet of all the organs of sense the eye is the most like the sun?

By far the most like.

And the power which the eye possesses is a sort of effluence which is dispensed from the sun?

Exactly.

Then the sun is not sight, but the author of sight who is recognized by sight.

True, he said.

And this is he whom I call the child of the good, whom the good begat in his own likeness, to be in the visible world, in relation to sight and the things of sight, what the good is in the intellectual world in relation to mind and the things of mind.

Will you be a little more explicit? he said.

Why, you know, I said, that the eyes, when a person directs them towards objects on which the light of day is no longer shining, but the moon and stars only, see dimly, and are nearly blind; they seem to have no clearness of vision in them?

Very true.

But when they are directed towards objects on which the sun shines, they see clearly and there is sight in them?

Certainly.

And the soul is like the eye: when resting upon that on which truth and being shine, the soul perceives and understands and is radiant with intelligence; but when turned towards the twilight of becoming and perishing, then she has opinion only, and goes blinking about, and is first of one opinion and then of another, and seems to have no intelligence?

Just so.

Now, that which imparts truth to the known and the power of knowing to the knower is what I would have you term the idea of good, and this you will deem to be the cause of science, and of truth in so far as the latter becomes the subject of knowledge; beautiful too, as are both truth and knowledge, you will be right in esteeming this other nature as more beautiful than either; and, as in the previous instance, light and sight may be truly said to be like the sun, and yet not to be the sun, so in this other sphere, science and truth may be deemed to be like the good, but not the good; the good has a place of honor yet higher.

What a wonder of beauty that must be, he said, which is the author of science and truth, and yet surpasses them in beauty; for you surely cannot mean to say that pleasure is the good?

God forbid, I replied; but may I ask you to consider the image in another point of view?

In what point of view?

You would say, would you not, that the sun is not only the author of visibility in all visible things, but of generation and nourishment and growth, though he himself is not generation?

Certainly.

In like manner the good may be said to be not only the author of knowledge to all things known, but of their being and essence, and yet the good is not essence, but far exceeds essence in dignity and power.

Glaucon said, with a ludicrous earnestness: By the light of heaven, how amazing!

Asserting the objective nature of beauty, truth, and goodness—as well as their interpenetration—Plato has just urged the primacy of the good as the source of both truth and beauty. The good is held to be the source of unity and harmony not only in human life, but in the universe as well. At this point (end of bk. VI, beginning bk. VII, the *Republic*, secs. 509–18, and 533; also, *q.v.* Plato D1) he discusses the divided line of truth, and the parable of the cave. These passages are to be found in the *Truth* volume of this series. We continue now with Plato's Seventh Letter which, using the circle as an example, argues for the objective status of all the forms, or essences, whether mathematical, physical, or valuational in nature.

Notice that while the circle is a "naturally flawless object," so are the "good and the beautiful and the just" as well as every quality of character. Notice, too, that upon the discovery of essence the mind is "flooded with light."

The Seventh Letter

(6) For everything that exists there are three classes of objects through which knowledge about it must come; the knowledge itself is a fourth; and we must put as a fifth entity the actual object of knowledge which is the true reality. We have then; first, a name; second, a description; third, an image; and fourth, a knowledge of the object. Take a particular case if you want to understand the meaning of what I have just said, then apply the theory to every object in the same way. There is something for instance called a circle, the name of which is the very word I just now uttered. In the second place there is a description of it which is composed of nouns and verbal expressions. For example the description of that which is named round and circumference and circle, would run as follows: the thing which has everywhere equal distances between its extremities and its center. In the third place there is the class of object which is drawn and erased and turned on the lathe and destroyed—processes which do not affect the real circle to which these other circles are all related, because it is different from them. In the fourth place there are knowledge and understanding and correct opinion concerning them; all of which we must set down as one thing more, that is found not in sounds nor in shapes of bodies, but in minds; whereby it evidently differs in its nature from the real circle and from the aforementioned three. Of all these four understanding approaches nearest in affinity and likeness to the fifth entity, while the others are more remote from it.

The same doctrine holds good in regard to shapes and surfaces, both straight and curved; in regard to the good and the beautiful and the just; in regard to all bodies artificial and natural; in regard to fire and water and the like; and in regard to every animal; and in regard to every quality of character; and in respect to all states active and passive. For if in the case of any of these a man does not somehow or other get hold of the first four, he will never gain a complete understanding of the fifth. Furthermore these four—[names, descriptions, bodily forms, concepts]—do as much to illustrate the particular quality of any object as they do to illustrate its essential reality because of the inadequacy of language. Hence no intelligent man will ever be so bold as to put into language those things which his reason has contemplated, especially not into a form that is unalterable,— which must be the case with what is expressed in written symbols.

⧬   ⧬   ⧬

Again, however, the meaning of what has just been said must be explained. Every circle that is drawn or turned on a lathe in actual operations, abounds in the opposite of the fifth entity, for it everywhere touches the straight,[1] while the real circle, I maintain, contains in itself neither much nor little of the opposite character. Names, I maintain, are in no case stable. Nothing prevents the things that are now called round from being called straight and the straight round; and those who have transposed the names and use them in the opposite way will find them no less stable than they are now. The same thing for that matter is true of a description, since it consists of nouns and of verbal expressions, so that in a description there is nowhere any sure ground that is sure enough. One might, however, speak forever about the inaccurate character of each of the four!

The important thing is that, as I said a little earlier, there are two things, the essential reality and the particular quality; and when the mind is in quest of knowledge not of the particular but of the essential, each of the four confronts the mind with the unsought (particular), whether in verbal or in bodily form. Each of the four makes the reality that is expressed in words or illustrated in objects liable to easy refutation by the evidence of the senses. The result of this is to make practically every man a prey to complete perplexity and uncertainty.

Now in cases where as a result of bad training we are not even accustomed to look for the real essence of anything but are satisfied to accept what confronts us in the phenomenal presentations, we are not rendered ridiculous by each other,—the examined by the examiners, who have the ability to handle the four with dexterity and to subject them to examination. In those cases, however, where we demand answers and proofs in regard to the fifth entity, anyone who pleases among those who have skill in confutation gains the victory and makes most of the audience think that the man who was first to speak or write or answer has no acquaintance with the matters of which he attempts to write or speak. Sometimes they are unaware that it is not the mind of the writer or speaker that fails in the test, but rather the character of the four,—since that is naturally defective. Consideration of all of the four in turn,—moving up and down from one to another,—barely begets knowledge of a naturally flawless object in a naturally flawless man. If a man is naturally defective,—and this is the natural state of most people's minds with regard to intelligence and to what are called morals,—while the objects he inspects are tainted with imperfection, not even Lynceus[2] could make such a one see.

To sum it all up in one word, natural intelligence and a good memory are equally powerless to aid the man who has not an inborn affinity with the subject. Without such endowments there is of course not the slightest possibility. Hence all who have no natural aptitude for and affinity with justice and all the other noble ideals, though in the study of other matters they may be both intelligent and retentive,—all those too who have affinity but are stupid and unretentive,—such will never any of them attain to an understanding of the most complete truth in regard to moral concepts. The study of virtue and vice must be accompanied by an inquiry into what is false and true of existence in general and must be carried on by constant practice throughout a long period, as I said in the beginning. Hardly after practising detailed comparisons of names and definitions and visual and other sense-perceptions, after scrutinizing them in benevolent disputation by the use of question and answer without jealousy, at last in a flash understanding of each blazes up, and the mind, as it exerts all its powers to the limit of human capacity, is flooded with light.

NOTES

1. Plato here refers to the fact that there is a straight line, which we call a tangent, related to every point on the circle.

2. Hero of legend, famed for sharp sight.

[*The Dialogues of Plato*, tr. B. Jowett, 2 vols. (New York: Random House, 1937; original copyright 1892). (1) *Philebus*, pp. 352–55. (2) *Ibid.*, pp. 395–403. (3) *Symposium*, pp. 330–31. (4) *Ibid.*, pp. 334–35. (5) *Republic*, bk. 6, pp. 768–70. (6) "Epistle VII," from *Thirteen Epistles of Plato*, tr. L. A. Post (England: Oxford at the Clarendon Press, 1925), pp. 95–99.]

5

Aristotle

384–322 B.C.E.

The Nicomachean Ethics

ON HAPPINESS

Although Aristotle's approach to the good in his *Nicomachean Ethics* stressed happiness (*eudaimonia*), the moral virtues come strongly into play. He presented a virtues approach to ethics, which involved the finding of a mean between extremes. Some of the qualities emerging from this approach would be instances of value but not ethics in the ordinary way of speaking, for example, liberality and pride. The moral virtues in usage, both narrow and broad, belong to the analysis of value; and Aristotle's support of happiness as final value must have been a factor in its wide acceptance as the final value of human life.

Also see Study Guide (4b5), pp. 32–33.

(1) *That at which all things aim.* Bk. 1, ch. 1.

Every art and every scientific inquiry, and similarly every action and purpose, may be said to aim at some good. Hence the good has been well defined as that at which all things aim. But it is clear that there is a difference in the ends; for the ends are sometimes activities, and sometimes results beyond the mere activities. Also, where there are certain ends beyond the actions, the results are naturally superior to the activities.

As there are various actions, arts, and sciences, it follows that the ends are also various. Thus health is the end of medicine, a vessel of ship-building, victory of strategy, and wealth of domestic economy. It often happens that there are a number of such arts or sciences which fall under a single faculty, as the art of making bridles, and all such other arts as make the instruments of horsemanship, under horsemanship, and this again as well as every military action under strategy, and in the same way other arts or sciences under other faculties. But in all these cases the ends of the architectonic arts or sciences, whatever they may be, are more desirable than those of the subordinate arts or sciences, as it is for the sake of the former that the latter are themselves sought after. It makes no difference to the argument whether the activities themselves are the ends of the actions, or something else beyond the activities as in the above-mentioned sciences.

If it is true that in the sphere of action there is an end which we wish for its own sake, and for the sake of which we wish everything else, and that we do not desire all things for the sake of something else (for, if that is so, the process will go on *ad infinitum*, and our desire will be idle and futile) it is clear that this will be the good or the supreme good. Does it not follow then that the knowledge of this supreme good is of great importance for the conduct of life, and that, *if we know it*, we shall be like archers who have a mark at which to aim, we shall have a better chance of attaining what we want? But, if this is the case, we must endeavor to comprehend, at least in outline, its nature, and the science or faculty to which it belongs.

It would seem that this is the most authoritative or architectonic science or faculty, and such is evidently the political; for it is the political science or faculty which determines what sciences are necessary in states, and what kind of sciences should be learnt, and how far they should be learnt by particular people. We perceive too that the faculties which are held in the highest esteem, *e.g.* strategy, domestic economy, and rhetoric, are subordinate to it. But as it makes use of the other practical sciences, and also legislates upon the things to be done and the things to be left undone, it follows that its end will comprehend the ends of all the other sciences, and will therefore be the true good of mankind. For although the good of an individual is identical with the good of a state, yet the good of the state, whether in attainment or in preservation, is evidently greater and more perfect. For while in an individual by himself it is something to be thankful for, it is nobler and more divine in a nation or state.

These then are the objects at which the present inquiry aims, and it is in a sense political inquiry.

(2) Bk. 1, ch. 2. But having said so much by way of preface as to the students of political science, the spirit in which it should be studied, and the object which we set before ourselves, let us resume our argument as follows:

As every knowledge and moral purpose aspires to some good, what is in our view the good at which the political science aims, and what is the highest of all practical goods? As to its name there is, I may say, a general agreement. The masses and the cultured classes agree in calling it happiness, and conceive that "to live well" or "to do well" is the same thing as "to be happy." But as to the nature of happiness they do not agree, nor do the masses give the same account of it as the philosophers. The former define it as something visible and palpable, *e.g.* pleasure, wealth, or honor; different people give different definitions of it, and often the same person gives different definitions at different times; for when a person has been ill, it is health, when he is poor, it is wealth, and, if he is conscious of his own ignorance, he envies people who use grand language above his own comprehension. Some philosophers[1] on the other hand have held that, besides these various goods, there is an absolute good which is the cause of goodness in them all. It would perhaps be a waste of time to examine all these opinions, it will be enough to examine such as are most popular or as seem to be more or less reasonable.

But we must not fail to observe the distinction between the reasonings which proceed from first principles and the reasonings which lead up to first principles. For Plato[2] was right in raising the difficult question whether the *true* way was from first principles or to first principles, as in the racecourse from the judges to the goal, or *vice versa*. We must begin then with such facts as are known. But facts may be known in two ways, *i.e.* either relatively to ourselves or absolutely. It is probable then that *we* must begin with such facts as are known to us, *i.e. relatively*. It is necessary therefore, if a person is to be a competent student of what is noble and just and of politics in general, that he should have received a good moral training. For the fact that a thing is so is a first principle or starting-point,[3] and, if the fact is sufficiently clear, it will not be necessary to go on to ask the reason of it. But a person who has received a good moral training either possesses first principles or will have no difficulty in acquiring them.

(3) Bk. 1, ch. 3. . . . it seems not unreasonable that people should derive their conception of the good or of happiness from men's lives. Thus ordinary or vulgar people conceive it to be pleasure, and accordingly approve a life of enjoyment. For there are practically three prominent lives, the sensual, the political, and, thirdly, the speculative. Now the mass of men present an absolutely slavish appearance, as choosing the life of brute beasts, but they meet with consideration because so many persons in authority share the tastes of Sardanapalus.[4] Cultivated and practical people, on the other hand, identify happiness with honor, as honor is the general end of political life. But this appears too superficial for our present purpose; for

honor seems to depend more upon the people who pay it than upon the person to whom it is paid, and we have an intuitive feeling that the good is something which is proper to a man himself and cannot easily be taken away from him. It seems too that the reason why men seek honor is that they may be confident of their own goodness. Accordingly they seek it at the hands of the wise and of those who know them well, and they seek it on the ground of virtue; hence it is clear that in their judgment at any rate virtue is superior to honor. It would perhaps be right then to look upon virtue rather than honor as being the end of the political life. Yet virtue again, it appears, lacks completeness; for it seems that a man may possess virtue and yet be asleep or inactive throughout life, and, not only so but he may experience the greatest calamities and misfortunes. But nobody would call such a life a life of happiness, unless he were maintaining a paradox. It is not necessary to dwell further on this subject, as it is sufficiently discussed in the popular philosophical treatises.[5] The third life is the speculative which we will investigate hereafter.[6]

The life of money-making is in a sense a life of constraint, and it is clear that wealth is not the good of which we are in quest; for it is useful in part as a means of something else. It would be a more reasonable view therefore that the things mentioned before, viz. *sensual pleasure, honor and virtue*, are ends that that wealth is [for], as they are things which are desired on their own account. Yet these too are apparently not ends, although much argument has been employed[7] to show that they are.

(4) Bk. 1, chs. 4–10. However these are questions which may be deferred to another occasion; but there is an objection to my arguments which suggests itself, viz. that the *Platonic* theory does not apply to every good, that the things which in themselves are sought after and welcomed are reckoned as one species and the things which tend to produce or in any sense preserve these or to prevent their opposites are reckoned as goods in a secondary sense as being means to these. It is clear then that there will be two kinds of goods, some being absolute goods, and others secondary. Let us then separate goods which are merely serviceable from absolute goods and consider if they are conceived as falling under a single idea. But what kind of things is it that may be defined as absolute goods? Will it be all such as are sought after independently of their consequences, *e.g.* wisdom, sight, and certain pleasures and honors? For granting that we seek after these sometimes as means to something else, still we may define them as absolute goods. Or is none of these things an absolute good, nor anything else except the idea? But then the type *or idea* will be purposeless, *i.e. it will*

not comprise any particulars. If, on the other hand, these things too are absolute goods, the conception of the good will necessarily appear the same in them all, as the conception of whiteness appears the same in snow and in white lead. But the conception of honor, wisdom and pleasure, are distinct and different in respect of goodness. "Good" then is not a common term falling under one idea. But in what sense is the term used? For it does not seem to be an accidental homonymy.[8] Is it because all goods issue from one source or all tend to one end; or is it rather a case of analogy? for as the sight is to the body, so is the mind to the soul, *i.e. the mind may be called the eye of the soul, and so on.* But it will perhaps be well to leave the subject for the present, as an exact discussion of it would belong rather to a different branch of philosophy. But the same is true of the idea; for even if there is some one good which is predicated of all these things, or some abstract and absolute good, it will plainly not be such as a man finds practicable and attainable, and therefore will not be such a good as we are in search of. It will possibly be held, however, that it is worthwhile to apprehend this *universal good,* as having a relation to the goods which are attainable and practicable; for if we have this as a model, we shall be better able to know the things which are good relatively to ourselves, and, knowing them, to acquire them. Now although there is a certain plausibility in this theory, it seems not to harmonize with scientific experience; for while all sciences aim at a certain good and seek to supply a deficiency, they omit the knowledge of the universal good. Yet it is not reasonable to suppose that what would be so extremely helpful is ignored, and not sought at all by artists generally. But it is difficult to see what benefit a cobbler or carpenter will get in reference to his art by knowing the absolute good, or how the contemplation of the absolute idea will make a person a better physician or general. For it appears that a physician does not regard health abstractedly, but regards the health of man or rather perhaps of a particular man, as he gives his medicine to individuals.

But leaving this subject for the present let us revert to the good of which we are in quest and consider what its nature may be. For it is clearly different in different actions or arts; it is one thing in medicine, another in strategy, and so on. What then is the good in each of these instances? It is presumably that for the sake of which all else is done. This in medicine is health, in strategy, victory, in domestic architecture, a house, and so on. But in every action and purpose it is the end, as it is for the sake of the end that people all do everything else. If then there is a certain end of all action, it will be to this which is the practicable good, and if there are several such ends it will be these.

Our argument has arrived by a different path at the same conclusion as before; but we must endeavor to elucidate it still further. As it appears that there are more ends than one and some of these, *e.g.* wealth, flutes, and instruments generally we desire as means to something else, it is evident that they are not all final ends. But the highest good is clearly something final. Hence if there is only one final end, this will be the object of which we are in search, and if there are more than one, it will be the most final of them. We speak of that which is sought after for its own sake as more final than that which is sought after as a means to something else; we speak of that which is never desired as a means to something else as more final than the beings which are desired both in themselves and as means to something else; and we speak of a thing as absolutely final, if it is always desired in itself and never as a means to something else.

It seems that happiness preeminently answers to this description, as we always desire happiness for its own sake and never as a means to something else, whereas we desire honor, pleasure, intellect, and every virtue, partly for their own sakes (for we should desire them independently of what might result from them) but partly also as being means to happiness, because we suppose they will prove the instruments of happiness. Happiness, on the other hand, nobody desires for the sake of these things, nor indeed as a means to anything else at all.

We come to the same conclusion if we start from the consideration of self-sufficiency, if it may be assumed that the final good is self-sufficient. But when we speak of self-sufficiency, we do not mean that a person leads a solitary life all by himself, but that he has parents, children, wife, and friends, and fellow-citizens in general, as man is naturally a social being. But here it is necessary to prescribe some limit; for if the circle be extended so as to include parents, descendants, and friends' friends, it will go on indefinitely. Leaving this point, however, for future investigation, we define the self-sufficient as that which, taken by itself, makes life desirable, and wholly free from want, and this is our conception of happiness.

Again, we conceive happiness to be the most desirable of all things, and that not merely as one among other good things. If it were one among other good things, the addition of the smallest good would increase its desirableness; for the accession makes a superiority of goods, and the greater of two goods is always the more desirable. It appears then that happiness is something final and self-sufficient, being the end of all action.

Perhaps, however, it seems a truth which is generally admitted, that happiness is the supreme good; what is wanted is to define its nature a little more clearly. The best way of arriving at such a definition will probably be to ascertain the function of Man. For, as with a flute-player, a statuary, or any artisan, or in fact anybody who has a definite function and action, his good-ness, or excellence seems to lie in his function, so it would seem to be with Man, if indeed he has a definite function. Can it be said then that, while a carpenter and a cobbler have definite functions and actions, Man, unlike them, is naturally functionless? The reasonable view is that, as the eye, the hand, the foot, and similarly each several part of the body has a definite function, so Man may be regarded as having a definite function apart from all these. What then, can this function be? It is not life; for life is apparently something which man shares with the plants; and it is something peculiar to him that we are looking for. We must exclude therefore the life of nutrition and increase. There is next what may be called the life of sensation. But this too, is apparently shared by Man with horses, cattle, and all other animals. There remains what I may call the practical life of the rational part of *Man's being.* But the rational part is twofold; it is rational partly in the sense of being obedient to reason, and partly in the sense of possessing reason and intelli-gence. The practical life too may be conceived of in two ways,[9] *viz., either as a moral state, or as a moral activity.* but we must understand by it the life of activity, as this seems to be the truer form of the conception.

The function of Man then is an activity of soul in accordance with reason, or not independently of reason. Again the functions of a person of a certain kind, and of such a person who is good of his kind *e.g.* of a harpist and a good harpist, are in our view generically the same, and this view is true of people of all kinds without exception, the superior excellence being only an addition to the function; for it is the function of a harpist to play the harp, and of a good harpist to play the harp well. This being so, if we define the function of Man as a kind of life, and this life as an activity of soul, or a course of action in conformity with reason, if the function of a good man is such activity or action of a good and noble kind, and if everything is suc-cessfully performed when it is performed in accordance with its proper excellence, it follows that the good of Man is an activity of soul in accor-dance with virtue or, if there are more virtues than one, in accordance with the best and most complete virtue. But it is necessary to add the words "in a complete life." For as one swallow or one day does not make a spring, so one day or a short time does not make a fortunate or happy man.

This may be taken as a sufficiently accurate sketch of the good; for it is right, I think, to draw the outlines first and afterwards to fill in the details. It would seem that anybody can carry on and complete what has been satisfactorily sketched in outline, and that time is a good inventor or cooperator in so doing. This is the way in which the arts have made their advances, as anybody can supply a deficiency.

But bearing in mind what has been already said, we must not look for the same degree of accuracy in all subjects; we must be content in each class of subjects with accuracy of such a kind as the subject-matter allows, and to such an extent as is proper to the inquiry. For while a carpenter and a geometrician both want to find a right angle, they do not want to find it in the same sense; the one wants only such an approximation to it as will serve his practical purpose, the other, as being concerned with truth, wants to know its nature or character. We must follow the same course in other subjects, or we shall sacrifice the main points to such as are subordinate. Again, we must not insist with equal emphasis in all subjects upon ascertaining the reason of things. We must sometimes *e.g.* in dealing with first principles be content with the proper evidence of a fact; the fact itself is a first point or principle. But there are various ways of discovering first principles; some are discovered by induction, others by perception, others by what may be called habituation, and so on. We must try to apprehend them all in the natural *or appropriate* way, and must take pains to define them satisfactorily, as they have a vital influence upon all that follows from them. For it seems that the first principle or beginning is more than half the whole, and is the means of arriving at a clear conception of many points which are under investigation.

In considering the first principle we must pay regard not only to the conclusion and the premisses of our argument, but also to such views as are popularly held about it. For while all experience harmonizes with the truth, it is never long before truth clashes with falsehood.

Goods have been divided into three classes, *viz.* external goods as they are called, goods of the soul and goods of the body. Of these three classes we consider the goods of the soul to be goods in the strictest or most literal sense. But it is to the soul that we ascribe psychical actions and activities. Thus our definition is a good one, at least according to this theory, which is not only ancient but is accepted by students of philosophy at the present time. It is right too, inasmuch as certain actions and activities are said to be the end; for thus it appears that the end is some good of the soul and not an external good. It is in harmony with this definition that the happy man should live well and do well, as happiness, it has been said, is in fact a kind of living and doing well.

It appears too that the requisite characteristics of happiness are all contained in the definition; for some people hold that happiness is virtue, others that it is prudence,[10] others that it is wisdom of some kind, others that it is these things or one of them conjoined with pleasure or not dissociated from pleasure, others again include external prosperity. Some of these views are held by many ancient thinkers, others by a few thinkers of high repute. It is probable that neither side is altogether wrong, they are both right.

Now the definition is in harmony with the view of those who hold that happiness is virtue or excellence of some sort; for activity in accordance with virtue implies virtue. But it would seem that there is a considerable difference between taking the supreme good to consist in acquisition or in use, in a moral state or in an activity. For a moral state, although it exists, may produce nothing good, *e.g.* if a person is asleep, or has in any other way become inactive. But this cannot be the case with an activity, as activity implies action and good action. As in the Olympian games it is not the most beautiful and strongest persons who receive the crown but they who actually enter the lists as combatants—for it is some of these who become victors—so it is they who act rightly that attain to what is noble and good in life. Again, their life is pleasant in itself. For pleasure is a psychical fact, and whatever a man is said to be fond of is pleasant to him, *e.g.* a horse to one who is fond of horses, a spectacle to one who is fond of spectacles, and similarly just actions to a lover of justice, and virtuous actions in general to a lover of virtue. Now most men find a sense of discord in their pleasures, because their pleasures are not such as are naturally pleasant. But to the lovers of nobleness natural pleasures are pleasant. It is actions in accordance with virtue that are naturally pleasant. Such actions then are pleasant both relatively to these persons and in themselves. Nor does their life need that pleasure should be attached to it as a sort of amulet; it possesses pleasure in itself. For it may be added that a person is not good, if he does not take delight in noble actions, as nobody would call a person just if he did not take delight in just actions or liberal if he did not take delight in liberal actions and so on. But if this is so, it follows that actions in accordance with virtue are pleasant in themselves. But they are also good and noble, and good and noble in the highest degree, if the judgment of the virtuous man upon them is right, his judgment being such as we have described. Happiness then is the best and noblest and pleasantest thing in the world, nor is there any such distinction between goodness, nobleness, and pleasure as the epigram at Delos suggests:

> "Justice is noblest, Health is best,
> To gain one's end is pleasantest."

For these are all essential characteristics of the best activities, and we hold that happiness consists in these or in one and the noblest of these. Still it is clear that happiness requires the addition of external goods, as we said; for it is impossible, or at least difficult for a person to do what is noble unless he is furnished with external means. For there are many things which can only be done through the instrumentality of friends or wealth or political power, and there are some things, the lack of which must mar felicity, *e.g.* noble birth, a prosperous family, and personal beauty. For a person is incapable of happiness if he is absolutely ugly in appearance, or low born, or solitary and childless, and perhaps still more so, if he has exceedingly bad children or friends, or has had good children or friends and has lost them by death. As we said, then, it seems that prosperity of this kind is an indispensable addition to virtue. It is for this reason that some persons identify good fortune, and others virtue, with happiness.

The question is consequently raised whether happiness is something that can be learnt or acquired by habit or discipline of any other kind, or whether it comes by some divine dispensation or even by chance.

Now if there is anything in the world that is a gift of the Gods to men, it is reasonable to suppose that happiness is a divine gift, especially as it is the best of human things. This however is perhaps a point which is more appropriate to another investigation than the present. But even if happiness is not sent by the Gods but is the result of virtue and of learning or discipline [of] some kind, it is apparently one of the most divine things in the world; for it would appear that that which is the prize and end of virtue is the supreme good and is in its nature divine and blessed. It will also be widely extended; for it will be capable of being produced in all persons, except such as are morally deformed, by a process of study or care. And if it is better that happiness should be produced in this way than by chance, it may reasonably be supposed that it is so produced as the order of things is the best possible in Nature and so too in art, and in causation generally, and most of all in the highest kind of causation. But it would be altogether inconsistent to leave what is greatest and noblest to chance. But the definition of *happiness* itself helps to clear up the question; for happiness has been defined as a certain kind of activity of the soul in accordance with virtue. Of the other goods, *i.e. of goods besides those of the soul*, such are necessary as antecedent conditions of happiness, others are in their nature co-operative and serviceable as instruments of happiness.

The conclusion at which we have arrived agrees with our original position. For we laid it down that the end of political science is the supreme good; and political science is concerned with nothing so much as with producing a certain character in the citizens or in other words with making them good, and capable of performing noble actions. It is reasonable then not to speak of an ox, or a horse, or any other animal as happy; for none of them is capable of participating in activity as so defined. For the same reason no child can be happy, as the age of a child makes it impossible for him to display this activity at present, and if a child is ever said to be happy, the ground of the felicitation is his promise, *rather than his actual performance.*

For happiness demands, as we said, a complete virtue and a complete life. For there are all sorts of changes and chances in life, and it is possible that the most prosperous of men will, in his old age, fall into extreme calamities as is told of Priam in the heroic legends. But if a person has experienced such chances, and has died a miserable death, nobody calls him happy.

Is it the case then that nobody in the world may be called happy so long as he is alive? Must we adopt Solon's[11] rule of looking to the end? and, if we follow Solon, can it be said that a man is really happy after his death? Surely such a view is wholly absurd, especially for us who define happiness as a species of activity. But if we do not speak of one who is dead as happy, and if Solon's meaning is not this but rather that it is only when a man is dead that it is safe to call him fortunate as being exempt at last from evils and calamities, this again is a view which is open to some objection. For it seems that one who is dead is capable of being affected both by good and by evil in the same way as one who is living but unconscious, *e.g.* by honors and dishonors and by the successes or reverses of his children and his descendants generally. But here again a difficulty occurs. For if a person has lived a fortunate life up to old age, and has died a fortunate death, it is possible that he may experience many vicissitudes of fortune in the persons of his descendants. Some of them may be good and may enjoy such a life as they deserve; others may be bad and may have a bad life.

It is clear, too, that descendants may stand in all sorts of different degrees of relationship to their ancestor. It would be an extraordinary result, if the dead man were to share the vicissitudes of their fortune and to become happy at one time and miserable at another, *as they became either happy or miserable.* But it would be equally extraordinary if the future descendants should not affect their parents at all or for a certain time. It will be best, however, to revert to the difficulty which was raised before, as it will perhaps afford an answer to the present question. If it is right to look to the end, and when the end comes to felicitate a person not as being fortunate but as having been so before, surely it is an extraordinary thing that at the time when he is happy we should not speak the truth about him, because we do not wish to call the living happy in view of the vicissitudes to which they are liable and because we have formed a conception of happiness as something that is permanent and exempt from the possibility of change and because the same persons are liable to many revolutions of fortune. For it is clear that, if we follow the changes of fortune, we shall often call the same person happy at one time, and miserable at another, representing the happy man as "a sort of chameleon without any stability of position." It cannot be right to follow the changes of fortune. It is not upon these that good or evil depends; they are necessary accessories of human life, as we said; but it is a man's activities in accordance with virtue that constitute his happiness and the opposite activities that constitute his misery. The difficulty which has now been discussed is itself a witness that this is the true view. For there is no human function so constant as the activities in accordance with virtue; they seem to be more permanent than the sciences themselves. Among these activities, too, it is the most honorable which are the most permanent, as it is in them that the life of the fortunate chiefly and most continuously consists. For this is apparently the reason why such activities are not liable to be forgotten.[12]

The element of permanency which is required will be found in the happy man, and he will preserve his character throughout life; for he will constantly or in a preeminent degree pursue such actions and speculations as accord with virtue; nor is there anybody who will bear the chances of life so nobly, with such a perfect and complete harmony, as he who is truly good and "foursquare without a flaw."[13] Now the events of chance are numerous and of different magnitudes. It is clear then that small incidents of good fortune, or the reverse, do not turn the scale of life, but that such incidents as are great and numerous augment the felicity of life, if they are fortunate, as they tend naturally to embellish it and the use of them is noble and virtuous, and on the other hand, if they are of a contrary character, mar and mutilate its felicity by causing pains and hindrances to various activities. Still even in these circumstances nobility shines out, when a person bears the weight of accumulated misfortunes with calmness, not from insensibility but from innate dignity and magnanimity.

But if it is the activities which determine the life, as we said, nobody who is fortunate can become miserable; for he will never do what is hateful and mean. For our conception of the truly good and sensible man is that he bears all the chances of life with decorum and always does what is noblest in the circumstances, as a good general uses the forces at his command to the best advantage in war, a good cobbler makes the best shoe with the leather that is given him, and so on through the whole series of the arts. If this is so, it follows that the happy man can never become miserable; I do not say that he will be fortunate, if he meets such chances of life as Priam.[14] Yet he will not be variable or liable to frequent change, as he will not be moved from his happiness easily or by ordinary misfortunes but only by such misfortunes as are great and numerous, and after them it will not be soon that he will regain his happiness but, if he regains it at all, it will be only in a long and complete period of time and after attaining in it to great and noble results.

We may safely then define a happy man as one whose activity accords with perfect virtue and who is adequately furnished with external goods, not for a casual period of time but for a complete or perfect lifetime. But perhaps we ought to add, that he will always live so, and will die as he lives; for it is not given us to foresee the future, but we take happiness to be an end, and to be altogether perfect and complete, and, this being so, we shall call people fortunate during their lifetime, if they possess and will possess these characteristics, but fortunate only so far as men may be fortunate.

(5) Bk. 1, ch. 13. Inasmuch as happiness is an activity of soul in accordance with complete or perfect virtue, it is necessary to consider virtue, as this will perhaps be the best way of studying happiness.

It appears that virtue is the object upon which the true statesman has expended the largest amount of trouble, as it is his wish to make the citizens virtuous and obedient to the laws. We have instances of such statesmen in the legislators of Crete and Lacedaemon and such other legislators as have resembled them. But if this inquiry is proper to political science, it will clearly accord with our original purpose to pursue it. But it is clear that it is human virtue which we have to consider; for the good of which we are in search is, as we said, human good, and the happiness, human happiness. By human virtue or excellence we mean not that of the body, but that of the soul, and by happiness we mean an activity of the soul.

If this is so, it is clearly necessary for statesmen to have some knowledge of the nature of the soul in the same way as it is necessary for one who is to treat the eye or any part of the body, to have some knowledge of it, and all the more as political science is better and more honorable than medical science. Clever doctors take a great deal of trouble to understand the body, and similarly the statesman must make a study of the soul. But he must study it with a view to his particular object and so far only as his object requires; for to elaborate the study of it further would, I think, be to aggravate unduly the labor of our present undertaking.

(6) *Virtue requires the mean between extremes.* Bk 2, ch. 1.

In Bk. 2 Aristotle distinguishes between intellectual and moral virtue. Intellectual virtue includes the theoretical and practical reason. Moral virtue concerns that part of the practical reason having to do with passions and actions which exemplify a mean between extremes. In this and the following sections moral virtue is examined.

Virtue or excellence being twofold, partly intellectual and partly moral, intellectual virtue is both originated and fostered mainly by teaching; it therefore demands experience and time. Moral[15] virtue on the other hand is the outcome of habit, and accordingly its name (ἠθικὴ ἀρετή) is derived by a slight deflexion from habit (ἔθος).[16] From this fact it is clear that no moral virtue is implanted in us by nature; a law of nature cannot be altered by habituation. Thus a stone naturally tends to fall downwards, and it cannot be habituated or trained to rise upwards, even if we were to habituate it by throwing it upwards ten thousand times; nor again can fire be trained to sink downwards, nor anything else that follows one natural law be habituated or trained to follow another. It is neither by nature then nor in defiance of nature that virtues are implanted in us. Nature gives us the capacity of receiving them, and that capacity is perfected by habit.

(7) *Application to individual cases.* Bk. II, chs. 6, 7, 8.

Notice in what follows how "courage," "liberty," "proper pride," "good-temperedness," "truthfulness," "ready wittedness," and "modesty," all fit the analysis of being in a mean state between extremes.

Book 2, ch. 6. Every science then performs its function well, if it regards the mean and refers the works which it produces to the mean. This is the reason why it is usually said of successful works that it is impossible to take anything from them or to add anything to them, which implies that excess or deficiency is fatal to excellence but that the mean state ensures it. Good artists too, as we say, have an eye to the mean in their works. But virtue, like Nature herself, is more accurate and better than any art; virtue therefore, will aim at the mean;—I speak of moral virtue, as it is moral virtue which is concerned with emotions and actions, and it is these which admit of excess and deficiency and the mean. Thus it is possible to go too far, or not to go far enough, in respect of fear, courage, desire, anger, pity, and pleasure and pain generally, and the excess and the deficiency are alike wrong; but to experience these emotions at the right times and on the right occasions and towards the right persons and for the right causes and in the right manner is the mean or the supreme good, which is characteristic of virtue. Similarly there may be excess, deficiency, or the mean, in regard to actions. But virtue is concerned with emotions and actions, and here excess is an error and deficiency a fault, whereas the mean is successful and laudable, and success and merit are both characteristics of virtue.

It appears then that virtue is a mean state, so far at least as it aims at the mean.

Again, there are many different ways of going wrong; for evil is in its nature infinite, to use the Pythagorean[17] figure, but good is finite. But there is only one possible way of going right. Accordingly the former is easy and the latter difficult; it is easy to miss the mark but difficult to hit it. This again is a reason why excess and deficiency are characteristics of vice and the mean state a characteristic of virtue.

"For good is simple, evil manifold."[18]

Virtue then is a state of deliberate moral purpose consisting in a mean that is relative to ourselves, the mean being determined by reason, or as a prudent man would determine it.

It is a mean state *firstly as lying* between two vices, the vice of excess on the one hand, and the vice of deficiency on the other, and secondly because, whereas the vices either fall short of or go beyond what is proper in the emotions and actions, virtue not only discovers but embraces the mean.

Accordingly, virtue, if regarded in its essence or theoretical conception, is a mean state, but, if regarded from the point of view of the highest good, or of excellence, it is an extreme.

But it is not every action or every emotion that admits of a mean state. There are some whose very name implies wickedness, as *e.g.* malice, shamelessness, and envy, among emotions, or adultery, theft, and murder, among actions. All these, and others like them, are censured as being intrinsically wicked, not merely the excesses or deficiencies of them. It is never possible then to be right in respect of them; they are always sinful. Right or wrong in such actions as adultery does not depend on our committing them with the right person, at the right time or in the right manner; on the contrary it is sinful to do anything of the kind at all. It would be equally wrong then to suppose that there can be a mean state or an excess or deficiency in unjust, cowardly or licentious conduct; for, if it were so, there would be a mean state of an excess or of a deficiency, an excess of an excess and a deficiency of a deficiency. But as in temperance and courage there can be no excess or deficiency because the mean is, in a sense, an extreme, so too in these cases there cannot be a mean or an excess or deficiency, but, however the acts may be done, they are wrong. For it is a general rule that an excess or deficiency does not admit of a mean state, nor a mean state of an excess or deficiency.

Ch. 7. But it is not enough to lay down this as a general rule; it is necessary to apply it to particular cases, as in reasonings upon actions general statements, although they are broader, are less exact than particular statements. For all action refers to particulars, and it is essential that our theories should harmonize with the particular cases to which they apply.

We must take particular virtues then from the catalogue *of virtues.*

In regard to feelings of fear and confidence, courage is a mean state. On the side of excess, he whose fearlessness is excessive has no name, as often happens, but he whose confidence is excessive is foolhardy, while he whose timidity is excessive and whose confidence is deficient is a coward.

In respect of pleasures and pains, although not indeed of all pleasures and pains, and to a less extent in respect of pains than of pleasures, the mean state is temperance, the excess is licentiousness. We never find people who are deficient in regard to pleasures; accordingly such people again have not received a name, but we may call them insensible.

As regards the giving and taking of money, the mean state is liberality, the excess and deficiency are prodigality and illiberality. Here the excess and deficiency take opposite forms; for while the prodigal man is excessive in spending and deficient in taking, the illiberal man is excessive in taking and deficient in spending.

(For the present we are giving only a rough and summary account *of the virtues*, and that is sufficient for our purpose; we will hereafter determine their character more exactly.)

In respect of money there are other dispositions as well. There is the mean state which is magnificence; for the magnificent man, as having to do with large sums of money, differs from the liberal man who has to do only with small sums; and the excess *corresponding to it* is bad taste or vulgarity, the deficiency is meanness. These are different from the excess and deficiency of liberality; what the difference is will be explained hereafter.

In respect of honor and dishonor the mean state is high-mindedness, the excess is what is called vanity, the deficiency little-mindedness. Corresponding to liberality, which, as we said, differs from magnificence as having to do *not with great but* with small sums of money, there is a moral state which has to do with petty honor and is related to high-mindedness which has to do with great honor; for it is possible to aspire to honor in the right way, or in a way which is excessive or insufficient, and if a person's aspirations are excessive, he is called ambitious, if they are deficient, he is called unambitious, while if they are between the two, he has no name. The dispositions too are nameless, except that the disposition of the ambitious person is called ambition. The consequence is that the extremes lay claim to the mean or intermediate place. We ourselves speak of one who observes the mean sometimes as ambitious, and at other times as unambitious; we sometimes praise an ambitious, and at other times an unambitious person. The reason for our doing so will be stated in due course, but let us now discuss the other virtues in accordance with the method which we have followed hitherto.

Anger, like other emotions, has its excess, its deficiency, and its mean state. It may be said that they have no names, but as we call one who observes the mean gentle, we will call the mean state gentleness. Among the extremes, if a person errs on the side of excess, he may be called passionate and his vice passionateness, if on that of deficiency, he may be called impassive and his deficiency impassivity.

There are also three other mean states with a certain resemblance to each other, and yet with a difference. For while they are all concerned with intercourse in speech and action, they are different in that one of them is concerned with truth in such intercourse, and the others with pleasantness, one with pleasantness in amusement and the other with pleasantness in the various circumstances of life. We must therefore discuss these states in order to make it clear that in all cases it is the mean state which is an object of praise, and the extremes are neither right nor laudable but censurable. It is true that these mean and extreme states are generally nameless, but we must do our best here as elsewhere to give them a name, so that our argument may be clear and easy to follow.

In the matter of truth then, he who observes the mean may be called truthful, and the mean state truthfulness. Pretense, if it takes the form of exaggeration, is boastfulness, and one who is guilty of pretense is a boaster; but if it takes the form of depreciation it is irony, and he who is guilty of it is ironical.

As regards pleasantness in amusement, he who observes the mean is witty, and his disposition wittiness; the excess is buffoonery, and he who is guilty of it a buffoon, whereas he who is deficient in wit may be called a boor and his moral state boorishness.

As to the other kind of pleasantness, *viz.* pleasantness in life, he who is pleasant in a proper way is friendly, and his mean state friendliness; but he who goes too far, if he has no ulterior object in view, is obsequious, while if his object is self-interest, he is a flatterer, and he who does not go far enough and always makes himself unpleasant is a quarrelsome and morose sort of person.

There are also mean states in the emotions[19] and in the expression of the emotions. For although modesty is not a virtue, yet a modest person is praised as if he were virtuous; for here too one person is said to observe the mean and another to exceed it, as *e.g.* the bashful man who is never anything but modest, whereas a person who has insufficient modesty or no modesty at all is called shameless, and one who observes the mean modest.

Righteous indignation, again, is a mean state between envy and malice. They are all concerned with the pain and pleasure which we feel at the fortunes of our neighbors. A person who is righteously indignant is pained at the prosperity of the undeserving; but the envious person goes further and is pained at anybody's prosperity, and the malicious person is so far from being pained that he actually rejoices at misfortunes.

We shall have another opportunity[20] however of discussing these matters. But in regard to justice as the word is used in various senses, we will afterwards[21] define those senses and explain how each of them is a mean state. And we will follow the same course with the intellectual virtues.[22]

There are then three dispositions, two being vices, viz. one the vice of excess and the other that of deficiency, and one virtue, which is the mean state between them; and they are all in a sense mutually opposed. For the extremes are opposed both to the mean and to each other, and the mean is opposed to the extremes. For as the equal if compared with the less is greater but if compared with the greater is less, so the mean states, whether in the emotions or in actions, if compared with the deficiencies, are excessive, but if compared with the excesses are deficient. Thus the courageous man appears foolhardy as compared with the coward, but cowardly as compared with the foolhardy. Similarly, the temperate man appears licentious as compared with the insensible but insensible as compared with the licentious, and the liberal man appears prodigal as compared with the illiberal, but illiberal as compared with the prodigal. The result is that the extremes mutually repel and reject the mean; the coward calls the courageous man foolhardy, but the foolhardy man calls him cowardly, and so on in the other cases.

But while there is this mutual opposition between the extremes and the mean, there is greater opposition between the two extremes than between either extreme and the mean; for they are further removed from each other than from the mean, as the great from the small and the small from the great than both from the equal. Again, while some extremes exhibit more or less similarity to the mean, as foolhardiness to courage and prodigality to liberality, there is the greatest possible dissimilarity between the extremes. But things which are furthest removed from each other are defined to be opposites; hence the further things are removed, the greater is the opposition between them.

It is in some cases the deficiency and in others the excess which is the more opposed to the mean. Thus it is not foolhardiness the excess, but cowardice the deficiency which is the more opposed to courage, nor is it insensibility the deficiency, but licentiousness the excess which is the more opposed to temperance. There are two reasons why this should be so. One lies in the nature of the thing itself; for as one of the two extremes is the nearer and more similar to the mean, it is not this extreme, but its opposite, that we chiefly set against the mean. For instance, as it appears that foolhardiness is more similar and nearer to courage than cowardice, it is cowardice that we chiefly set against courage; for things which are further removed from the mean seem to be more opposite to it. This being one reason which lies in the nature of the thing itself, there is a second which lies in our own nature. It is the things to which we ourselves are naturally more inclined that appear more opposed to the mean. Thus we are ourselves naturally more inclined to pleasures *than to their opposites*, and are more prone therefore to licentiousness than to decorum. Accordingly we speak of those things, in which we are more likely to run to great lengths, as being more opposed to the mean. Hence it follows that licentiousness which is an excess is more opposed to temperance than insensibility.

It has now been sufficiently shown that moral virtue is a mean state, and in what sense it is a mean state; it is a mean state as lying between two vices, a vice of excess on the one side and a vice of deficiency on the other, and as aiming at the mean in the emotions and actions.

That is the reason why it is so hard to be virtuous; for it is always hard work to find the mean in anything, *e.g.* it is not everybody, but only a man of science, who can find the mean or center[23] of a circle. So too anybody can get angry—that is an easy matter—and anybody can give or spend money, but to give it to the right persons, to give the right amount of it and to give it at the right time and for the right cause and in the right way, this is not what anybody can do, nor is it easy. That is the reason why it is rare and laudable and noble to do well. Accordingly one who aims at the mean must begin by departing from that extreme which is the more contrary to the mean; he must act in the spirit of Calypso's[24] advice,

"Far from this smoke and swell keep thou thy bark,"

for of the two extremes one is more sinful than the other. As it is difficult then to hit the mean exactly, we must take the second-best course,[25] as the saying is, and choose the lesser of two evils, and this we shall best do in the way that we have described, *i.e. by steering clear of the evil which is further from the mean.* We must also observe the things to which we are ourselves particularly prone, as different natures have different inclinations, and we may ascertain what these are by a consideration of our feelings of pleasure and pain. And then we must drag ourselves in the direction opposite to them; for it is by removing ourselves as far as possible from what is wrong that we shall arrive at the mean, as we do when we pull a crooked stick straight.

But in all cases we must especially be on our guard against what is pleasant and against pleasure, as we are not impartial judges of pleasure. Hence our attitude towards pleasure must be like that of the elders of the people in the *Iliad* towards Helen, and we must never be afraid of applying the words they use[26]; for if we dismiss pleasure as they dismissed Helen, we shall be less likely to go wrong. It is by action of this kind, to put it sum-marily, that we shall best succeed in hitting the mean.

It may be admitted that this is a difficult task, especially in particular cases. It is not easy to determine *e.g.* the right manner, objects, occasions, and duration of anger. There are times when we ourselves praise people who are deficient in anger, and call them gentle, and there are other times when we speak of people who exhibit a savage temper as spirited. It is not however one who deviates a little from what is right, but one who deviates a great deal, whether on the side of excess or of deficiency, that is cen-sured; for he is sure to be found out. Again, it is not easy to decide theo-retically how far and to what extent a man may go before he becomes cen-surable, but neither is it easy to define theoretically anything else within the region of perception; such things fall under the head of particulars, and our judgment of them depends upon our perception.

So much then is plain, that the mean state is everywhere laudable, but that we ought to incline at one time towards the excess and at another towards the deficiency; for this will be our easiest manner of hitting the mean, or in other words of attaining excellence.

(8) *Justice as a mean between extremes.* Bk. 5, ch. 1.

In Bks. 3 and 4 Aristotle has developed his mean between extremes analysis of the examples given above (as well as some others). In Bk. 5 he turns to the value term "justice." He separates his discussion however from "complete justice," a term he thinks identical to "complete virtue," a justice which is the whole of virtue as "complete injustice" is the whole of vice. His interest in this book is "particular justice." This is jus-tice as part of virtue, as "particular injustice" is a part of vice. Particular justice and particular injustice, like his earlier examples, fit the mean between extremes analysis. There are two forms of particular justice (and injustice). One is distributive, the other is corrective.

We come now to investigate justice and injustice. We have to consider what is the character of the actions with which they deal, what is the sense in which justice is a mean state, and what are the extremes between which the just is a mean. In our investigation we will follow the same plan as in the virtues already described.

We see that everybody who uses the term "justice" means by it the moral state which makes people capable of doing what is just, and which makes them just in action and in intention. In the same way injustice is the moral state which makes them unjust in action and in intention. Let us begin then by assuming this rough definition of justice and injustice. *We regard justice as one moral state and injustice as another.*

(9) Distributive justice. Bk. 5, chs. 6–7.

As the person who is unjust is unfair, and the thing which is unjust is unfair, it is clear that there is a certain mean in respect of unfairness, or inequality. This mean is that which is fair or equal; for whatever be the nature of an action that admits of excess or defect, it admits also of fairness or equality.

If then that which is unjust is unfair, that which is just is fair, as indeed every one sees without argument.

But since that which is fair or equal is a mean between two extremes, that which is just will in a certain sense be a mean. But fairness or equality implies two persons or things at least. It follows therefore that that which is just is a mean, that it is fair or equal and that it is relative to certain persons. It follows also that, inasmuch as it is a mean, it is a mean between certain extremes, *viz.* excess and defect, and that inasmuch as it is just, it is relative to certain persons. But, if so, then that which is just must imply four terms at least; for the persons relatively to whom it is just are two, and the things in which it consists are two likewise. Also, if the persons are equal, the things will be equal; for as one thing is to the other thing, so is one person to the other person. For if the persons are not equal, they will not have equal shares; in fact the source of battles and complaints is either that people who are equal have unequal shares, or that people who are not equal have equal shares, distributed to them. The same truth is clearly seen from the principle of merit; for everybody admits that justice in distributions is determined by merit of some sort; only people do not all understand the same thing by merit. The democrats understand freedom, the oligarchs wealth or nobility, and the aristocrats virtue.

Justice then is a sort of proportion; for proportion is not peculiar to abstract quantity,[27] but belongs to quantity generally, proportion being equality of ratios and implying four terms at least.

Now it is plain that discrete proportion implies four terms; but the same is true of continuous proportion; for in continuous proportion one of the terms is used as two, and is repeated. Thus as A is to B, so is B to C[28]; here B is repeated; consequently if B be set down twice, the terms of the proportion will be four.

That which is just then requires four terms at least, and an equality of ratio between them, the persons and the things being similarly divided.[29] As then the term A is to the term B, so will C be to D, and consequently *alternando* as A is to C, so will B be to D. The whole therefore will bear the same ratio to the whole *i.e. A + C will be to B + D as A is to B or C to D*[30]; but this is the combination which the distribution effects, and, if the terms be thus united, it is a just combination.

The conjunction therefore of *A* with *C* and of *B* with *D* is what is just in distribution, and this justice is a mean between the violations of proportion; for that which is proportionate is a mean, and that which is just is proportionate. Mathematicians call this kind of proportion geometrical; for in geometrical proportion the whole is to the whole as each of the separate terms is to each.[31] But this proportion is not continuous, as no one arithmetical term can stand both for person and for thing.

That which is just then in this sense is that which is proportionate, and that which is unjust is that which is disproportionate. It follows that this disproportion may take the form either of excess or defect; and this is actually the case, for the author of the injustice has too much, and the victim has too little, of the good. In regard to evil the contrary is the case; for the lesser evil in comparison with the greater counts as a good, as the lesser evil is more desirable than the greater, and that which is desirable is a good, and that which is more desirable is a greater good.

This then, is one form of justice *i.e. of particular justice.*

(10) Corrective justice. Bk. 5, ch. 7.

The remaining form of justice is the corrective, which occurs in private transactions whether voluntary or involutary.

This justice is different in kind from the former. For distributive justice in dealing with the public funds invariably follows the proportion which has been described, *i.e. geometrical proportion*, as even if the distribution be made *to two or more people* out of the public funds, it will be in accordance with the ratio of the contributions which they have severally made.[32] Also the injustice which is opposite to this form of justice is the violation of *geometrical* proportion. But the justice which exists in private transactions, although in a sense it is fair or equal, and the corresponding injustice is unfair or unequal, follows not geometrical but arithmetical proportion.[33] For it makes no difference here whether it be a virtuous man who defrauded a bad man, or a bad man who defrauded a virtuous man, or whether it be a virtuous or a bad man who committed adultery; the law looks only to the degree of the injury, it treats the parties as equal, and asks only if one is the author and the other the victim of injustice or if the one inflicted and the other has sustained an injury. Injustice then in this sense is unfair or unequal, and the endeavor of the judge[34] is to equalize it; for even when one person deals a blow and the other receives it, or one person kills and the other is killed, the suffering and the action are divided into unequal parts, and it is the effort of the judge to restore equality by the penalty which he inflicts, as the penalty is so much subtracted from the profit. For the term "profit" is applied generally to such cases, although it is sometimes not strictly appropriate; thus we speak of the "profit" of one who inflicts a blow, or the "loss" of one who suffers it, but it is when the suffering is assessed *in a court of law* that the prosecutor gets profit, and the guilty person loss. That which is fair or equal then is the mean between excess and defect. But profit and loss are excess and defect, although in opposite senses, the excess of good and the defect of evil being profit, and the excess of evil and the defect of good being loss. The mean between them is, as we said, the equal, which we call just. Hence corrective justice will be the mean between profit and loss.

(11) Bk. 5, ch. 9. The nature of the just and the unjust has now been described. The definitions which have been given make it clear that just conduct is a mean between committing and suffering injustice; for to commit injustice is to have too much, and to suffer it is to have too little. But justice is a mean state, not in the same sense as the virtues already described, but rather as aiming at the mean, while injustice aims at the extremes. It is justice which entitles the just man to be regarded as capable of deliberately effecting what is just, and of making a distribution whether between himself and somebody else, or between two other people, not in such a way as to give himself too large, and his neighbor too small a share of what is desirable, and conversely to give himself too small and his neighbor too large a share of what is injurious, but to give both himself and his neighbor such a share as is proportionately equal, and to do the same when the distribution is between other people. Injustice on the contrary aims at that which is unjust; but that which is unjust is disproportionate excess and defect of what is profitable or injurious. Hence injustice is excess and defect, inasmuch as it aims at excess and defect, *viz.* excess of what is absolutely profitable, and defect of what is injurious in one's own case, while in the cases of other people, although they are generally similar, the violation of proportion may take the form either of excess or of defect. But the defect of unjust action is to suffer injustice, the excess is to inflict it.

This then may be taken as a sufficient account of the nature of justice and injustice respectively, and similarly of that which is just or unjust in general.

NOTES

1. Aristotle is thinking of the Platonic "ideas."

2. The reference is probably not to any special passage in the dialogues of Plato, but to the general drift or scope of the Socratic dialectics.

3. Aristotle's reasoning depends in part on the double meaning of ἀρχή *viz.* (1) starting-point or beginning, (2) first principle or axiomatic truth.

4. The most luxurious, and the last, Assyrian monarch.

5. The "popular philosophical treatises" τὰ ἐγκύκλια θιλοσοθήματα as they are called περὶ οὐρανοῦ i. ch. 9, p. 279 A30 represent, as I suppose, the discussions and conclusions of thinkers outside the Aristotelian school and are in fact the same as the ἐξῶτερικοὶ λόγοι.

6. The investigation of the speculative life occurs in Book x.

7. The usage of Aristotle is in favor of taking καταβέβληνται to mean "has been employed" rather than "has been wasted"; see especially περὶ Κόσμον ch. 6, p. 397 B19.

8. What is meant by an "accidental homonymy" or equivocation is easily seen in the various senses of a single English word such as *bull*.

9. In other words life may be taken to mean either the mere possession of certain faculties or their active exercise.

10. The difference between φρόνησιό "prudence" or "practical wisdom" and σοφία "speculative" or "theoretical wisdom" is commonly assumed by Aristotle.

11. Herodotus 1. ch. 32 is the authority for the celebrated warning which Solon is said to have addressed to Croesus.

12. Aristotle means that it is comparatively easy to forget scientific truths, when they have once been learnt, but it is difficult, if not impossible, to lose the habit of virtuous activity. In other words, he means that knowledge is less stable, and therefore less valuable, than character.

13. The phrase "foursquare without a flaw" is taken from Simonides, as Plato says in his *Protagoras* p. 339, B, where the passage in which the phrase occurs is quoted at length. *Cp. Rhetoric* 3, ch. 11 p. 1411 B27. In a similar, but not identical sense a modern poet speaks of the Great Duke of Wellington as
"that tower of strength
Which stood foursquare to all the winds that blew."

14. Among his tragedies in the final year of the Trojan War were the deaths of his thirteen sons. [Ed.]

15. The student of Aristotle must familiarize himself with the conception of intellectual as well as of moral virtues, although it is not the rule in modern philosophy to speak of the "virtues" of the intellect.

16. The approximation of ἔΘος (habit) and ἤθος (character) cannot be represented in English.

17. The Pythagoreans, starting from the mystical significance of number, took the opposite principles of "the finite" (τὸ πέρας or τὸ πεπερασμένον), and "the infinite" (τὸ ἄπειρον) to represent good and evil.

18. A line—perhaps Pythagorean—of unknown authorship.

19. The distinction, it seems, is between those mean or intermediate states (μεσότητες) which take the form of action and those which are simply emotional.

20. In Book 3, ch. 9—end of Book 4.

21. In Book 5.

22. In Book 6.

23. Aristotle does not seem to be aware that the center (τὸ μέσον) of a circle is not really comparable to the mean (τὸ μέσον) between the vices.

24. *Odyssey* 12. 219, 220; but it is Odysseus who speaks there, and the advice has been given him not by Calypso but by Circe (*ibid.*, 101–10).

25. The Greek proverb means properly "We must take to the oars, if sailing is impossible."

26. The reference is to the *Iliad*, Bk. 3, ll. 156–60 where the elders murmur "softly to each other" that neither side can be blamed for going to war over a woman so like an immortal goddess; yet she should be allowed to "go away in the ships" since her presence is likely to bring "a grief to us and our children" (tr. Richard Lattimore, University of Chicago Press, 1951).[Ed.]

27. "Abstract quantity" is, Sir A. Grant says, "number expressed in ciphers." It is *e.g.* the number 2, not two horses or two carts, etc.

28, If $A : B :: B : C$ be taken as the example of continuous proportion, $A : B :: C : D$ will be an example of discrete proportion.

29. *I.e.* so that person should be to person, as thing to thing.

30. In the supposed instance A and B are persons, C and D are things, and the combination consists in adding C (thing) to A (person) and D (thing) to B (person).

31. *I.e.* $A + C : B + D :: A : B$ or $C : D$.

32. The meaning is that, if A pays a larger income tax than B, he will receive a larger share of such public property as may be distributed.

33. If in geometrical proportion $2 : 4 :: 3 : 6$, in arithmetical proportion $2 : 4 :: 4 : 6$, 4 being the arithmetical mean between 2 and 6.

34. As the Athenian δικαστής was partly judge and partly juror, it is necessary, in every case of translating it, to use the English word which best represents the particular functions denoted by the Greek.

[*The Nicomachean Ethics*, tr. J. E. C. Welldon (Amherst, N.Y.: Prometheus Books, 1987) (1) Bk. 1, ch. 1, pp. 9–11. (2) Bk. 1, ch. 2, pp. 13–14. (3) Bk. 1, ch. 3, pp. 15–16. (4) Bk. 1, chs. 4–11, pp. 18–35. (5) Bk. 1, ch. 13, pp. 38–39. (6) Bk 2, ch. 1, pp. 42–43. (7) Bk. 2, chs. 6–9, pp. 54–65. (8) Bk. 5 ch. 1, p. 142. (9) Bk 5, chs. 6–7, pp. 150–53. (10) Bk. 5, ch. 7, pp. 153–55. (11) Bk. 5, ch. 9, pp. 163–64.]

6

Epicurus

341–270 B.C.E.

Diogenes Laertius, *Lives of Eminent Philosophers*

Epicurus is preeminent among those who esteem pleasure (from the Greek *hedone*) to be our final good. Pleasure is our final good because we are built that way. His view survives only in the summary of Diogenes Laertius.

Also see Study Guide (4b6), pp. 33–34.

Pleasure our first and kindred good

(1) Pleasure is our first and kindred good. It is the starting-point of every choice and of every aversion, and to it we come back, inasmuch as we make feeling the rule by which to judge of every good thing. And since pleasure is our first and native good, for that reason we do not choose every pleasure whatsoever, but ofttimes pass over many pleasures when a greater annoyance ensues from them. And ofttimes we consider pains superior to pleasures when submission to the pains for a long time brings us as a consequence a greater pleasure. While therefore all pleasure because it is naturally akin to us is good, not all pleasure is choiceworthy, just as all pain is an evil and yet not all pain is to be shunned. It is, however, by measuring one against another, and by looking at the conveniences and inconveniences, that all these matters must be judged. Sometimes we treat the good as an evil, and the evil, on the contrary, as a good. Again, we regard independence of outward things as a great good, not so as in all cases to use little, but so as to be contented with little if we have not much, being honestly persuaded that they have the sweetest enjoyment of luxury who stand least in need of it, and that whatever is natural is easily procured and only the vain and worthless hard to win. Plain fare gives as much pleasure as a costly diet,

when once the pain of want has been removed while bread and water confer the highest possible pleasure when they are brought to hungry lips. To habituate one's self, therefore, to simple and inexpensive diet supplies all that is needful for health, and enables a man to meet the necessary requirements without shrinking, and it places us in a better condition when we approach at intervals a costly fare and renders us fearless of fortune.

When we say, then, that pleasure is the end and aim, we do not mean the pleasures of the prodigal or the pleasures of sensuality, as we are understood to do by some through ignorance, prejudice, or wilful misrepresentation. By pleasure we mean the absence of pain in the body and of trouble in the soul. It is not an unbroken succession of drinking-bouts and of revelry, not sexual love, not the enjoyment of the fish and other delicacies of a luxurious table, which produce a pleasant life; it is sober reasoning, searching out the grounds of every choice and avoidance, and banishing those beliefs through which the greatest tumults take possession of the soul. Of all this the beginning and the greatest good is prudence. Wherefore prudence is a more precious thing even than philosophy; from it spring all the other virtues, for it teaches that we cannot lead a life of pleasure which is not also a life of prudence, honor, and justice; nor lead a life of prudence, honor, and justice, which is not also a life of pleasure. For the virtues have grown into one with a pleasant life, and a pleasant life is inseparable from them.

❧   ❧   ❧

(2) Principal Doctrines[1]

1. The blessed and immortal is itself free from trouble nor does it cause trouble for anyone else; therefore, it is not constrained either by anger or by favor. For such sentiments exist only in the weak.

2.[2] Death is nothing to us. For what has been dispersed has no sensation. And what has no sensation is nothing to us.

3. The limit of the extent of pleasure is the removal of all pain. Wherever pleasure is present, for however long a time, there can be no pain or grief, or both at once.

4. Pain does not dwell continuously in the flesh. Extreme pain is present but a very brief time, and that which barely exceeds bodily pleasure continues no more than a few days. But chronic illness allows greater pleasure than pain in the flesh.

5.[3] It is impossible to live pleasantly without living prudently, well, and justly, nor is it possible to live prudently, well, and justly without living pleasantly. The man for whom this latter condition is impossible cannot live prudently, well, or justly; he for whom the former is impossible, cannot live pleasantly.

6. Whatever you can provide yourself with to secure protection from men is a natural good.

7. Some men wished to become esteemed and admired by everyone, thinking that in this way they would procure for themselves safety from others. Therefore, if the life of such men is safe, they have received the good that comes from nature. If it is not safe, they do not have that for which they struggled at first by natural instinct.

8. No pleasure is evil in itself; but the means of obtaining some pleasures bring in their wake troubles many times greater than the pleasures.

9. If every pleasure were condensed[4] and existed for a long time throughout the entire organism or its most important parts, pleasures would never differ from one another.

10. If the things that beget pleasure in dissolute individuals could dispel their minds' fears about the heavens, death, and pain, and could still teach them the limits of desires, we would have no grounds for finding fault with the dissolute, since they would be filling themselves with pleasures from every source and in no way suffering from pain or grief, which are evil.

11. If apprehensions about the heavens and our fear lest death concern us, as well as our failure to realize the limits of pains and desires, did not bother us, we would have no need of natural science.

12. It is impossible for anyone to dispel his fear over the most important matters, if he does not know what is the nature of the universe but instead suspects something that happens in myth. Therefore, it is impossible to obtain unmitigated pleasure without natural science.

13. There is no benefit in securing protection from men if things above and beneath the earth and indeed all the limitless universe are made matters for suspicion.

14. The most perfect means of securing safety from men, which arises, to some extent, from a certain power to expel, is the assurance that comes from quietude and withdrawal from the world.

15. Natural wealth is limited and easily obtained; the riches of idle fancies go on forever.

16. In few instances does chance intrude upon the wise man, but reason has administered his greatest and most important affairs, and will continue to do so throughout his whole life.

17. The just man is most free of perturbation, while the unjust man is full of the greatest disturbance.

18. The pleasure in the flesh will not be increased when once the pain resulting from want is taken away, but only varied. The limit of understanding as regards pleasure is obtained by a reflection on these same pleasures and the sensations akin to them, which used to furnish the mind with its greatest fears.

19. Infinite time contains the same amount of pleasure as finite time, if one measures the limits of pleasure by reason.

20. The flesh considers the limits of pleasure to be boundless, and only infinite time makes it possible. But the mind, having gained a reasonable understanding of the end and limit of the flesh, and having expelled fears about eternity, furnishes the complete life, and we no longer have any need for time without end. But the mind does not flee from pleasure nor, when circumstances bring about the departure from life, does it take its leave as though falling short somehow of the best life.

21. He who understands the limits of life knows how easy it is to remove the pain that results from want and to make one's whole life complete. As a result, he does not need actions that bring strife in their wake.

22. We must take into account both the underlying purpose and all the evidence of clear perception, to which we refer our opinions. Otherwise, everything will be filled with confusion and indecision.

23. If you do battle with all your sensations, you will be unable to form a standard for judging even which of them you judge to be false.

24. If you reject any sensation and you do not distinguish between the opinion based on what awaits confirmation and evidence already available based on the senses, the feelings, and every intuitive faculty of the mind, you will send the remaining sensations into a turmoil with your foolish opinions, thus driving out every standard for judging. And if, among the perceptions based on opinion, you affirm both that which awaits confirmation and that which does not, you will fail to escape from error, since you will have retained every ground for dispute in judgment concerning right and wrong.

25. If you do not on every occasion refer each of your actions to the end ordained by nature, but instead stop short at something else when considering whether to go after something or avoid it, your actions will not be in keeping with the principles you profess.

26. Those desires that do not lead to pain, if they are not fulfilled, are not necessary. They involve a longing that is easily dispelled, whenever it is difficult to fulfill the desires or they appear likely to lead to harm.

27. Of all the things that wisdom provides for living one's entire life in happiness, the greatest by far is the possession of friendship.

28. The same knowledge that makes one confident that nothing

dreadful is eternal or long-lasting, also recognizes in the face of these limited evils the security afforded by friendship.

29. Of the desires some are natural and necessary while others are natural but unnecessary. And there are desires that are neither natural nor necessary but arise from idle opinion.

30. If there is intense striving after those physical desires that do not lead to pain if unfulfilled, this is because they arise from idle opinion; they fail to be dispelled, not because of their own nature but because of the vain fancies of humankind.

31. Natural justice is a pledge guaranteeing mutual advantage, to prevent one from harming others and to keep oneself from being harmed.

32. For those living creatures that are unable to form compacts not to harm others or to be harmed, there is neither justice nor injustice. It is the same for all tribes of men unable or unwilling to form compacts not to do harm or be harmed.

33. There is no such thing as "justice in itself"; it is, rather, always a certain compact made during men's dealings with one another in different places, not to do harm or to be harmed.

34. Injustice is not evil in itself but in the fear and apprehension that one will not escape from those appointed to punish such actions.

35. It is impossible for the one who commits some act in secret violation of the compacts made among men not to do harm or to be harmed, to remain confident that he will escape notice, even if for the present he escapes detection a thousand times. For right up to the day of his death, it remains unclear whether he will escape detection.

36. Broadly considered, justice is the same for all, because it is a kind of mutual benefit in men's interactions with one another. But in individual countries and circumstances, justice turns out not to be the same for all.

37. Among the measures regarded as just, that which is proven to be beneficial in the business of men's dealings with one another, has the guarantee of justice whether it is the same for all or not. If someone makes a law which does not result in advantage for men's dealings with each other, it no longer has the nature of justice. Even if advantage in the matter of justice is variable but nonetheless conforms for a certain length of time to the common notion people have of it, no less for that period is it just in the opinion of those who do not confuse themselves with words but look straight at the facts.

38. Where actions that were considered just are shown not to fit the conception (of justice) in actual practice—provided circumstances are not altered—they are not just. But where, once events have changed, the same actions once held to be just are no longer advantageous, they were just at the

time when they brought advantage to citizens' dealings with one another; but later they were no longer just, when they brought no advantage.

39. The man who has best settled the feeling of disquiet that comes from external circumstances is he who has made those things he can of the same kin as himself; and what he cannot, at least not alien. Whatever he cannot do even this to he avoids all contact with, and banishes whatever it is advantageous to treat in this way.

40. Those who possess the power of securing themselves completely from their neighbors, live most happily with one another, since they have this constant assurance. And after partaking of the fullest intimacy, they do not mourn a friend who dies before they do, as though there were need for pity.

NOTES

1. These follow a brief passage in Diogenes Laertius' *Lives* (10.135–138), in which he describes how Epicurus' teachings about pleasure differ from those of the Cyrenaics, and then introduces the *Principal Doctrines*.

2. Cf. the letter to Menoeceus, sec. 124.

3. Cf the letter to Menoeceus, sec. 132.

4. By "condensed" here, Epicurus means "maximized."

[Diogenes Laertius, *Lives of Eminent Philosophers*, The Loeb Classical Library, tr. R. D. Hicks (Cambridge: Harvard University Press, 1925), vol. 2. (1) Pp. 655–57. (2). "Principal Doctrines" section of *The Essential Epicurus*, tr. and ed. E. O'Connor (Amherst, N.Y.: Prometheus Books, 1993), pp. 69–76.]

7

Stoic Philosophy

(A) EPICTETUS, 60–138
FROM *THE DISCOURSES, THE MANUAL (OR ENCHEIRIDION),
AND FRAGMENTS*

The position of Epictetus emerges rather clearly from his criticism of what he believes Epicurus to have held. His discourses contain two extended passages of criticism. We include both.

Also see Study Guide (4b7), p. 34.

Criticism of Epicureanism

(1) . . . Epicurus, when he wishes to do away with the natural fellowship of men with one another, at the same time makes use of the very principle that he is doing away with. For what does he say? "Be not deceived, men, nor led astray, nor mistaken; there is no natural fellowship with one another among rational beings; believe me. Those who say the contrary are deceiving you and leading you astray with false reasons." Why do *you* care, then? Allow us to be deceived. Will you fare any the worse, if all the rest of us are persuaded that we do have a natural fellowship with one another, and that we ought by all means to guard it? Nay, your position will be much better and safer. Man, why do you worry about us, why keep vigil on our account, why light your lamp, why rise betimes, why write such big books? Is it to keep one or another of us from being deceived into the belief that the gods care for men, or is it to keep one or another of us from supposing that the nature of the good is other than pleasure? For if this is so, off to your couch and sleep, and lead the life of a worm, of which you have

judged yourself worthy; eat and drink and copulate and defecate and snore. What do you care how the rest of mankind will think about these matters, or whether their ideas be sound or not? For what have you to do with us? Come, do you interest yourself in sheep because they allow themselves to be shorn by us, and milked, and finally to be butchered and cut up? Would it not be desirable if men could be charmed and bewitched into slumber by the Stoics and allow themselves to be shorn and milked by you and your kind? Is not this something that you ought to have said to your fellow Epicureans only and to have concealed your views from outsiders, taking special pains to persuade them, of all people, that we are by nature born with a sense of fellowship, and that self-control is a good thing, so that everything may be kept for you? Or ought we to maintain this fellowship with some, but not with others? With whom, then, ought we to maintain it? With those who reciprocate by maintaining it with us, or with those who are transgressors of it? And who are greater transgressors of it than you Epicureans who have set up such doctrines?

What, then, was it that roused Epicurus from his slumbers and compelled him to write what he did? What else but that which is the strongest thing in men—nature, which draws a man to do her will though he groans and is reluctant? "For," says she, "since you hold these antisocial opinions, write them down and bequeathe them to others and give up your sleep because of them and become in fact yourself the advocate to denounce your own doctrines."

(2) I greatly fear that a noble-spirited young man may hear these statements and be influenced by them, or, having been influenced already, may lose all the germs of the nobility which he possessed; that we may be giving an adulterer grounds for brazening out his acts; that some embezzler of public funds may lay hold of a specious plea based upon these theories; that someone who neglects his own parents may gain additional affrontery from them.

What, then, in your opinion is good or bad, base or noble? This or that? What then? Is there any use in arguing further against any of these persons, or giving them a reason, or listening to one of theirs, or trying to convert them? By Zeus, one might much rather hope to convert a filthy degenerate than men who have become so deaf and blind!

(3) When the Imperial Bailiff, who was an Epicurean, came to visit him, Epictetus said: It is proper for us laymen to make inquiry of you philosophers what the best thing in the world is—just as those who have come to a strange town make inquiry of the citizens and people who are familiar with the place—so that, having learned what it is, we may go in

quest of it ourselves and behold it, as do strangers with the sights in the cities. Now that three things belong to man, soul, and body, and things external, hardly anyone denies; all you have to do, then, is to answer the question, Which is the best? What are we going to tell men? The flesh? And was it for this that Maximus[1] sailed all the way to Cassiope during the winter with his son, to see him on his way? Was it to have pleasure in the flesh? When the other had denied that and said "God forbid!" Epictetus continued: Is it not proper to have been very zealous for that which is best?—It is certainly most proper.—What have we better, then, than the flesh?—The soul, said he.—Are the goods of the best thing better, or those of the inferior?—Those of the best thing.—Do goods of the soul belong in the sphere of the moral purpose, or do they not?—To the sphere of the moral purpose.—Is the pleasure of the soul, therefore, something that belongs in this sphere?—He agreed.—At what is this produced? At itself? But that is inconceivable. For we must assume that there is already in existence a certain antecedent essence of the good, by partaking of which we shall feel pleasure of soul.—He agreed to this also.—At what, then, are we going to feel this pleasure of soul? If it is at the goods of the soul, the essence of the good has already been discovered. For it is impossible that one thing be good, and yet that it is justifiable for us to take delight in something else; nor again, that when the antecedent is not good the consequent be good; because, in order to justify the consequent, the antecedent must be good. But say not so, you Epicureans, if you are in your right mind; for you will be saying what is inconsistent both with Epicurus and with the rest of your doctrines. The only thing left for you to say is that pleasure of soul is pleasure in the things of the body, and then *they* become matters of prime importance, and the true nature of the good.

That is why Maximus acted foolishly if he made his voyage for the sake of anything but the flesh, that is, for the sake of anything but the best. And a man acts foolishly too, if, when he is judge and able to take the property of other men, he keeps his hands off it. But, if you please, let us consider this point only, that the stealing be done secretly, safely, without anybody's knowledge. For even Epicurus himself does not declare the act of theft evil, but only getting caught, and merely because it is impossible to feel certain that one will not be detected, he says, "Do not steal." But I tell you that if it is done adroitly and circumspectly, we shall escape detection; besides that, we have influential friends in Rome, both men and women; and the Greeks are a feeble folk, none of them will have the courage to go up to Rome for that purpose. Why refrain from your own good? This is foolish, it is silly. And again, I shall not believe you, even if you tell me that you do refrain. For just as it is impossible to assent to what is seen to be false, and to reject what is true, so it is impossible to reject what is seen to be good. Now wealth is a good, and when it comes to pleasures is, so to speak, the thing most productive of them. Why should you not acquire it? And why should we not seduce our neighbor's wife, if we can escape detection? And if her husband talks nonsense, why should we not break his neck to boot? That is, if you wish to be a proper sort of philosopher, a perfect one, consistent with your own doctrines. If not, you will be no better than we who bear the name of Stoics; for we too talk of one thing and do another. We talk of the noble and do the base; but you will be perverse in the opposite way, laying down base doctrines, and doing noble deeds.

In the name of God, I ask you, can you imagine an Epicurean State? One man says, "I do not marry." "Neither do I," says another, "for people ought not to marry." No, nor have children; no, nor perform the duties of a citizen. And what, do you suppose, will happen then? Where are the citizens to come from? Who will educate them? Who will be superintendent of the *ephebi*,² or gymnasium director? Yes, and what will either of these teach them? What the young men of Lacedaemon or Athens were taught? Take me a young man; bring him up according to your doctrines. Your doctrines are bad, subversive of the State, destructive to the family, not even fit for women. Drop these doctrines, man. You live in an imperial State; it is your duty to hold office, to judge uprightly, to keep your hands off the property of other people; no woman but your wife ought to look handsome to you, no boy handsome, no silver plate handsome, no gold plate. Look for doctrines consistent with these principles of conduct, doctrines which will enable you to refrain gladly from matters so persuasive to attract and to overpower a man. If, however, in addition to the persuasive power of the things just mentioned, we shall have gone ahead and invented also some such doctrine as this of yours, which helps to push us on into them, and gives them additional strength, what is going to happen?

⁓   ⁓   ⁓

. . . in the case of man, it is not his material substance that we should honor, his bits of flesh, but the principal things. What are these? The duties of citizenship, marriage, begetting children, reverence to God, care of parents, in a word, desire, avoidance, choice, refusal, the proper performance of each one of these acts, and that is, in accordance with our nature. And what is our nature? To act as free men, as noble, as self-respecting. Why, what other living being blushes, what other comprehends the impression of shame? And it is our nature to subordinate pleasure to these duties as their servant, their minister, so as to arouse our interest and keep us acting in accordance with nature.

The things to which one ought to pay attention.

(4) What are the things, then, to which I ought to pay attention?—First, these general principles, and you ought to have them at your command, and without them neither go to sleep, nor rise up, nor drink, nor eat, nor mingle with men; I mean the following: No man is master of another's moral purpose; and: In its sphere alone are to be found one's good and evil. It follows, therefore, that no one has power either to procure me good, or to involve me in evil, but I myself alone have authority over myself in these matters. Accordingly, when these things are secure for me, what excuse have I for being disturbed about things external? What kind of tyrant inspires fear, what kind of disease, or poverty, or obstacle?—But I have not pleased So-and-so.—He is not my function, is he? He is not my judgment, is he?—No.—Why, then, do I care any longer?—But he has the reputation of being somebody.—He and those who think so highly of him will have to see to that, but I have one whom I must please, to whom I must submit, whom I must obey, that is, God, and after Him, myself. God has commended me to myself, and He has subjected to me alone my moral purpose, giving me standards for the correct use of it; and when I follow these standards, I pay heed to none of those who say anything else, I give not a thought to anyone in arguments with equivocal premises. Why, then, in the more important matters am I annoyed by those who censure me? What is the reason for this perturbation of spirit? Nothing but the fact that in this field I lack training. For, look you, every science is entitled to despise ignorance and ignorant people, and not merely the sciences, but also the arts. Take any cobbler you please, and he laughs the multitude to scorn when it comes to his own work; take any carpenter you please.

First, therefore, we ought to have these principles at command, and to do nothing apart from them, but keep the soul intent upon this mark; we must pursue none of the things external, none of the things which are not our own, but as He that is mighty has ordained; pursuing without any hesitation the things that lie within the sphere of the moral purpose, and all other things as they have been given us. And next we must remember who we are, and what is our designation, and must endeavor to direct our actions, in the performance of our duties, to meet the possibilities of our social relations. We must remember what is the proper time for song, the proper time for play, and in whose presence; also what will be out of place;

lest our companions despise us, and we despise ourselves; when to jest, and whom to laugh at, and to what end to engage in social intercourse, and with whom; and, finally, how to maintain one's proper character in such social intercourse. But whenever you deviate from any one of these principles, immediately you suffer loss, and that not from anywhere outside, but from the very nature of the activity.

What then? Is it possible to be free from fault altogether? No, that cannot be achieved, but it *is* possible ever to be intent upon avoiding faults. For we must be satisfied, if we succeed in escaping at least a few faults by never relaxing our attention. But now, when you say, "Tomorrow I will pay attention," I would have you know that this is what you are saying: "Today I will be shameless, tactless, abject; it will be in the power of other men to grieve me; I will get angry today, I will give way to envy." Just see all the evils that you are allowing yourself! But if it is good for you to pay attention tomorrow, how much better is it today! If it is to your interest tomorrow, it is much more so today, that you may be able to do the same tomorrow also, and not put it off again, this time to the day after tomorrow.

The principal task in life

(5) . . . the principal task in life is this: distinguish matters and weigh them one against another, and say to yourself, "Externals are not under my control; moral choice is under my control. Where am I to look for the good and the evil? Within me, in that which is my own." But in that which is another's never employ the words "good" or "evil," or "benefit" or "injury," or anything of the sort.

What then? Are these externals to be used carelessly? Not at all. For this again is to the moral purpose an evil and thus unnatural to it. They must be used carefully, because their use is not a matter of indifference, and at the same time with steadfastness and peace of mind, because the material is indifferent. For in whatever really concerns us, there no man can either hinder or compel me. The attainment of those things in which I can be hindered or compelled is not under my control and is neither good nor bad, but the use which I make of them is either good or bad, and that is under my control. It is, indeed, difficult to unite and combine these two things—the carefulness of the man who is devoted to material things and the steadfastness of the man who disregards them, but it is not impossible. Otherwise happiness were impossible. But we act very much as though we were on a voyage. What is possible for me? To select the helmsman, the sailors, the day, the moment. Then a storm comes down upon us. Very well, what further concern have I? For my part has been fulfilled. The business belongs to someone else, that is, the helmsman. But, more than that, the ship goes down. What, then, have I to do? What I can; that is the only thing I do; I drown without fear, neither shrieking nor crying out against God, but recognizing that what is born must also perish. For I am not eternal, but a man; a part of the whole, as an hour is part of a day. I must come on as the hour and like an hour pass away. What difference, then, is it to me how I pass away, whether by drowning or by a fever? For by something of the sort I must needs pass away.

Excellence

(6) Be not elated at any excellence which is not your own. If the horse in his elation were to say, "I am beautiful," it could be endured; but when you say in your elation, "I have a beautiful horse," rest assured that you are elated at something good which belongs to a horse. What, then, is your own? The use of external impressions. Therefore, when you are in harmony with nature in the use of external impressions, then be elated; for then it will be some good of your own at which you will be elated.

The good

(7) The subject-matter with which the good and excellent man has to deal is his own governing principle, that of a physician and the masseur is the body, of a farmer is his farm; but the function of the good and excellent man is to deal with his impressions in accordance with nature. Now just as it is the nature of every soul to assent to the true, dissent from the false, and to withhold judgment in a matter of uncertainty, so it is its nature to be moved with desire toward the good, with aversion toward the evil, and feel neutral toward what is neither evil nor good. For just as neither the banker nor the greengrocer may legally refuse the coinage of Caesar, but if you present it, whether he will or no, he must turn over to you what you are purchasing with it, so it is also with the soul. The instant the good appears it attracts the soul to itself, while the evil repels the soul from itself. A soul will never refuse a clear sense-impression of good, any more than a man will refuse the coinage of Caesar. On this concept of the good hangs every impulse to act both of man and of God.

That is why the good is preferred above every form of kinship. My father is nothing to me, but only the good. "Are you so hard-hearted?" Yes, that is my nature. This is the coinage which God has given me. For that reason, if the good is something different from the noble and the just, then father and brother and country and all relationships simply disappear. But shall I neglect my good, so that you may have it, and shall I make way for you? What for? "I am your father." But not a good. "I am your brother." But not a good. If, however, we define the good as consisting in a right moral purpose, then the mere preservation of the relationships of life becomes a good; and furthermore, he who gives up some of the externals achieves the good. "My father is taking away my money." But he is doing you no harm. "My brother is going to get the larger part of the farm." Let him have all he wants. That does not help him at all to get a part of your modesty, does it, or of your fidelity, or of your brotherly love? Why, from a possession of this kind who can eject you? Not even Zeus. Nay, nor did He ever wish to, but this matter He put under my control, and He gave it to me even as He had it Himself, free from hindrance, compulsion, restraint.

(8) "What sort of a thing do you imagine the good to be? Serenity, happiness, freedom from restraint. Come, do you not imagine it to be something naturally great? Something precious? Something not injurious? In what kind of subject-matter for life ought one to seek serenity, and freedom from restraint? In that which is slave, or in that which is free?" "In the free." "Is the paltry body which you have, then, free or is it a slave?" "We know not." "You do not know that it is a slave of fever, gout, ophthalmia, dysentery, a tyrant, fire, iron, everything that is stronger?" "Yes, it is their servant." "How, then, can anything that pertains to the body be unhampered? And how can that which is naturally lifeless, earth, or clay, be great or precious? What then? Have you nothing that is free?" "Perhaps nothing." "And who can compel you to assent to that which appears to you to be false?" "No one." "And who to refuse assent to that which appears to you to be true?" "No one." "Here, then, you see that there *is* something within you which is naturally free. But to desire, or to avoid, or to choose, or to refuse, or to prepare, or to set something before yourself—what man among you can do these things without first conceiving an impression of what is profitable, or what is not fitting?" "No one." "You have, therefore, here too, something unhindered and free. Poor wretches, develop this, pay attention to this, seek here your good."

Freeing oneself

(9) And how shall I free myself?—Have you not heard over and over again that you ought to eradicate desire utterly, direct your aversion towards the things that lie within the sphere of the moral purpose, and these things only, that you ought to give up everything, your body, your property, your reputation, your books, turmoil, office, freedom from office? For if once you swerve aside from this course, you are a slave, you are a subject, you have become liable to hindrance and to compulsion,

you are entirely under the control of others. Nay, the word of Cleanthes is ready at hand,

Lead thou me on, O Zeus, and Destiny.[3]

The good man invincible

(10) . . . in the early days not only had labor been expended upon maintaining the governing principle in a state of accord with nature, but there was also progress along that line. Do not, therefore, substitute one thing for the other, and do not expect, when you devote labor to one thing, to be making progress in another. But see whether any one of us who is devoting himself to keeping in a state of conformity with nature, and to spending his life so, fails to make progress. For you will find that there is none of whom that is true.

The good man is invincible; naturally, for he enters no contest where he is not superior. "If you want my property in the country," says he, "take it; take my servants, take my office, take my paltry body. But you will not make my desire fail to get what I will, nor my aversion fall into what I would avoid." This is the only contest into which the good man enters, one, namely, that is concerned with the things which belong in the province of the moral purpose; how, then, can he help but be invincible?

Serenity

(11) There is but one way to serenity (keep this thought ready for use at dawn, and by day, and at night), and that is to yield up all claim to the things that lie outside the sphere of the moral purpose, to regard nothing as your own possession; to surrender everything to the Deity, to Fortune; to yield everything to the supervision of those persons whom even Zeus has made supervisors; and to devote yourself to one thing only, that which is your own, that which is free from hindrance, and to read referring your reading to this end, and so to write and so to listen.

(12) . . . one ought none the less to prepare oneself for this also, that is, to be able to be self-sufficient, to be able to commune with oneself; even as Zeus communes with himself, and is at peace with himself, and contemplates the character of his governance, and occupies himself with ideas appropriate to himself, so ought we also to be able to converse with ourselves, not to be in need of others, not to be at a loss for some way to spend our time; we ought to devote ourselves to the study of the divine governance, and of our own relation to all other things; to consider how we used to act toward the things that happen to us, and how we act now; what the

things are that still distress us; how these too can be remedied, or how removed; if any of these matters that I have mentioned need to be brought to perfection, to perfect them in accordance with the principle of reason inherent in them.

Behold now, Caesar seems to provide us with profound peace, there are no wars any longer, nor battles, no brigandage on a large scale, nor piracy, but at any hour we may travel by land, or sail from the rising of the sun to its setting. Can he, then, at all provide us with peace from fever too, and from shipwreck too, and from fire, or earthquake, or lightning? Come, can he give us peace from love? He cannot. From sorrow? From envy? He cannot—from absolutely none of these things. But the doctrine of the philosophers promises to give us peace from these troubles too. And what does it say? "Men, if you heed me, wherever you may be, whatever you may be doing, you will feel no pain, no anger, no compulsion, no hindrance, but you will pass your lives in tranquillity and in freedom from every disturbance." When a man has this kind of peace proclaimed to him, not by Caesar—why, how could *he* possibly proclaim it?—but proclaimed by God through the reason, is he not satisfied, when he is alone? When he contemplates and reflects, "Now no evil can befall me, for me there is no such thing as a brigand, for me there is no such thing as an earthquake, everything is full of peace, everything full of tranquillity; every road, every city, every fellow-traveller, neighbor, companion, all are harmless. Another, whose care it is, supplies food; Another supplies raiment; Another has given senses; Another preconceptions. Now whenever He does not provide the necessities for existence, He sounds the recall; He has thrown open the door and says to you, "Go." Where? To nothing you need fear, but back to that from which you came, to what is friendly and akin to you, to the physical elements. What there was of fire in you shall pass into fire, what there was of earth into earth, what there was of spirit into spirit, what there was of water into water. There is no Hades, nor Acheron, nor Cocytus, nor Pyriphlegethon, but everything is filled with gods and divine powers."[4] A man who has this to think upon, and who beholds the sun, and moon, and stars, and enjoys land and sea, is no more forlorn than he is without help. "Why, what then? What if someone should attack me when I am alone and murder me?" Fool, not murder you but your trivial body.

Keeping festival

(13) Bearing all this in mind, rejoice in what you have and be satisfied with what the moment brings. If you see any of the things that you have learned and studied thoroughly coming to fruition for you in action, rejoice

in these things. If you have put away or reduced a malignant disposition, and reviling, or impertinence, or foul language, or recklessness, or negligence; if you are not moved by the things that once moved you, or at least not to the same degree, then you can keep festival day after day; today because you behaved well in this action, tomorrow because you behaved well in another. How much greater cause for thanksgiving is this than a consulship or a governorship! These things come to you from your own self and from the gods. Remember who the Giver is, and to whom He gives, and for what end. If you are brought up in reasonings such as these, can you any longer raise the questions where you are going to be happy, and where you will please God?

Death

(14) As for me, I would fain that death overtook me occupied with nothing but my own moral purpose, trying to make it tranquil, unhampered, unconstrained, free. This is what I wish to be engaged in when death finds me so that I may be able to say to God, "Have I in any respect transgressed Thy commands? Have I in any respect misused the resources which Thou gavest me, or used my senses to no purpose, or my preconceptions? Have I ever found any fault with Thee? Have I blamed Thy governance at all ? I fell sick, when it was Thy will; so did other men, but I willingly. I became poor, it being Thy will, but with joy. I have held no office, because Thou didst not will it, and I never set my heart upon office. Hast Thou ever seen me for that reason greatly dejected ? Have I not ever come before Thee with a radiant countenance, ready for any injunctions or orders Thou mightest give? And now it is Thy will that I leave this festival; I go, I am full of gratitude to Thee that Thou hast deemed me worthy to take part in this festival with Thee, and to see Thy works, and to understand Thy governance." Be this my thought, this my writing, this my reading, when death comes upon me.

NOTES

1. A distinguished man of the time, not otherwise identified.
2. Those arriving at man's estate *i.e.* age eighteen in Athens.
3. From a celebrated hymn.
4. A doctrine ascribed to Thales, *Diog. Laert.* 1, 27.

[*Epictetus, the Discourses as Reported by Arian, the Manual, and Fragments,* tr. W. A. Oldfather (Cambridge: Harvard University Press, 1925), 2 vols. (1) Vol. 1, bk. 2. 20. pp. 373–75. (2) Ibid., p. 383. (3) Vol. 2, bk. 3. 6. pp. 49–57. (4)

Ibid., bk. 4. 12. pp. 425–29. (5) Vol. 1, bk. 2. 5. pp. 239–41. (6) Ibid., "The Encheiridian," 6. vol. 2, p. 489. (7) Ibid., bk. 3. 2. pp. 29–31. (8) Ibid., bk. 3. 22. pp. 145–47. (9) Ibid., bk. 4. 4. pp. 325–27. (10) Ibid., bk. 3. 6. p. 47. (11) Ibid., bk. 4. 4. pp. 327–29. (12) Ibid., bk. 3. 13. pp. 89–93. (13) Ibid., bk. 4. 4. pp. 329–31. (14) Ibid., bk. 3. 5. pp. 41–43.]

(B) MARCUS AURELIUS, 121–180
FROM *THE COMMUNINGS (OR MEDITATIONS)*

Agreeing with Epictetus in general, Marcus Aurelius believed that the life in accordance with reason is valid even if there is no universal reason, if the gods have no concern with us (sec. 9), if it is all atoms; still, one's interest agrees with one's nature, and that is both rational and civic. Notice his view in bk. 5. 18 (sec. 6) that nothing befalls one beyond one's capacity to bear. Finally note (sec. 13) his support for the third definition of freedom (in agreement with Epictetus).

Also see Study Guide (4b7), p. 34.

Ten propositions, and four perversions, of reason to keep before one

(1) Bk. 2. 18. Firstly: Consider your relation to mankind and that we came into the world for the sake of one another; and taking another point of view, that I have come into it to be set over men, as a ram over a flock or a bull over a herd. Start at the beginning from this premiss: If not atoms, then an all-controlling Nature. If the latter, then the lower are for the sake of the higher and the higher for one another.

Secondly: What sort of men they are at board and in bed and elsewhere? Above all how they are the self-made slaves of their principles, and how they pride themselves on the very acts in question.

Thirdly: That if they are acting rightly in this, there is no call for us to be angry. If not rightly, it is obviously against their will and through ignorance. For it is against his will that every soul is deprived, as of truth, so too of the power of dealing with each man as is his due. At any rate, such men resent being called unjust, unfeeling, avaricious, and in a word doers of wrong to their neighbors.

Fourthly: That you too do many a wrong thing yourself and are much as others are, and if you do refrain from certain wrongdoings, you have a disposition inclinable thereto even supposing that through cowardice or a regard for your good name or some such base consideration you do not actually commit them.

Fifthly: That you have not even proved that they are doing wrong, for many things are done even "by way of policy."[1] Speaking generally a man must know many things before he can pronounce an adequate opinion on the acts of another.

Sixthly: When you are above measure angry or even out of patience, recall that man's life is momentary, and in a little while we shall all have been laid out.

Seventhly: That in reality it is not the acts men do that vex us—for they belong to the domain of *their* ruling Reason—but the opinions we form of those acts. Eradicate these, be ready to discard your conclusion that the act in question is a calamity, and your anger is at an end. How then eradicate these opinions? By realizing that no act of another debases us. For unless that alone which debases is an evil, you too must perforce do many a wrong thing and become a brigand or any sort of man.

Eighthly: Think how much more grievous are the consequences of our anger and vexation at such actions than are the acts themselves which arouse that anger and vexation.

Ninthly: That kindness is irresistible, be it but sincere and no mock smile or a mask assumed. For what can the most unconscionable of men do to you, if you persist in being kindly to him, and when a chance is given exhort him mildly and, at the very time when he is trying to do you harm, quietly teach him a better way thus: *Nay, my child, we have been made for other things. I shall be in no wise harmed, but you are harming yourself, my child.* Show him delicately and without any personal reference that this is so, and that even honeybees do not act thus nor any creatures of gregarious instincts. But you must do this not in irony or by way of rebuke, but with kindly affection and without any bitterness at heart, not as from a master's chair, nor yet to impress the bystanders, but as if he were indeed alone even though others are present.

Think then of these nine heads, taking them as a gift from the Muses, and begin at last to be a *man* while life is yours. But beware of flattering men no less than being angry with them. For both these are nonsocial and conducive of harm. In temptations to anger a precept ready to your hand is this: to be wroth is not manly, but a mild and gentle disposition, as it is more human, so it is more masculine. Such a man, and not he who gives way to anger and discontent, is endowed with strength and sinews and manly courage. For the nearer such a mind attains to a passive calm,[2] the nearer is the man to strength. As grief is a weakness, so also is anger. In both it is a case of a wound and a surrender.

But take if you will as a tenth gift from Apollo, the Leader of the Muses, this, that to expect the bad not to do wrong is worthy of a madman; for that is to wish for impossibilities. But to acquiesce in their wronging others, while expecting them to refrain from wronging you, is unfeeling and despotic.

19. Against four perversions of the ruling Reason you should above all keep unceasing watch, and, once detected, wholly abjure them, saying in each case to yourself: *This thought is not necessary; this is destructive of human fellowship; this could be no genuine utterance from the heart.*—And not to speak from the heart, what is it but a contradiction in terms?—The fourth case is that of self-reproach,³ for that is an admission that the divine part of you has been worsted by and acknowledges its inferiority to the body, the baser and mortal partner, and to its gross notions.

20. Your soul and all the fiery part that is blended with you, though by Nature ascensive, yet in submission to the system of the Universe are held fast here in your compound personality. And the entire earthy part too in you and the humid, although naturally descensive, are yet upraised and take up a station not their natural one. Thus indeed we find the elements also in subjection to the Whole and, when set anywhere, remaining there under constraint until the signal sound for their release again therefrom.

Is it not then a paradox that the intelligent part alone of you should be rebellious and quarrel with its station? Yet is no constraint laid upon it but only so much as is in accordance with its nature. Howbeit it does not comply and takes a contrary course. For every motion towards acts of injustice and licentiousness, towards anger and grief and fear, but betokens one who cuts himself adrift from Nature. Aye and when the ruling Reason in a man is vexed at anything that befalls, at that very moment it deserts its station. For it was not made for justice alone, but also for piety and the service of God. And in fact the latter are included under the idea of a true fellowship, and indeed are prior to the practice of justice.

21. He who has not ever in view one and the same goal of life cannot be throughout his life one and the same. Nor does that which is stated suffice, there needs to be added what that goal should be. For just as opinion as to all the things that in one way or another are held by the mass of men to be good is not uniform, but only as to certain things, such, that is, as affect the common weal, so must we set before ourselves as our goal the common and civic weal. For he who directs all his individual impulses towards this goal will render his actions homogeneous and thereby be ever consistent with himself.

(2) Bk 2. 5. Every hour make up your mind sturdily as a Roman and a man to do what you have in hand with scrupulous and unaffected dignity and love of your kind and independence and justice; and to give yourself rest from all other impressions. And you will give yourself this, if you do execute every act of your life as though it were your last, divesting yourself of all aimlessness and all passionate antipathy to the convictions of reason, and all hypocrisy and self-love and dissatisfaction with your allotted share. You see how few are the things, by mastering which a man may lead a life of tranquillity and godlikeness; for the Gods also will ask no more from him who keeps these precepts.

≈   ≈   ≈

7. Do those things draw you at all away, which befall you from without? Make then leisure for yourself for the learning of some good thing more, and cease being carried aside hither and thither. But therewith must you take heed of the other error. For they too are triflers, who by their activities have worn themselves out in life without even having an aim whereto they can direct every impulse, aye and even every thought.

(3) Bk 4. 1. That which holds the mastery within us, when it is in accordance with Nature, is so disposed towards what befalls, that it can always adapt itself with ease to what is possible and granted us. For it is wedded to no definite material, but, though in the pursuit of its high aims it works under reservations, yet it converts into material for itself any obstacle that it meets with, just as fire when it gets the mastery of what is thrown in upon it. A little flame would have been stifled by it, but the blazing fire instantly assimilates what is cast upon it and, consuming it, leaps the higher in consequence.

2. Take no act in hand aimlessly or otherwise than in accordance with the true principles perfective of the art.

3. Men seek out retreats for themselves in the country, by the seaside, on the mountains, and you too are wont to long above all for such things. But all this is unphilosophical to the last degree, when you can at a moment's notice retire into yourself. For nowhere can a man find a retreat more full of peace or more free from care than his own soul—above all if he have that within him, a steadfast look at which and he is at once in all good ease, and by good ease I mean nothing other than good order. Make use then of this retirement continually and regenerate yourself. Let your axioms be short and elemental, such as when set before you will at once rid

you of all trouble, and send you away with no discontent at those things to which you are returning.

Why with what are you discontented? The wickedness of men? Take this conclusion to heart, that rational creatures have been made for one another; that forbearance is part of justice; that wrongdoing is involuntary; and think how many ere now, after passing their lives in implacable enmity, suspicion, hatred, and at daggers drawn with one another, have been laid out and burnt to ashes—think of this, I say, and at last stay your fretting. But are you discontented with your share in the whole? Recall the alternative: *Either Providence or Atoms!* and the abundant proofs there are that the Universe is as it were a state. But is it the affections of the body that shall still lay hold on you? Bethink you that the Intelligence, when it has once abstracted itself and learnt its own power, has nothing to do with the motions smooth or rough of the vital breath. Bethink you too of all that you have heard and subscribed to about pleasure and pain.

But will that paltry thing, Fame, pluck you aside? Look at the swift approach of complete forgetfulness, and the void of infinite time on this side of us and on that, and the empty echo of acclamation, and the fickleness and uncritical judgment of those who claim to speak well of us, and the narrowness of the arena to which all this is confined. For the whole earth is but a point, and how tiny a corner of it is this the place of our sojourning! and how many therein and of what sort are the men who shall praise you.

From now therefore bethink you of the retreat into this little plot that is yourself. Above all distract not yourself, be not too eager, but be your own master, and look upon life as a man, as a human being, as a citizen, as a mortal creature. But among the principles readiest to your hand, upon which you shall pore, let there be these two. One, that objective things do not lay hold of the soul, but stand quiescent without; while disturbances are but the outcome of that opinion which is within us. A second, that all this visible world changes in a moment, and will be no more; and continually bethink you to the changes of how many things you have aleady been a witness. "The Universe—mutation: Life—opinion."[4]

4. If the intellectual capacity is common to us all, common too is the reason, which makes us rational creatures. If so, that reason also is common which tells us to do or not to do. If so, law also is common. If so, we are citizens. If so, we are fellow-members of an organized community. If so, the Universe is as it were a state—for of what other single polity can the whole race of mankind be said to be fellow-members?—and from it, this common State, we get the intellectual, the rational, and the legal instinct, or whence do we get them? For just as the earthy part has been portioned off for me

from some earth, and the watery from another element, and the aerial[5] from some source, and the hot and fiery from some source of its own—for nothing comes from the nonexistent, any more than it disappears into nothingness—so also the intellect has undoubtedly come from somewhere.

5. Death like birth is a secret of Nature—a combination of the same elements, a breaking up into the same—and not at all a thing in fact for any to be ashamed of, for it is not out of keeping with an intellectual creature or the reason of his equipment.

6. Given such men, it was in the nature of the case inevitable that their conduct should be of this kind. To wish it otherwise, is to wish that the fig-tree had no acrid juice. As a general conclusion call this to mind, that within a very short time both you and he will be dead, and a little later not even your names will be left behind you.

7. Efface the opinion, *I am harmed*, and at once the feeling of being harmed disappears; efface the feeling, and the harm disappears at once.

8. That which does not make a man himself worse than before cannot make his life worse either, nor injure it whether from without or within.

9. The nature of the general good could not but have acted so.

10. Note that all that befalls befalls justly. Keep close watch and you will find this true, I do not say, as a matter of sequence merely but as a matter of justice also, and as would be expected from One whose dispensation is based on desert. Keep close watch, then, as you have begun, and whatsoever you do, do it as only a good man should in the strictest sense of that word. In every sphere of activity safeguard this.

11. Harbor no such opinions as he holds who does you violence, or as he would have you hold. See things in all their naked reality.

12. You should have these two readinesses always at hand; the one which prompts you to do only what your reason in its royal and lawmaking capacity shall suggest for the good of mankind; the other to change your mind if one be near to set you right, and convert you from some vain conceit. But this conversion should be the outcome of a persuasion in every case that the thing is just or to the common interest—and some such cause should be the only one—not because it is seemingly pleasant or popular.

13. Have you reason? *I have.* Why then not use it? For if this performs its part, what else would you have?

14. You have subsisted as part of the Whole. You shall vanish into that which begat you or rather you shall be taken again into its Seminal Reason[6] by a process of change.

15. Many little pellets of frankincense fall upon the same altar, some are cast on it sooner, some later: but it makes no difference.

16. Before ten days are past, you shall rank as a god with those who hold you now a wild beast or an ape, if you but turn back to your axioms and your reverence of reason.

17. Behave not as though you had ten thousand years to live. Your doom hangs over you. While you live, while you may, become good.

18. What richness of leisure does he gain who has no eye for his neighbor's words or deeds or thoughts, but only for his own doings, that they be just and righteous! Verily it is not for the good man to peer about into the blackness of another's heart, but to "run straight for the goal with never a glance aside."

19. He whose heart flutters for after-fame does not reflect that very soon every one of those who remember him, and he himself, will be dead, and their successors again after them, until at last the entire recollection of the man will be extinct, handed on as it is by links that flare up and are quenched. But put the case that those who are to remember are even immortal and the remembrance immortal, what then is that to you? To the dead man, I need scarcely say, the praise is nothing, but what is it to the living, except, indeed, in a subsidiary way. For you reject the bounty of nature unseasonably in the present, and cling to what others shall say of you hereafter.[7]

20. Everything, which has any sort of beauty of its own, is beautiful of itself, and looks no further than itself, not counting praise as part of itself. For indeed that which is praised is made neither better nor worse thereby. This is true also of the things that in common parlance are called beautiful, such as material things and works of art. Does, then, the truly beautiful need anything beyond? Nay, no more than law, than truth, than kindness, than modesty. Which of these owes its beauty to being praised, or loses it by being blamed? What! Does an emerald forfeit its excellence by not being praised? Does gold, ivory, purple, a lyre, a poniard, a floweret, a shrub?

⧼   ⧼   ⧼

24. *If you would be tranquil in heart,* says the Sage,[8] *do not many things.* Is not this a better maxim? do but what is needful, and what the reason of a living creature born for a civic life demands, and as it demands. For this brings the tranquillity which comes of doing few things no less than of doing them well. For nine-tenths of our words and deeds being unnecessary, if a man retrench there, he will have more abundant leisure and fret the less. Wherefore forget not on every occasion to ask yourself, *Is this one of the unnecessary things?* But we must retrench not only actions but thoughts which are unnecessary, for then neither will superfluous actions follow.

25. Try living the life of the good man who is more than content with what is allotted to him out of the whole, and is satisfied with his own acts as just and his own disposition as kindly: see how that answers.

26. Have you looked on that side of the picture? Look now on this! Fret not yourself, study to be simple. Does a man do wrong? The wrong rests with him. Has something befallen you? It is well. Everything that befalls was from the beginning destined and spun for you as your share out of the Whole. To sum up, life is short. Make profit of the present by right reasoning and justice. In your relaxation be sober.

31. Cherish the art, though humble, that you have learned, and take your rest therein; and pass through the remainder of your days as one that with his whole soul has given all that is his in trust to the Gods, and has made of himself neither a tyrant nor a slave to any man.

(4) Bk 5.5. Sharpness of wit men cannot praise you for.[9] Granted! Yet there are many other qualities of which you cannot say: *I had not that by nature.*

Well then, display those which are wholly in your power, sterling sincerity, dignity, endurance of toil, abstinence from pleasure. Grumble not at your lot, be content with little, be kindly, independent, frugal, serious, high-minded. Do you not see how many virtues it is in your power to display now, in respect of which you can plead no natural incapacity or incompatibility, and yet you are content still with a lower standard? Or are you forced to be discontented, to be grasping, to flatter, to inveigh against the body, to play the toady and the braggart, and to be so unstable in your soul, because forsooth you have no natural gifts? By the Gods, *No!* but long before now could you have shaken yourself free from all this and have lain under the imputation only, if it must be so, of being somewhat slow and dull of apprehension. And this too you must amend with training and not ignore your dullness or be in love with it.

(5) Bk. 5. 8. Take much the same view of the accomplishment and consummation of what Nature approves as of your health, and so welcome whatever happens, should it even be somewhat distasteful, because it contributes to the health of the Universe and the well-faring and well-doing of Zeus himself. For he had not brought this on a man, unless it had brought welfare to the Whole. For take any nature you will, it never brings upon that which is under its control anything that does not conduce to its interests.

For two reasons then it behooves you to acquiesce in what befalls: one, that it was for you it took place, and was prescribed for you, and had reference in some sort to you, being a thread of destiny spun from the first for you[10] from the most ancient causes; the other, that even what befalls each individual is the cause of the well-faring, of the consummation and by heaven of the very permanence of that which controls the Universe. For the perfection of the Whole is impaired, if you cut off ever so little of the coherence and continuance of the Causes no less than of the parts. And you do cut them off, as far as lies with you, and bring them to an end, when you murmur.

(6) Bk. 5. 16. The character of your mind will be such as is the character of your frequent thoughts, for the soul takes its dye from the thoughts. Dye her then with a continuous succession of such thoughts as these: Where life is possible, there it is possible also to live well.—*But the life is life in a Court.* Well, in a Court too it is possible to live well. And again: A thing is drawn towards that for the sake of which it has been made, and its end lies in that towards which it is drawn and, where its end lies, there lie also its interest and its good. The Good, then, for a rational creature is fellowship with others. For it has been made clear long ago that we were constituted for fellowship. Or was it not obvious that the lower were for the sake of the higher and the higher for the sake of one another? And living things are higher than lifeless, and those that have reason than those that have life only.

17. To crave impossibilities is lunacy; but it is impossible for the wicked to act otherwise.

18. Nothing befalls anyone that he is not fitted by nature to bear. Others experience the same things as you, but either from ignorance that anything has befallen them, or to manifest their greatness of mind, they stand firm and get no hurt. A strange thing indeed that ignorance and vanity should prove stronger than wisdom.

(7) Bk. 5. 27. Walk with the Gods! And he does walk with the Gods, who lets them see his soul invariably satisfied with its lot and carrying out the will of that "genius," a particle of himself, which Zeus has given to every man as his captain and guide—and this is none other than each man's intelligence and reason.

(8) Bk. 6. 30. See thou be not *Caesarified*, nor take that dye, for there is the possibility.[11] So keep yourself a simple and good man, uncorrupt, dignified, plain, a friend of justice, god-fearing, gracious, affectionate, manful in doing your duty. Strive to be always such as Philosophy minded to make

you. Revere the Gods, save mankind. Life is short. This only is the harvest of earthly existence, a righteous disposition and social acts.

Do all things as a disciple of Antoninus.[12] Think of his constancy in every act rationally undertaken, his invariable equability, his piety, his serenity of countenance, his sweetness of disposition, his contempt for the bubble of fame, and his zeal for getting a true grasp of affairs. How he would never on any account dismiss a thing until he had first thoroughly scrutinized and clearly conceived it; how he put up with those who found fault with him unfairly, finding no fault with them in return; how he was never in a hurry; how he gave no ear to slander, and with what nicety he tested dispositions and acts; was no imputer of blame, and no craven, not a suspicious man, nor a sophist, what little sufficed him whether for lodging or bed, dress, food, or attendance; how fond he was of work, and how long-suffering; how he would remain the whole day at the same occupation, owing to his spare diet not even requiring to relieve nature except at the customary time; and how loyal he was to his friends and always the same; and his forbearance towards those who openly opposed his views, and his pleasure when anyone pointed out something better; and how god-fearing he was and yet not given to superstition. Take heed to all this, that your last hour come upon you as much at peace with your conscience as he was.

(9) Bk. 6. 44. If the Gods have taken counsel about me and the things to befall me, doubtless they have taken good counsel. For it is not easy even to imagine a God without wisdom. And what motive could they have impelling them to do me evil? For what advantage could thereby accrue to them or to the Universe which is their special care? But if the Gods have taken no counsel for me individually, yet they have in any case done so for the interests of the Universe, and I am bound to welcome and make the best of those things also that befall as a necessary corollary to those interests. But if so be they take counsel about nothing at all—an impious belief—in good sooth let us have no more of sacrifices and prayers and oaths, nor do any other of these things every one of which is a recognition of the Gods as if they were at our side and dwelling amongst us—but if so be, I say, they do not take counsel about any of our concerns, it is still in my power to take counsel about myself, and it is for me to consider my own interest.[13] And that is to every man's interest which is agreeable to his own constitution and nature. But my nature is rational and civic; my city and country, as Antoninus, is Rome; as a man, the world. The things then that are of advantage to these communities, these, and no other, are good for me.

45. All that befalls the Individual is to the interest of the Whole also.

So far, so good. But further careful observation will show you that, as a general rule, what is to the interest of one man is also to the interest of other men. But in this case the word *interest* must be taken in a more general sense as it applies to intermediate[14] things.

＊ ＊ ＊

48. When you would cheer your heart, think upon the good qualities of your associates; as for instance, this one's energy, that one's modesty, the generosity of a third, and some other trait of a fourth. For nothing is so cheering as the images of the virtues mirrored in the characters of those who live with us, and presenting themselves in as great a throng as possible. Have these images then ever before your eyes.

49. Are you not aggrieved, at being so many pounds in weight and not three hundred? Then why be aggrieved if you have only so many years to live and no more? For as you are contented with the amount of matter allotted you, so be content also with the time.

＊ ＊ ＊

(10) Bk. 8. 57. Love only what befalls you and is spun for you by fate. For what can be more befitting for you?

58. In every contingency keep before your eyes those who, when these same things befell them, were straightway aggrieved, estranged, rebellious. Where are they now? Nowhere! What then? Would you too be like them? Why not leave those alien deflections to what deflects and is deflected by them, and devote yourself wholly to the question how to turn these contingencies to the best advantage? For then will you make a noble use of them, and they shall be thy raw material. Only in thought and will take heed to be beautiful to yourself in all that you do. And remember, in rejecting the one and using the other, that the thing which matters is the aim of the action.

59. Look within. Within is the fountain of Good,[15] ready always to well forth if you will always delve.

Bk. 3. 16. . . . there is left as the characteristic of the good man to delight in and to welcome what befalls and what is being spun for him by destiny; and not to sully the divine "genius" that is enthroned in his bosom, nor yet to perplex it with a multitude of impressions, but to maintain it to the end in a gracious serenity, in orderly obedience to God, uttering no word that is not true and doing no deed that is not just. But if all men disbelieve in his living a simple and modest and cheerful life, he is not wroth with any of them, nor swerves from the path which leads to his life's goal, whither he must go pure, peaceful, ready for release, needing no force to bring him into accord with his lot.

60. The body too should be firmly set and suffer no distortion in movement or bearing. For what the mind effects in the face, by keeping it composed and well-favored, should be looked for similarly in the whole body. But all this must be secured without conscious effort.

61. The business of life is more akin to wrestling than dancing, for it requires of us to stand ready and unshakeable against every assault however unforeseen.

(11) Bk. 8. 1. . . . past experience tells you how much you have gone astray, nor anywhere lighted upon the true life; no, not in the subtleties of logic, or in wealth or fame or enjoyment, or *anywhere*. Where then is it to be found? In doing that which is the quest of man's nature. How then shall a man do this? By having axioms as the source of his impulses and actions. What axioms? On the nature of Good and Evil, showing that nothing is for a man's good save what makes him just, temperate, manly, free; nor anything for his ill that makes him not the reverse of these.

(12) Bk. 8. 10. Repentance is a sort of self-reproach at some useful thing passed by; but the good must needs be a useful thing, and ever to be cultivated by the true good man; but the true good man would never regret having passed a pleasure by. Pleasure therefore is neither a useful thing nor a good.

⋙　⋙　⋙

12. When you are loth to get up, call to mind that the due discharge of social duties is in accordance with your constitution and in accordance with man's nature, while even irrational animals share with us the faculty of sleep; but what is in accordance with the nature of the individual is more congenial, more closely akin to him, aye and more attractive.

⋙　⋙　⋙

16. Remember that neither a change of mind nor a willingness to be set right by others is inconsistent with true freedom of will. For yours alone is the active effort that effects its purpose in accordance with your impulse and judgment, aye and your intelligence also.

17. If the choice rests with you, why do the thing? if with another, whom do you blame? Atoms or Gods? To do either would be crazy folly. No one is to blame. For if you can, set the offender right. Failing that, at least set the thing itself right. If that too be impracticable, what purpose is served bv imputing blame? For without a purpose nothing should be done.

≈ ≈ ≈

19. Every thing, be it a horse, be it a vine, has come into being for some end. Why wonder? Helios himself will say: *I exist to do some work;* and so of all the other Gods. For what then do you exist? For pleasure? Surely it is not to be thought of.

(13) Bk. 8. 54. Be no longer content merely to breathe in unison with the all-embracing air, but from this moment think also in unison with the all-embracing Intelligence. For that intelligent faculty is everywhere diffused and offers itself on every side to him that can take it in no less than the aerial to him that can breathe.

≈ ≈ ≈

56. To my power of choice[16] the power of choice of my neighbor is as much a matter of indifference as is his vital breath and his flesh. For however much we may have been made for one another, yet our ruling Reason is in each case master in its own house. Else might my neighbor's wickedness become my bane; and this was not God's will, that another might not have my unhappiness in his keeping.

(14) Bk. 10. 8. Assuming for yourself the appellations, a good man, a modest man, a truth teller, wise of heart, sympathetic of heart, great of heart, take heed you be not new-named. And if you should forfeit these titles, e'en make haste to get back to them. And bear in mind that *wise of heart* was meant to signify for you a discerning consideration of every object and a thoroughness of thought; *sympathetic of heart,* a willing acceptance of all that the Universal Nature allots you; *great of heart* an uplifting of our mental part above the motions smooth or rough of the flesh, above the love of empty fame, the fear of death, and all other like things. Only keep yourself entitled to these appellations, not itching to receive them from others, and then you will be a new man and enter on a new life.

❧   ❧   ❧

When will you find your delight in simplicity? *When* in dignity? *When* in the knowledge of each separate thing, what it is in its essence, what place it fills in the Universe, how long it is formed by Nature to subsist, what are its component parts, to whom it can pertain, and who can bestow and take it away?

❧   ❧   ❧

16. Put an end once for all to this discussion of what a good man should be, and be one.

(15) Bk. 9. 5. What is your vocation? To be a good man. But how be successful in this save by assured conceptions on the one hand of the universal Nature and on the other of the special constitution of man?

NOTES

1. Or, *"with an eye to circumstances," "with some further end in view,"* knowledge of which would justify the action or show its necessity.

2. The Stoic.

3. Marcus reproaches himself when nineteen years old for backwardness in philosophy.

4. A maxim of Democrates, a Pythagorean.

5. Lit. *the pneumatic.*

6. The primal Fire and the eternal Reason are one and the same, and held to contain the seed of all things.

7. Marcus is perhaps finding real fault with himself for caring so much what people said of him.

8. Democritus.

9. The author here speaks of himself.

10. Or, from above.

11. More of a possibility for Marcus Aurelius than for most people. [Ed.]

12. His adoptive father.

13. Gods taking counsel about nothing at all would be like the indifferent Epicurean gods. Or he may be hinting at a contrast he uses from time to time, as in bk. 9, 39: Either one intelligent source, or atoms "and nothing but a medley and dispersion." The contrast here is between "a well-arranged order of things, or a

maze." In the latter case he is still hopeful that even if all things are "separated and dispersed" they "are still in sympathetic connexion" (Bk. 6. 27). Even in a chaotic universe, the reason of one's nature remains valid. [Ed.]

14. *I.e.* indifferent, neither good nor bad.

15. We supplement the idea of the good with a passage from Bk. 3. 16.

16. Not distinguishable from the "ruling Reason." This places the view in the third definition of freedom. But if one has the power to follow or not to follow the ruling reason, a bit of the first definition enters—true also of 8.16–17 in (12) above. [Ed.]

[*The Communings with Himself of Marcus Aurelius Antoninus, Emperor of Rome*, tr. C. R. Haines (Cambridge, Mass.: Harvard University Press, 1916). (1) Bk. 9. 18–21, pp. 307–15. (2) Bk. 2. 5, 7, p. 31. (3) Bk. 4. 1–20, 24–26, 31, pp. 67–85. (4) Bk. 5. 5, p. 103. (5) Bk. 5. 8, pp. 107–109. (6) Bk. 5. 16–718, pp. 115–17. (7) Bk. 5. 27, p. 123. (8) Bk. 6. 30, pp. 145–47. (9) Bk. 6. 44–45, 48–49, pp. 155–59. (10) Bk. 7. 58, 59 and bk. 3. 16, 60–61, p. 189 (and 65). (11) Bk. 8. 1, pp. 199–201. (12) Bk. 8. 10, 12, 16–17, 19, pp. 203–207. (13) Bk. 8. 54, 56, p. 237. (14) Bk. 10. 8, 9, 16, pp. 267–75. (15) Bk. 5, p. 295.]

8

Jesus

4 B.C.E.–29 C.E.

The Sayings Gospel Q

Our concern is with the system of values endorsed by Jesus. In order to feature his values we have selected passages from "Q." "Q" stands for the German "*quelle*" (source), and is used to refer to a remarkable series of passages in Matthew and Luke, so nearly identical that scholars believe the authors of Matthew and Luke had a common written source before them. Readers can test that identity for themselves, since the editors of the Polebridge edition of this material have placed the passages in a double column, the first for Luke, the second for Matthew. Q is, then, earlier than Matthew and Luke, and is a "sayings" gospel. Since the sayings of Jesus circulated earlier, and independently of the later encasing narrative material, one can believe with some confidence that these sayings are as close as one can come to the authentic words of Jesus. Notice that Matthew and Luke sometimes disagree on statements of Q, notably, for example, in Luke 6:20–21, and Matt 5:3 and 5:6. The Gospel of Thomas is another early sayings Gospel. When this Gospel is compared to Q, it becomes clear that in case of disagreement Luke's rendering is to be preferred to that of Matthew. The Polebridge translation is closer to ordinary speech than others. As in the case of Buddha (*q.v.* SG4b1, R1) sayings and teachings are taken to be early and authentic. The first Christian Council was held at Nicaea in 325 C.E. The concerns of both this Council and its successors were doctrinal, not concerned with scriptural authenticity. Q and Thomas are important elements in the contemporary effort to discover the early and authentic teachings of Jesus.

Also see Study Guide (4b8), pp. 34–35.

(1) *Inaugural sermon*
Luke 6:12, 17, 20 / Matt. 5:1–2

5:1Taking note of the crowds,

12During that time,
it so happened that he went out to the mountain to pray, and spent the night in prayer to God.

he climbed up the mountain,

17On the way down with them, Jesus stopped at a level place. There was a huge crowd of his disciples and a great throng of people from all Judea and Jerusalem and the coast of Tyre and Sidon.

and when he had sat down, his disciples came to him.

20Then he would look squarely at his disciples and say:

2He then began to speak, and

this is what he would teach them:

Congratulations
Luke 6:20–26 / Matt. 5:3, 6, 4, 11–12

"Congratulations, you poor!

3"Congratulations to the poor in spirit!

God's domain belongs to you.

Heaven's domain belongs to them.

21Congratulations, you hungry!

6Congratulations to those who hunger and thirst for justice!

You will have a feast.
Congratulations, you who weep now!
You will laugh.

They will have a feast.
4Congratulations to those who grieve!
They will be consoled.

22Congratulations to you when people hate you, and when they ostracize you and denounce you

11Congratulations to you

when they denounce you and persecute you

and scorn your name as evil,

and spread malicious gossip about you

because of the son of Adam!

because of me.

6:20b
//Th54
cf. Lk6:24
6:21a
//Th69:2
Cf.Lk6:25a
6:21b
Cf. Lk6:25b
6:22-23
Cf.Lk6:26
6:22
//Th68
1Pet4:14
Cf.Th69:1
1Pet3:14
⤳Is66:5

²³Rejoice on that day,
and jump for joy!
Just remember,
your compensation
is great in heaven.
Recall that their ancestors treated
the prophets the same way.

¹²Rejoice
and be glad!

Your compensation
is great in heaven.
Recall that this is how they
persecuted the prophets
who preceded you.

²⁴*Damn you rich!*
You already have your consolation.
²⁵*Damn you who are well-fed now!*
You will know hunger.
Damn you who laugh now!
You will learn to weep and grieve.
²⁶*Damn you when everybody*
speaks well of you!
Recall that their ancestors treated
the phony prophets the same way.

Love of enemies
Luke 6:27–36 / Matt. 5:44, 39–42; 7:12; 5:46–47, 45, 48

²⁷But to you who listen I say,
love your enemies,
do favors for those who hate you,
²⁸bless those who curse you,
pray for your abusers.

⁴⁴But I tell you:
Love your enemies

and pray for your persecutors.

6:23
Cf. QI1:47-51
13:34-35;
1Pet4:13;
① Acts7:52

²⁹When someone strikes you
on the cheek,
offer the other as well.

³⁹When someone slaps you
on the right cheek,
turn the other as well.

6:28b
//GOxy
12246:1,
Rom12:14;
cf. 1Pet3:9

If someone takes
away your coat
don't prevent that person from
taking your shirt along with it.

⁴⁰If someone is determined
to sue you for your shirt,
let that person have your coat
along with it.

6:29a
⭢Prv1911,
20:22, 24:29;
Lam 3:30

⁴¹*Further, when anyone conscripts*
you for one mile, go along an extra
mile.

6:30
Cf. Lk6:34
Th95;
⭢Prv25:21

³⁰Give to everyone who begs
from you;

⁴²Give to the one who begs
from you;

6:27=Matt 5:44 Some mss add "bless those who curse you, do good to those who hate you"
after *love your enemies.*

and when someone takes your things,
don't ask for them back.

who tries to borrow from you.

and don't turn away the one
who tries to borrow from you.
7 [12]Consider this:

[31]Treat people the way
you want them to treat you.

Treat people in ways
you want them to treat you.
This sums up the whole of the
Law and the Prophets.
5[46] "Tell me,

[32]"If you love those who love you,
what merit is there in that?

if you love those who love you,
why should you be commended
for that?

After all, even sinners love those
who love them.
[33]And if you do good to those
who do good to you,
what merit is there in that?

Even the toll collectors do
as much, don't they?
[47]And if you greet only
your friends,
what have you done that is
exceptional?

After all,
even sinners do as much.
[34]If you lend to those from whom
you hope to gain, what merit is
there in that? Even sinners lend to
sinners, in order to get as much in
return.
[35]But love your enemies,
and do good, and lend,
expecting nothing in return.
Your reward will be great,
and you'll be children
of the Most High.

Even the pagans do as much,
don't they?

[45]You'll then become children
of your Father in the heavens.
(God) causes the sun to rise on
both the bad and the good,

As you know, he is generous
to the ungrateful and the wicked.

and sends rain on both the just
and the unjust.
[48]To sum up,

6:31
Cf. Th6:3
Rom13:10,
Tob4:15
6:35c
⮑Sir4:10

6:31 The "Golden Rule" is based on, but reverses, the ancient principle of retaliation. The Golden Rule antedates Jesus, and is found in various forms in Chinese, Indian, Greek, Persian, Jewish and Arabic sources.

6:32 *Sinner* was used for Jews who disregarded OT Law; they were thus the practical equivalent of Gentiles (non-Jews).

6:35 Several mss have "despairing of no one" instead of *expecting nothing in return*.

³⁶Be as compassionate

                             you are to be as liberal
                             in your love

as your Father is."   as your heavenly Father is."

On judging
Luke 6:37–38 / Matt 7:1–2

³⁷"Don't pass judgment,   ¹"Don't pass judgment,
and you won't be judged;   so you won't be judged.
                             ²Don't forget, the judgment you
                             hand out will be the judgment
                             you get back.

don't condemn,
and you won't be condemned;
forgive, and, you'll be forgiven.
³⁸Give, and it will be given to you:
they will put in your lap
a full measure, packed down,
sifted and overflowing.
For the standard you apply will   And the standard you apply will
be the standard applied to you."   be the standard applied to you."

Blind guides
Luke 6:39–40 / Matt 15:14; 10:24–25

                             ¹⁴"They are blind guides
                             of blind people!
         ³⁹"Can one blind person   If one blind person
6:36   guide another?   guides another,
⟲Dt18:13   Won't they both end up   both will end up
(LXX)
Lv19:2   in some ditch?   in some ditch.
6:37   ⁴⁰Students are not above   10 ²⁴Students are not above
//Mary9:12
6:38b   their teachers.   their teachers,
//Mk4:24   nor slaves above their masters.
⟲Sir35:10
6:39   But those who are fully taught   ²⁵It is appropriate for students
//Th34   will be like their teachers."   to be like their teachers and
6:40   slaves to be like their masters."
Cf. Jn13:16a,
15:20;
DSav20:1c

6:38b A common Jewish saying.

On pretense
Luke 6:41–42 / Matt 7:3–5

[41]"Why do you notice the sliver in your friend's eye, but overlook the timber in your own? [42]How can you say to your friend, "Friend, let me get the sliver in your eye," when you don't notice the timber in your own? You phony, first take the timber out of your own eye, and then you'll see well enough to remove the sliver in your friend's eye."	[3]"Why do you notice the sliver in your friend's eye, but overlook the timber in your own? [4]How can you say to your friend, "Let me get the sliver out of your eye," when there is that timber in your own? [5]You phony, first take the timber out of your own eye and then you'll see well enough to remove the sliver from your friend's eye."

Tree & fruit
Luke 6:43–45 / Matt 7:16–20; 12:33–35

v. 44	[16]"You'll know who they are by what they produce. Since when do people pick grapes from thorns or figs from thistles? [17]Every healthy tree produces choice fruit, but the rotten tree produces spoiled fruit.
[43]"A choice tree does not produce rotten fruit, any more than a rotten tree produces choice fruit;	[18]A healthy tree cannot produce spoiled fruit, any more than a rotten tree can produce choice fruit. [19]Every tree that does not produce choice fruit gets cut down and tossed on the fire. [20]Remember you'll know who they are by what they produce.
[44]for each tree is known by its fruit. Figs are not gathered from thorns, nor are grapes picked from	v. 16

6:41-42
//Th26
6:43-45
//Th45;
ⓂMt3:7-10,
12:33-35,
21:33-43
6:44a
↺Sir27:6,
6:44b
//Jas3:12

brambles.
v. 43a–b

12 [33]If you make the tree choice,
its fruit will be choice;
if you make the tree rotten,
its fruit will be rotten.

v. 44a

After all, the tree is known
by its fruit.
[34]You spawn of Satan, how can
your speech be good when you
are corrupt?

v. 45c

As you know, the mouth gives
voice to what the heart is full of.

[45]The good person produces good
from the fund of good in the
heart,
and the evil person produces
evil from the evil within.
As you know, the mouth gives
voice to what the heart is full of.

[35]The good person produces good
things out of a fund of good;

and the evil person produces
evil things out of a fund of evil."
v. 34b

Foundations
Luke 6:46/Matt 7:21, 24–27

[46]"Why do you call
me 'Master, master,'

[21]"Not everyone who addresses
me as 'Master, master,'
will get into Heaven's domain—
only those who carry out the will
of my Father in heaven.

and not do what I tell you?
[47]Everyone who comes to me
and pays attention to my words
and acts on them—
I'll show you what such a person
is like:
[48]That one is like a person
building a house, who dug deep
and laid the foundation
on bedrock;

when a flood came,

[24]Everyone who pays attention
to these words of mine
and acts on them

will be like a shrewd builder

who erected a house
on bedrock.
[25]Later the rain fell,
and the torrents came,

6:45
Cf. Mt12:37,
1Sm24:14,
Prv12:14
6:46
//EgerG3:5
6:47-49
⊃Ps1; Jer17:
5-8; Sir22:16,
27:3

6:47–49 Like some other Jewish sayings collections, the Q Sermon on the Mount/Plain concludes with a comparison with a ruined house; see also Job 3–27; Prov 1–9; 22:17–24:22.

the torrent slammed against that house, and the winds blew and pounded that house,

but could not shake it, because it was well built. yet it did not collapse, since its foundation rested on bedrock.

⁴⁹But the one who listens (to my words) and doesn't act (on them) is like a person who built a house on the ground without a foundation;

²⁶Everyone who listens to these words of mine and doesn't act on them will be like a careless builder, who erected a house on the sand.

²⁷When the rain fell, when the torrent slammed against it, and the torrents came,

and the winds blew and pounded that house, it collapsed immediately. it collapsed. And so the ruin of that house was total." Its collapse was colossal."

(2) *Ask, seek, knock*
Luke 11:9–13 / Matt 7:7–11

⁹"Ask—it'll be given to you; seek—you'll find; knock—it'll be opened for you. ¹⁰Rest assured: everyone who asks receives; everyone who seeks finds; and for the one who knocks it is opened.

⁷"Ask—it'll be given to you; seek—you'll find; knock—it'll be opened for you. ⁸Rest assured: everyone who asks receives; everyone who seeks finds; and for the one who knocks it is opened.

⁹Who among you would hand a son a stone when it's bread he's asking for?

¹¹Which of you fathers would hand his son a snake when it's fish he's asking for? ¹²Or a scorpion when it's an egg he's asking for?

¹⁰Again, who would hand him a snake when it's fish he's asking for?

Of course no one would!

¹³So if you, worthless as you are,

¹¹So if you, worthless as you are,

11:9-10
//Jn15:7,
16:23-24;
Th2:1-2;
92:1;94;
cf. Mk11:24;
Mt18:19, 21:22;
Jn15:16;
1Jn3:22;
⟳Prv8:17
11:10
//Mary4:7;
GHeb6b;
cf. DSav7:2,
11:5

know how to give your children
good gifts,
isn't it much more likely
that the heavenly Father
will give holy spirit to those
who ask him?"

know how to give your children
good gifts,
isn't it much more likely
that your Father in the heavens
will give good things to those
who ask him?"

(3) *Return of an unclean spirit*
Luke 11:24–26 / Matt 12:43–45

[24]"When an unclean spirit
leaves a person,
it wanders through waterless
places in search of a resting place.
When it doesn't find one,
it says,
"I will go back to the home I left."
[25]It then returns
and finds it swept
and refurbished.
[26]Next, it goes out
and brings back seven
other spirits more vile than itself,
who enter
and settle in there.
So that person ends up worse off
than when he or she started."

[41]"When an unclean spirit
leaves a person,
it wanders through waterless
places in search of a resting place.
When it doesn't find one,
[44]it then says,
"I will return to the home I left."
It then returns
and finds it empty, swept,
and refurbished.
[45]Next, it goes out
and brings back with it seven
other spirits more vile than itself,
who enter
and settle in there.
So that person ends up worse off
than when he or she started.
That's how it will be for
this perverse generation."

(4) *Lamp & bushel*
Luke 11:33 / Matt 5:15

11:24-26
①2Esd7:78-80
11:26b
①2Pet2:20
11:33
//Mk4:21,
Lk8:16,
Th33:2-3

[33]"No one lights a lamp
and then puts it in a cellar
or under a bushel basket,
but rather on a lampstand,
so that those who come in
can see the light."

[15]"Nor do people light a lamp

and put it under a bushel basket
but rather on a lampstand,
where it sheds light for everyone
in the house."

11:24 The *home* is the person from whom the demon was exorcised.

Eye & light
Luke 11:34–36 / Matt 6:22–23

³⁴"Your eye is the body's lamp.   ²²"The eye is the body's lamp.
                                         It follows that
When your eye is clear,   if your eye is clear,
your whole body is flooded   your whole body will be flooded
with light.   with light.
When your eye is clouded,   ²³If your eye is clouded,
your body is shrouded   your whole body will be shrouded
in darkness.   in darkness.
"Take care, then, that the light   If, then, the light
within you is not darkness.   within you is darkness,
                                         how dark that can be!"

³⁶*If then your whole body is flooded*
with light, and no corner of it is
darkness, it will be completely illu-
minated as when a lamp's rays
engulf you."

(5) *God & sparrows*
Luke 12:4–7 / Matt 10:28–31

⁴"I tell you, my friends,
don't fear those   ²⁸"Don't fear those
who kill the body,   who kill the body
and after that can do no more.   but cannot kill the soul;
⁵I'll show you
whom you ought to fear:
fear the one who can kill   instead, you ought to fear
                                         the one who can destroy
and then has authority to   both the soul and the body
cast into Gehenna.   in Gehenna.
Believe me,
that's the one you should fear!
⁶What do sparrows cost?   ²⁹What do sparrows cost?
A dime a dozen?   A penny apiece?
Yet not one of them is overlooked   Yet not one of them will fall
by God.   to the earth without the consent

11:34
//Th24:3, 61:5;
DSav6:1–2;
Mary7:4
11:35
Cf. Jn11:10,
Th70:2
12:5
⊃Ps119:120

11:34 The condition of the eye is described by a word (*haplous*) whose meaning is unclear;
it can be "single," "simple," 'sincere," "generous," or "sound."

of your Father.
[7]In fact,
even the hairs of your head
have all been counted.
Don't be so timid:
You're worth more
than a flock of sparrows."

[30]As for you,
even the hairs on your head
have all been counted.
[31]So, don't be so timid:
you're worth more
than a flock of sparrows."

(6) *On anxieties*
Luke 12:22–31 / Matt 6:25–33

[22]He said to his disciples,
"That's why I tell you:
Don't fret about life
—what you're going eat
or about your body
—what you're going wear.
[23]Remember,
there is more to living
than food and clothing.

[25]"That's why I tell you:
Don't fret about your life
—what you're going eat
and drink—or about your body
—what you're going wear.

There is more to living
than food and clothing,
isn't there?

[24]Think about the crows:

they don't plant or harvest,
they don't have storerooms
or barns.
Yet God
feeds them.
You're worth a lot more
than the birds!
[25]Can any of you add
an hour to life
by fretting about it?
[26]So if you can't do a little thing
like that,
why worry about the rest?
[27]Think about
how the lilies grow:
they don't slave

[26]Take a look at the birds
of the sky:
they don't plant or harvest,
or gather into barns.

Yet your heavenly Father
feeds them.
You're worth more
than they, aren't you?
[27]Can any of you add
one hour to life
by fretting about it?

[28]Why worry about clothes?
Notice
how the wild lilies grow:
they don't slave

12:7a
//Lk21:18,
Acts27:34b;
cf. 1Sm14:45,
2Sm14:11,
1Kgs1:52
12:7b
⊕Mt12:12
12:22
//Th36
12:24a
⊕Jb12:7-8;
Ps147:9,
Jb38:41
12:24b
TQ12:6-7
12:25
//GrTh36:3-4
12:27
//GrTh36:2

12:5 A warning to fear God, who has power to cast one into Gehenna, the valley of fire (see Matt 5:22; Jas 3:6). Gehenna is Greek for Valley of Hinnom, south of Jerusalem; probably because of Jer 19:1–10, it became a metaphor for the place God would punish the wicked.
12:27 A few mss add "or weave" after *never* spin.

and they never spin.
Yet let me tell you,
even Solomon at the height
of his glory
was never decked out like
one of them.
²⁸If God dresses up the grass
in the field,
which is here today
and tomorrow is tossed
into an oven,
it is surely more likely
(that God cares for) you,
you who don't take anything
for granted!

²⁹And don't be constantly
on the lookout for
what you're going to eat
and what you're going to drink.

Don't give it a thought.
³⁰These are all things
the world's pagans seek,
and your Father
is aware
that you need them.
³¹Instead, you are to seek
(God's) domain,

and these things will come
to you as a bonus."

and they never spin.
²⁹Yet let me tell you,
even Solomon at the height
of his glory
was never decked out like
one of them.
³⁰If God dresses up the grass
in the field,
which is here today
and tomorrow is thrown
into an oven,
won't (God care for) you
even more,
you who don't take anything
for granted?
³¹So don't fret.
Don't say,

'What am I going to eat?'
or 'What am I going to drink?'
or 'What am I going to wear?'

³²These are all things
pagans seek.
After all, your heavenly Father
is aware
that you need them.
"You are to seek
(God's) domain,
and his justice first,
and all these things will come
to you as a bonus."

On possessions
Luke 12:33–34 / Matt 6:19–21

³³"Sell your belongings,
and donate to charity;

make yourselves purses

¹⁹"Don't acquire possessions
here on earth,
where moths
and insects eat away
and where robbers break in
and steal.

12:29
↻Q10:4
12:30
↻Q11:13
12:31
Cf. Rom14:17;
↻Mt19:29,
Lk18:29b-30
12:33
//Th76:3;
cf. Mk10:21,
Mt19:21,
Jas5:2-3;
TLk12:16-21,
18:22; Tob4:9,
12:8-9

that don't wear out,
with inexhaustible wealth
in heaven,
where no robber can get to it
and no moth can destroy it.

[20]Instead, gather your nest egg
in heaven,

where neither moths
nor insects eat away
and where no robbers break in
or steal.

[34]As you know,
what you treasure
is your heart's true measure."

[21]As you know,
what you treasure
is your heart's true measure."

[Jesus. Selections from *The Sayings Gospel Q* from Robert J. Miller, ed., *The Complete Gospels: Annotated Scholars Version*, third edition. (A Polebridge Press Book, Harper San Francisco, A Division of Harper Collins Publishers, 1994.) (1) Pp. 256–61. (2) P. 270. (3) P. 273. (4) Pp. 275–76. (5) P. 280. (6) Pp. 282–84.]

9

Baruch (Benedict) Spinoza

1632–1677

On the Improvement of the Understanding

A short essay on value is included in a longer essay on the understanding. Although Spinoza stresses wisdom as the chief value in
human life, the final value is happiness or, as he puts it, "true happiness." Many of his values agree with those of the Stoics.

Also see Study Guide (4b9), pp. 35–36.

On wisdom

(1) After experience had taught me that all the usual surroundings of
social life are vain and futile; seeing that none of the objects of my fears contained in themselves anything either good or bad, except in so far as the mind
is affected by them, I finally resolved to inquire whether there might be some
real good having power to communicate itself, which would affect the mind
singly, to the exclusion of all else: whether, in fact, there might be anything
of which the discovery and attainment would enable me to enjoy continuous, supreme, and unending happiness. I say "I *finally* resolved," for at first
sight it seemed unwise willingly to lose hold on what was sure for the sake of
something then uncertain. I could see the benefits which are acquired
through fame and riches, and that I should be obliged to abandon the quest
of such objects, if I seriously devoted myself to the search for something different and new. I perceived that if true happiness chanced to be placed in the
former I should necessarily miss it; while if, on the other hand, it were not so
placed, and I gave them my whole attention, I should equally fail.

I therefore debated whether it would not be possible to arrive at the
new principle, or at any rate at a certainty concerning its existence,
without changing the conduct and usual plan of my life; with this end in

view I made many efforts, but in vain. For the ordinary surroundings of life which are esteemed by men (as their actions testify) to be the highest good, may be classed under the three heads—Riches, Fame, and the Pleasures of Sense: with these three the mind is so absorbed that it has little power to reflect on any different good. By sensual pleasure the mind is enthralled to the extent of quiescence, as if the supreme good were actually attained, so that it is quite incapable of thinking of any other object; when such pleasure has been gratified it is followed by extreme melancholy, whereby the mind, though not enthralled, is disturbed and dulled.

The pursuit of honors and riches is likewise very absorbing, especially if such objects be sought simply for their own sake, inasmuch as they are then supposed to constitute the highest good. In the case of fame the mind is still more absorbed, for fame is conceived as always good for its own sake, and as the ultimate end to which all actions are directed. Further, the attainment of riches and fame is not followed as in the case of sensual pleasures by repentance, but, the more we acquire, the greater is our delight, and, consequently, the more are we incited to increase both the one and the other; on the other hand, if our hopes happen to be frustrated we are plunged into the deepest sadness. Fame has the further drawback that it compels its votaries to order their lives according to the opinions of their fellow-men, shunning what they usually shun, and seeking what they usually seek.

When I saw that all these ordinary objects of desire would be obstacles in the way of a search for something different and new—nay, that they were so opposed thereto, that either they or it would have to be abandoned, I was forced to inquire which would prove the most useful to me: for, as I say, I seemed to be willingly losing hold on a sure good for the sake of something uncertain. However, after I had reflected on the matter, I came in the first place to the conclusion that by abandoning the ordinary objects of pursuit, and betaking myself to a new quest, I should be leaving a good, uncertain by reason of its own nature, as may be gathered from what has been said, for the sake of a good not uncertain in its nature (for I sought for a fixed good), but only in the possibility of its attainment.

Further reflection convinced me, that if I could really get to the root of the matter I should be leaving certain evils for a certain good. I thus perceived that I was in a state of great peril, and I compelled myself to seek with all my strength for a remedy, however uncertain it might be; as a sick man struggling with a deadly disease, when he sees that death will surely be upon him unless a remedy be found, is compelled to seek such a remedy with all his strength, inasmuch as his whole hope lies therein. All the objects pursued by the multitude not only bring no remedy that tends to preserve our being, but even act as hindrances, causing the death not seldom of those who possess them, and always of those who are possessed by them. There are many examples of men who have suffered persecution even to death for the sake of their riches, and of men who in pursuit of wealth have exposed themselves to so many dangers, that they have paid away their life as a penalty for their folly. Examples are no less numerous of men, who have endured the utmost wretchedness for the sake of gaining or preserving their reputation. Lastly, there are innumerable cases of men, who have hastened their death through overindulgence in sensual pleasure. All these evils seem to have arisen from the fact, that happiness or unhappiness is made wholly to depend on the quality of the object which we love. When a thing is not loved, no quarrels will arise concerning it—no sadness will be felt if it perishes—no envy if it is possessed by another—no fear, no hatred, in short no disturbances of the mind. All these arise from the love of what is perishable, such as the objects already mentioned. But love towards a thing eternal and infinite feeds the mind wholly with joy, and is itself unmingled with any sadness, wherefore it is greatly to be desired and sought for with all our strength. Yet it was not at random that I used the words, "If I could go to the root of the matter," for, though what I have urged was perfectly clear to my mind, I could not forthwith lay aside all love of riches, sensual enjoyment, and fame. One thing was evident, namely, that while my mind was employed with these thoughts it turned away from its former objects of desire, and seriously considered the search for a new principle; this state of things was a great comfort to me, for I perceived that the evils were not such as to resist all remedies. Although these intervals were at first rare, and of very short duration, yet afterwards, as the true good became more and more discernible to me, they became more frequent and more lasting; especially after I had recognized that the acquisition of wealth, sensual pleasure, or fame, is only a hindrance, so long as they are sought as ends not as means; if they be sought as means, they will be under restraint, and, far from being hindrances, will further not a little the end for which they are sought, as I will show in due time.

I will here only briefly state what I mean by true good, and also what is the nature of the highest good. In order that this may be rightly understood, we must bear in mind that the terms good and evil are only applied relatively, so that the same thing may be called both good and bad, according to the relations in view, in the same way as it may be called perfect or imperfect. Nothing regarded in its own nature can be called perfect or imperfect; especially when we are aware that all things which come to pass, come to pass according to the eternal order and fixed laws of nature. However, human weakness cannot attain to this order in its own thoughts, but meanwhile man conceives a human character much more stable than his own, and sees that there is no reason why he should not himself acquire such a character. Thus he is led to seek for means which will bring him to this pitch of perfection, and calls everything which will serve as such means a true good. The chief good is that he should arrive, together with other individuals if possible, at the possession of the aforesaid character. What that character is we shall show in due time, namely, that it is the knowledge of the union existing between the mind and the whole of nature. This, then, is the end for which I strive, to attain to such a character myself, and to endeavor that many should attain to it with me. In other words, it is part of my happiness to lend a helping hand, that many others may understand even as I do, so that their understanding and desire may entirely agree with my own. In order to bring this about, it is necessary to understand as much of nature as will enable us to attain to the aforesaid character, and also to form a social order such as is most conducive to the attainment of this character by the greatest number with the least difficulty and danger. We must seek the assistance of Moral Philosophy[1] and the Theory of Education; further, as health is no insignificant means for attaining our end, we must also include the whole science of Medicine, and, as many difficult things are by contrivance rendered easy, and we can in this way gain much time and convenience, the science of Mechanics must in no way be despised. But, before all things, a means must be devised for improving the understanding and purifying it, as far as may be at the outset, so that it may apprehend things without error, and in the best possible way.

Thus it is apparent to everyone that I wish to direct all sciences to one end and aim,[2] so that we may attain to the supreme human perfection which we have named; and, therefore, whatsoever in the sciences does not serve to promote our object will have to be rejected as useless. To sum up the matter in a word, all our actions and thoughts must be directed to this one end. Yet, as it is necessary that while we are endeavoring to attain our purpose, and bring the understanding into the right path, we should carry on our life, we are compelled first of all to lay down certain rules of life as provisionally good, to wit the following:—

I. To speak in a manner intelligible to the multitude, and to comply with every general custom that does not hinder the attainment of our purpose. For we can gain from the multitude no small advantages, provided that we strive to accommodate ourselves to its understanding as far as possible: moreover, we shall in this way gain a friendly audience for the reception of the truth.

II. To indulge ourselves with pleasures only in so far as they are necessary for preserving health.

III. Lastly, to endeavour to obtain only sufficient money or other commodities to enable us to preserve our life and health, and to follow such general customs as are consistent with our purpose.

Having laid down these preliminary rules, I will betake myself to the first and most important task, namely, the amendment of the understanding, and the rendering it capable of understanding things in the manner necessary for attaining our end.

In order to bring this about, the natural order demands that I should here recapitulate all the modes of perception, which I have hitherto employed for affirming or denying anything with certainty, so that I may choose the best, and at the same time begin to know my own powers and the nature which I wish to perfect.

Reflection shows that all modes of perception or knowledge may be reduced to four:—

I. Perception arising from hearsay or from some sign which everyone may name as he pleases.

II. Perception arising from mere experience—that is, from experience not yet classified by the intellect, and only so called because the given event has happened to take place, and we have no contradictory fact to set against it, so that it therefore remains unassailed in our mind.

III. Perception arising when the essence of one thing is inferred from another thing, but not adequately; this comes[3] when from some effect we gather its cause, or when it is inferred from some general proposition that some property is always present.

IV. Lastly, there is the perception arising when a thing is perceived solely through its essence, or through the knowledge of its proximate cause.

All these kinds of perception I will illustrate by examples. By hearsay I know the day of my birth, my parentage, and other matters about which I have never felt any doubt. By mere experience I know that I shall die, for this I can affirm from having seen that others like myself have died, though all did not live for the same period, or die by the same disease. I know by mere experience that oil has the property of feeding fire, and water of extinguishing it. In the same way I know that a dog is a barking animal, man a rational animal, and in fact nearly all the practical knowledge of life.

We deduce one thing from another as follows: when we clearly perceive that we feel a certain body and no other, we thence clearly infer that the mind is united to the body,[4] and that their union is the cause of the given sensation; but we cannot thence absolutely understand the nature of the sensation and the union.[5] Or after I have become acquainted with the nature of vision, and know that it has the property of making one and the same thing appear smaller when far off than when near, I can infer that the sun is larger than it appears, and can draw other conclusions of the same kind.

Lastly, a thing may be perceived solely through its essence; when, from the fact of knowing something, I know what it is to know that thing, or when, from knowing the essence of the mind, I know that it is united to the body. By the same kind of knowledge we know that two and three make five, or that two lines each parallel to a third, are parallel to one another, &c. The things which I have been able to know by this kind of knowledge are as yet very few.

NOTES

1. N.B. I do no more here than enumerate the sciences necessary for our purpose; I lay no stress on their order.

2. There is for the sciences but one end, to which they should all be directed.

3. In this case we do not understand anything of the cause from the consideration of it in the effect. This is sufficiently evident from the fact that the cause is only spoken of in very general terms, such as—there exists then something; there exists then some power, &c.; or from the fact that we only express it in a negative manner—it is not this or that, &c. In the second case something is ascribed to the cause because of the effect, as we shall show in an example, but only a property, never the essence.

4. From this example may be clearly seen what I have just drawn attention to. For through this union we understand nothing beyond the sensation, the effect, to wit, from which we inferred the cause of which we understand nothing.

5. A conclusion of this sort, though it be certain, is yet not to be relied on without great caution; for unless we are exceedingly careful we shall forthwith fall into error. When things are conceived thus abstractedly, and not through their true essence, they are apt to be confused by the imagination. For that which is in itself one, men imagine to be multiplex. To those things which are conceived abstractedly, apart, and confusedly, terms are applied which are apt to become wrested from their strict meaning, and bestowed on things more familiar; whence it results that these latter are imagined in the same way as the former to which the terms were originally given.

[The first part of the essay "On the Improvement of the Understanding" from *The Chief Works of Spinoza*, vol. 2, tr. R. H. M. Elwes (New York: Dover Publications, Inc., 1951). (1) Pp. 3–9.]

10

Andrew Carnegie

1835–1919

The Gospel of Wealth

A professed advocate of social Darwinism (*q.v.* D 1, 3), Carnegie recorded in his *Autobiography*, after reading Darwin and Spencer: " . . . the light came as in a flood and all was clear. Not only had I got rid of theology and the supernatural, but I had found the truth of evolution. 'All is well since all grows better' became my motto . . . " (Introduction, *The Gospel of Wealth*, p. xi). His manner of combining the "struggle for survival" with philanthropy was shared by John D. Rockefeller and other American industrialists.

Also see Study Guide (4b10), pp. 36–37.

(1) The contrast between the palace of the millionaire and the cottage of the laborer with us today measures the change which has come with civilization. This change, however, is not to be deplored, but welcomed as highly beneficial. It is well, nay, essential, for the progress of the race that the houses of some should be homes for all that is highest and best in literature and the arts, and for all the refinements of civilization, rather than that none should be so. Much better this great irregularity than universal squalor. Without wealth there can be no Mæcenas. The "good old times" were not good old times. Neither master nor servant was as well situated then as today. A relapse to old conditions would be disastrous to both—not the least so to him who serves—and would sweep away civilization with it. But whether the change be for good or ill, it is upon us, beyond our power to alter, and, therefore, to be accepted and made the best of. It is a waste of time to criticize the inevitable.

It is easy to see how the change has come. One illustration will serve for almost every phase of the cause. In the manufacture of products we have the whole story. It applies to all combinations of human industry, as stimulated and enlarged by the inventions of this scientific age. Formerly, articles were manufactured at the domestic hearth, or in small shops which formed part of the household.

❧ ❧ ❧

The inevitable result of such a mode of manufacture was crude articles at high prices. Today the world obtains commodities of excellent quality at prices which even the preceding generation would have deemed incredible. In the commercial world similar causes have produced similar results, and the race is benefited thereby. The poor enjoy what the rich could not before afford. What were the luxuries have become the necessaries of life. The laborer has now more comforts than the farmer had a few generations ago. The farmer has more luxuries than the landlord had, and is more richly clad and better housed. The landlord has books and pictures rarer and appointments more artistic than the king could then obtain.

❧ ❧ ❧

The price which society pays for the law of competition, like the price it pays for cheap comforts and luxuries, is also great; but the advantages of this law are also greater still than its cost—for it is to this law that we owe our wonderful material development, which brings improved conditions in its train. But, whether the law be benign or not, we must say of it, as we say of the change in the conditions of men to which we have referred: It is here; we cannot evade it; no substitutes for it have been found; and while the law may be sometimes hard for the individual, it is best for the race, because it insures the survival of the fittest in every department. We accept and welcome, therefore, as conditions to which we must accommodate ourselves, great inequality of environment; the concentration of business, industrial and commercial, in the hands of a few; and the law of competition between these, as being not only beneficial, but essential to the future progress of the race. Having accepted these, it follows that there must be great scope for the exercise of special ability in the merchant and in the manufacturer who has to conduct affairs upon a great scale. That this talent for organization and management is rare among men is proved by the fact that it invariably secures enormous rewards for its possessor, no matter where or under what laws or conditions. The experienced in affairs always rate the MAN whose services can be obtained as a partner as not only the first consideration, but such as render the question of his capital scarcely worth considering: for able men soon create capital; in the hands of those without the special talent required, capital soon takes wings. Such men become interested in firms or corporations using millions; and, estimating only simple interest to be made upon the capital invested, it is inevitable that their income must exceed their expenditure and that they must, therefore, accumulate wealth. Nor is there any middle ground which such men can occupy, because the great manufacturing or commercial concern which does not earn at least interest upon its capital soon becomes bankrupt. It must either go forward or fall behind; to stand still is impossible. It is a condition essential to its successful operation that it should be thus far profitable, and even that, in addition to interest on capital, it should make profit. It is a law, as certain as any of the others named, that men possessed of this peculiar talent for affairs, under the free play of economic forces must, of necessity, soon be in receipt of more revenue than can be judiciously expended upon themselves; and this law is as beneficial for the race as the others.

Objections to the foundations upon which society is based are not in order, because the condition of the race is better with these than it has been with any other which has been tried. Of the effect of any new substitutes proposed we cannot be sure. The Socialist or Anarchist who seeks to overturn present conditions is to be regarded as attacking the foundation upon which civilization itself rests, for civilization took its start from the day when the capable, industrious workman said to his incompetent and lazy fellow, "If thou dost not sow, thou shalt not reap," and thus ended primitive Communism by separating the drones from the bees. One who studies this subject will soon be brought face to face with the conclusion that upon the sacredness of property civilization itself depends—the right of the laborer to his hundred dollars in the savings bank, and equally the legal right of the millionaire to his millions. Every man must be allowed "to sit under his own vine and fig tree, with none to make afraid," if human society is to advance, or even to remain so far advanced as it is. To those who propose to substitute Communism for this intense Individualism, the answer therefore is: The race has tried that. All progress from that barbarous day to the present time has resulted from its displacement. Not evil, but good, has come to the race from the accumulation of wealth by those who have had the ability and energy to produce it. But even if we admit for a moment that it might be better for the race to discard its present foundation, Individualism,—that it is a nobler ideal that man should labor, not for himself alone, but in and for a brotherhood of his fellows, and share with them all in common, realizing Swedenborg's idea of heaven,[1] where, as he says, the angels derive their happiness, not from laboring for self, but for each other,—even admit all this, and a sufficient answer is, This is not evolution, but revolution. It necessitates the changing of human nature itself—a work of eons, even if it were good to change it, which we cannot know.

It is not practicable in our day or in our age. Even if desirable theoretically, it belongs to another and long-succeeding sociological stratum. Our duty is with what is practicable now—with the next step possible in our day and generation. It is criminal to waste our energies in endeavoring to uproot, when all we can profitably accomplish is to bend the universal tree of humanity a little in the direction most favorable to the production of good fruit under existing circumstances. We might as well urge the destruction of the highest existing type of man because he failed to reach our ideal as to favor the destruction of Individualism, Private Property, the Law of Accumulation of Wealth, and the Law of Competition; for these are the highest result of human experience, the soil in which society, so far, has produced the best fruit. Unequally or unjustly, perhaps, as these laws sometimes operate, and imperfect as they appear to the Idealist, they are, nevertheless, like the highest type of man, the best and most valuable of all that humanity has yet accomplished.

We start, then, with a condition of affairs under which the best interests of the race are promoted, but which inevitably gives wealth to the few. Thus far, accepting conditions as they exist, the situation can be surveyed and pronounced good. The question then arises,—and if the foregoing be correct, it is the only question with which we have to deal,—What is the proper mode of administering wealth after the laws upon which civilization is founded have thrown it into the hands of the few? And it is of this great question that I believe I offer the true solution. It will be understood that fortunes are here spoken of, not moderate sums saved by many years of effort, the returns from which are required for the comfortable maintenance and education of families. This is not wealth, but only competence, which it should be the aim of all to acquire, and which it is for the best interests of society should be acquired.

Three Modes for Disposing of Surplus Wealth

There are but three modes in which surplus wealth can be disposed of. It can be left to the families of the decedents; or it can be bequeathed for public purposes; or, finally, it can be administered by its possessors during their lives. Under the first and second modes most of the wealth of the world that has reached the few has hitherto been applied. Let us in turn consider each of these modes. The first is the most injudicious.

≈   ≈   ≈

... the question which forces itself upon thoughtful men in all lands is, Why should men leave great fortunes to their children? If this is done from affection, is it not misguided affection? Observation teaches that, generally speaking, it is not well for the children that they should be so burdened. Neither is it well for the State.

≈   ≈   ≈

... looking at the usual result of enormous sums conferred upon legatees, the thoughtful man must shortly say, "I would as soon leave to my son a curse as the almighty dollar," and admit to himself that it is not the welfare of the children, but family pride, which inspires these legacies.

As to the second mode, that of leaving wealth at death for public uses, it may be said that this is only a means for the disposal of wealth, provided a man is content to wait until he is dead before he becomes of much good in the world. Knowledge of the results of legacies bequeathed is not calculated to inspire the brightest hopes of much posthumous good being accomplished by them. The cases are not few in which the real object sought by the testator is not attained, nor are they few in which his real wishes are thwarted. In many cases the bequests are so used as to become only monuments of his folly. It is well to remember that it requires the exercise of not less ability than that which acquires it, to use wealth so as to be really beneficial to the community. Besides this, it may fairly be said that no man is to be extolled for doing what he cannot help doing, nor is he to be thanked by the community to which he only leaves wealth at death. Men who leave vast sums in this way may fairly be thought men who would not have left it at all had they been able to take it with them.

≈   ≈   ≈

There remains, then, only one mode of using great fortunes; but in this we have the true antidote for the temporary unequal distribution of wealth, the reconciliation of the rich and the poor—a reign of harmony, another ideal, differing, indeed, from that of the Communist in requiring only the further evolution of existing conditions, not the total overthrow of our civilization. It is founded upon the present most intense Individualism, and the race is prepared to put it in practice by degrees whenever it pleases. Under its sway we shall have an ideal State, in which the surplus wealth of the few will become, in the best sense, the property of the many, because administered for the common good; and this wealth, passing through the hands of the few, can be made a much more potent force for the elevation of our race than if distributed in small sums to the people themselves. Even the poorest can be made to see this, and to agree that great sums gathered by some of their fellow-citizens and spent for public purposes, from which the masses reap the principal benefit, are more valuable to them than if scattered among themselves in trifling amounts through the course of many years.

(2) Poor and restricted are our opportunities in this life, narrow our horizon, our best work most imperfect; but rich men should be thankful for one inestimable boon. They have it in their power during their lives to busy themselves in organizing benefactions from which the masses of their fellows will derive lasting advantage, and thus dignify their own lives. The highest life is probably to be reached, not by such imitation of the life of Christ as Count Tolstoi gives us, but, while animated by Christ's spirit, by recognizing the changed conditions of this age, and adopting modes of expressing this spirit suitable to the changed conditions under which we live, still laboring for the good of our fellows, which was the essence of his life and teaching, but laboring in a different manner.

This, then, is held to be the duty of the man of wealth: To set an example of modest, unostentatious living, shunning display or extravagance; to provide moderately for the legitimate wants of those dependent upon him; and, after doing so, to consider all surplus revenues which come to him simply as trust funds, which he is called upon to administer, and strictly bound as a matter of duty to administer in the manner which, in his judgment, is best calculated to produce the most beneficial results for the community—the man of wealth thus becoming the mere trustee and agent for his poorer brethren, bringing to their service his superior wisdom, experience, and ability to administer, doing for them better than they would or could do for themselves.

In bestowing charity, the main consideration should be to help those who will help themselves; to provide part of the means by which those who desire to improve may do so; to give those who desire to rise the aids by which they may rise; to assist, but rarely or never to do all. Neither the individual nor the race is improved by almsgiving. Those worthy of assistance, except in rare cases, seldom require assistance.

The really valuable men of the race never do, except in case of accident or sudden change. Every one has, of course, cases of individuals brought to his own knowledge where temporary assistance can do genuine good, and these he will not overlook. But the amount which can be wisely given by the individual for individuals is necessarily limited by his lack of knowledge of the circumstances connected with each. He is the only true reformer who is as careful and as anxious not to aid the unworthy as he is to aid the worthy, and, perhaps, even more so, for in almsgiving more injury is probably done by rewarding vice than by relieving virtue.

. . . the best means of benefiting the community is to place within its reach the ladders, upon which the aspiring can rise—free libraries, parks, and means of recreation, by which men are helped in body and mind; works of art, certain to give pleasure and improve the public taste; and public institutions of various kinds, which will improve the general condition of the people; in this manner returning their surplus wealth to the mass of their fellows in the forms best calculated to do them lasting good.

Thus is the problem of rich and poor to be solved. The laws of accumulation will be left free, the laws of distribution free. Individualism will continue, but the millionaire will be but a trustee for the poor, intrusted for a season with a great part of the increased wealth of the community, but administering it for the community far better than it could or would have done for itself. The best minds will thus have reached a stage in the development of the race in which it is clearly seen that there is no mode of disposing of surplus wealth creditable to thoughtful and earnest men into whose hands it flows, save by using it year by year for the general good. This day already dawns.

Such, in my opinion is the true gospel concerning wealth, obedience to which is destined some day to solve the problem of the rich and the poor, and to bring "Peace on earth, among men good will."

(3) Bearing in mind these considerations, let us endeavor to present some of the best uses to which a millionaire can devote the surplus of which he should regard himself as only the trustee.

First. Standing apart by itself there is the founding of a university by men enormously rich, such men as must necessarily be few in any country.

Second. The result of my own study of the question, What is the best gift which can be given to a community? is that a free library occupies the first place, provided the community will accept and maintain it as a public institution, as much a part of the city property as its public schools, and, indeed, an adjunct to these.

(4) *Third.* We have another most important department in which great sums can be worthily used—the founding or extension of hospitals, medical colleges, laboratories, and other institutions connected with the alleviation of human suffering, and especially with the prevention rather than with the cure of human ills.

Fourth. In the very front rank of benefactions public parks should be placed, always provided that the community undertakes to maintain, beautify, and preserve them inviolate. No more useful or more beautiful monument can be left by any man than a park for the city in which he was born or in which he has long lived, nor can the community pay a more graceful tribute to the citizen who presents it than to give his name to the gift.

(5) *Fifth.* We have another good use for surplus wealth in providing our cities with halls suitable for meetings of all kinds, and for concerts of elevating music. Our cities are rarely possessed of halls for these purposes, being in this respect also very far behind European cities.

Sixth. In another respect we are still much behind Europe. A form of benevolence which is not uncommon there is providing swimming-baths for the people. The donors of these have been wise enough to require the city benefited to maintain them at its own expense, and as proof of the contention that everything should never be done for any one or for any community, but that the recipients should invariably be called upon to do a part, it is significant that it is found essential for the popular success of these healthful establishments to exact a nominal charge for their use.

Seventh. Churches as fields for the use of surplus wealth have purposely been reserved for the last, because, these being sectarian, every man will be governed in his action in regard to them by his own attachments; therefore gifts to churches, it may be said, are not, in one sense, gifts to the community at large, but to special classes. Nevertheless, every millionaire may know of a district where the little cheap, uncomfortable, and altogether unworthy wooden structure stands at the crossroads, in which the whole neighborbood gathers on Sunday, and which, independently of the form of the doctrines taught, is the center of social life and source of neighborly feeling. The administrator of wealth makes a good use of a part of his surplus if he replaces that building with a permanent structure of brick, stone, or granite, up whose sides the honeysuckle and columbine may climb, and from whose tower the sweet-tolling bell may sound. The millionaire should not figure how cheaply this structure can be built, but how perfect it can be made. If he has the money, it should be made a gem, for the educating influence of a pure and noble specimen of architecture, built, as the pyramids were built, to stand for ages, is not to be measured by dollars.

     ≈   ≈   ≈

. . . (an) enchanting realm which lies far from the material and prosaic conditions which surround him in this workaday world—a real world, this new realm, vague and undefined though its boundaries be. Once within its magic circle, its denizens live there an inner life more precious than the external, and all their days and all their ways, their triumphs and their trials, and all they see, and all they hear, and all they think, and all they do, are hallowed by the radiance which shines from afar upon this inner life, . . . all right within.

     ≈   ≈   ≈

Many other avenues for the wise expenditure of surplus wealth might be indicated. I enumerate but a few—a very few—of the many fields which are open, and only those in which great or considerable sums can be judiciously used. It is not the privilege, however, of millionaires alone to work for or aid measures which are certain to benefit the community. Every one who has but a small surplus above his moderate wants may share this privilege with his richer brothers, and those without surplus can give at least a part of their time, which is usually as important as funds, and often more so.

NOTE

1. Carnegie is referring to Emanuel Swedenborg's (1688–1772) mystic theology expressed in his work *Heaven and Hell.*

[Andrew Carnegie. "The Gospel of Wealth," from *The Gospel of Wealth and Other Timely Essays*, ed. E. C. Kirkland (Cambridge, Mass.: Belknap Press of Harvard University, 1962). (1) Pp. 14–23. (2) Pp. 25–29. (3) Pp. 32–36. (4) Pp. 40–41. (5) Pp. 44–46.]

11

Thomas Hill Green

1836–1882

Prolegomena to Ethics

The first of the nineteenth-century British idealists, Green believed self-realization, understood as a principle of perfection operating in man, to be the ultimate good of human life. For Green the principle of perfection was a sign of divinity. He argued that the Utilitarian principle of a greatest sum of pleasures was both meaningless and unworkable.

Also see Study Guide (4b11), p. 37.

The Good as Human Perfection

(1) According to the doctrine of this treatise, as we have previously endeavored to state it, there is a principle of self-development in man, independent of the excitement of new desires by those new imaginations, which presuppose new experiences, of pleasure. In virtue of this principle he anticipates experience. In a certain sense he makes it, instead of merely waiting to be made by it. He is capable of being moved by an idea of himself, as becoming that which he has it in him to be—an idea which does not represent previous experience, but gradually brings an experience into being, gradually creates a filling for itself, in the shape of arts, laws, institutions, and habits of living, which, so far as they go, exhibit the capabilities of man, define the idea of his end, afford a positive answer to the otherwise unanswerable question, what in particular it is that man has it in him to become. The action of such an idea in the individual accounts for two things which, upon the Hedonistic supposition, are equally unaccountable. It accounts for the possibility of the question, Why should I trouble about making myself or my

neighbors other than we are? and, given the question, it accounts for an answer being rendered to it, in the shape of a real initiation of effort for the improvement of human life.

The supposition, therefore, of a free or self-objectifying spiritual agency in human history is one to which a fair analysis of human history inevitably leads us. But it remains to be asked by what rule the effort is to be guided, which we suppose the idea of a possible human perfection thus to initiate. That idea, according to our view, is primarily in man unfilled and unrealized; and within the experience of men it is never fully realized, never acquires a content adequate to its capacity. There are arts and institutions and rules of life, in which the human spirit has so far incompletely realized its idea of a possible Best; and the individual in whom the idea is at work will derive from it a general injunction to further these arts, to maintain and, so far as he can, improve these institutions. It is when this general injunction has to be translated into particulars that the difficulty arises. How is the essential to be distinguished from the unessential and obstructive, in the processes through which an effort after the perfection of man may be traced? How are the arts to become a more thorough realization of the ideal which has imperfectly expressed itself in them?

How are the institutions of social life, and the rules of conventional morality, to be cleared of the alien growths which they owe to the constant cooperation of selfish passions with interest in common good, and which render them so imperfectly organic to the development of the human spirit? Above all, how is this or that individual—circumstanced as he is, and endowed, physically and mentally, as he is—to take part in the work? When he is called upon to decide between adherence to some established rule of morality and service to a particular person, or to face some new combination of circumstances to which recognized rules of conduct do not seem to apply, how is he to find guidance in an idea which merely moves him to aim at the best and highest in conduct?

(2) Though the idea of an absolutely perfect life, however, cannot be more to us than the idea that there must be such a life, as distinct from an idea of what it is—and we may admit this while holding that this idea is in a supreme sense formative and influential—it does not follow that there is any difficulty in conceiving very definitely a life of the individual and of society more perfect, because more completely fulfilling the vocation of individual and society, than any which is being lived. There may have been a period in the history of our race when the idea of a possible perfection was a blindly moving influence; when it had not yet taken sufficient effect

in the ordering of life and the formation of virtues for reflection on these to enable men to say what it would be to be more perfect. But we are certainly not in that state now. We all recognize, and perhaps in some fragmentary way practice, virtues which both carry in themselves unfulfilled possibilities, and at the same time plainly point out the direction in which their own further development is to be sought for. It has already been sought in this treatise to trace the ideal of the cardinal virtues, as recognized by the conscience of Christendom. In none of these would the man who came nearest the ideal "count himself to have attained," nor would he have any difficulty in defining the path of his further attainment. No one is eager *enough* to know what is true or make what is beautiful; no one ready *enough* to endure pain and forgo pleasure in the service of his fellows; no one impartial *enough* in treating the claims of another exactly as his own. Thus to have more "intellectual excellence"; to be more brave, temperate, and just, in the sense in which any one capable of enquiring what it is to be more perfect would now understand these virtues, is a sufficient object for him to set before himself by way of answer to the question, so far as it concerns him individually; while a state of society in which these virtues shall be more generally attainable and attained, is a sufficient account of the more perfect life considered as a social good.

It would seem then that, though statements at once positive and instructive as to the absolutely Best life may be beyond our reach, yet, by help of mere honest reflection on the evidence of its true vocation which the human spirit has so far yielded in arts and sciences, in moral and political achievement, we can know enough of a better life than our own, of a better social order than any that now is, to have an available criterion of what is good or bad in law and usage, and in the tendencies of men's actions. The working theory of the end, which we derive from the doctrine that the ultimate good for man must be some full development of the human spirit in character and conduct, may be represented by some such question as the following: Does this or that law or usage, this or that course of action—directly or indirectly, positively or as a preventive of the opposite—contribute to the better-being of society, as measured by the more general establishment of conditions favorable to the attainment of the recognized excellences and virtues, by the more general attainment of those excellences in some degree, or by their attainment on the part of some persons in higher degree without detraction from the opportunities of others? In order to put this question we must, no doubt, have a definite notion of the direction in which the "Summum Bonum" is to be sought, but not of what its full attainment would actually be; and this, it will be found, is all that we need or can obtain for our guidance in estimating the value of laws and institutions, actions and usages, by their effects. It will do nothing indeed to help us in ascertaining what the effects of any institution or action really are. No theory whatever of the "Summum Bonum," Hedonistic or other, can avail for the settlement of this question, which requires analysis of facts and circumstances, not consideration of ends. But it will sufficiently direct us in regard to the kind of effects we should look out for in our analysis, and to the value we should put upon them when ascertained.

"Greatest Pleasure" Not the Ultimate Good

(3) We are brought, then, to this point. The Utilitarian theory of ultimate good, if founded upon the Hedonistic theory of motives, we have found to be "intrinsically unavailable for supplying motive or guidance to a man who wishes to make his life better," because that theory of motives, when argued out, appears to exclude, not indeed the hope on the part of the individual that his own life and that of mankind may become better, *i.e.* more pleasant, but the belief that it can rest with him to exercise any initiative, whether in the way of resistance to inclination or of painful interference with usage, which may affect the result. We saw reason to think that this logical consequence of the theory tended to have at least a weakening influence upon life and conduct, and that there was accordingly a practical reason for seeking a substitute in another theory of ultimate good. But the question now arises whether this substitute shall be sought, according to the previous argument of this treatise, in a theory which would place the "Summum Bonum" in a perfection of human life, not indeed positively definable by us, but having an identity with the virtuous life actually achieved by the best men, as having for its principle the same will to be perfect; or rather in a revision of the Utilitarian theory, which shall make it independent of the Hedonistic theory of motives, while retaining the account of the "Summum Bonum" as a maximum of possible pleasure. We will endeavor to consider candidly what the latter alternative has to recommend it.

It is noticeable in the first place that, if the Utilitarian doctrine of the chief good as criterion—the doctrine that the greatest possible sum of pleasures is the end by reference to which the value of actions is to be tested—is dissociated from the Hedonistic doctrine of motives, though it may be cleared from liability to bad practical effects, it has also lost what has been in fact its chief claim to the acceptance of ordinary men. The process of its acceptance has been commonly this. Because there is pleasure in all satisfaction of desire, men have come to think that the object of desire is always some pleasure; that every good is a pleasure. From this the inference is natural enough that a greatest possible sum of pleasures is a greatest possible good—at any rate till it is pointed out that the possibility of desiring a sum of pleasures, which never can be enjoyed as a sum, would not follow from the fact that the object of desire was always some imagined pleasure. But once drop the notion that pleasure is the sole thing desired, and the question arises why it should be deemed that which "in our calm moments" is to be counted the sole thing desirable, so that the value of all which men do or which concerns them is to be measured simply by its tendency to produce pleasure. We suppose ourselves now to be arguing with men who admit the possibility of disinterested motives, who value character according as it is habitually actuated by them; who neither understand by such motives desires for that kind of pleasure of which the contemplation of another's pleasure is the condition, nor allow themselves to suppose that, granting benevolence to be always a desire to produce pleasure, it is therefore a desire for (*i.e.* to enjoy) pleasure. Why, we ask such persons, do you take that to be the one thing ultimately desirable, which you not only admit to be not the sole thing desired, but which you admit is not desired in those actions which you esteem the most?

It may be surmised that the chief attraction which the Hedonistic criterion has had for such persons has lain in its apparent definiteness. The conception of the "Summum Bonum," as consisting in a greatest possible net sum of pleasures, has seemed to afford a much more positive and intelligible criterion than the conception of a full realization of human capacities, which we admit to be only definable by reflection on the partial realization of those capacities in recognized excellences of character and conduct. It promises an escape, too, from the circle in which, as already observed, we seem to move, when we say that we ought to do so and so because it is virtuous or noble to do it, and then have to explain what is virtuous or noble as what we ought to do. A "Summum Bonum" consisting of a greatest possible sum of pleasures is supposed to be definite and intelligible, because every one knows what pleasure is. But in what sense does every one know it? If only in the sense that every one can imagine the renewal of some pleasure which he has enjoyed, it may be pointed out that pleasures, not being enjoyable in a sum—to say nothing of a greatest possible sum—cannot be imagined in a sum either. Though this remark, however, might be to the purpose against a Hedonist who held that desire could only be excited by imagined pleasure, and yet that a greatest sum of pleasure was an object of desire, it is not to the purpose against those who merely look on the greatest sum of pleasures as the true criterion, without holding that desire is only excited by imagination of pleasure. They will reply that, though we may not be able, strictly speaking, to imagine a sum of pleasures, every one knows what it is. Every one knows the difference between enjoying a longer succession of pleasures and a shorter one, a succession of more intense and a succession of less intense pleasures, a succession of pleasures less interrupted by pain and one more interrupted. In this sense every one knows the difference between enjoying a larger sum of pleasures and enjoying a smaller sum. He knows the difference also between a larger number of persons or sentient beings and a smaller one. He attaches therefore a definite meaning to the enjoyment of a greater net amount of pleasure by a greater number of beings, and has a definite criterion for distinguishing a better action from a worse, in the tendency of the one, as compared with the other, to produce a greater amount of pleasure to a greater number of persons.

The ability, however, to compare a larger sum of pleasure with a smaller in the sense explained—as we might compare a longer time with a shorter—is quite a different thing from ability to conceive a greatest possible sum of pleasures, or to attach any meaning to that phrase. It seems, indeed, to be intrinsically as unmeaning as it would be to speak of a greatest possible quantity of time or space. The sum of pleasures plainly admits of indefinite increase, with the continued existence of sentient beings capable of pleasure. It is greater today than it was yesterday, and, unless it has suddenly come to pass that experiences of pain outnumber experiences of pleasure, it will be greater tomorrow than it is today; but it will never be complete while sentient beings exist. To say that ultimate good is a greatest possible sum of pleasures, strictly taken, is to say that it is an end which forever recedes; which is not only unattainable but from the nature of the case can never be more nearly approached; and such an end clearly cannot serve the purpose of a criterion, by enabling us to distinguish actions which bring men nearer to it from those that do not. Are we then, since the notion of a greatest possible sum of pleasures is thus unavailable, to understand that in applying the Utilitarian criterion we merely approve one action in comparison with another, as tending to yield more pleasure to more beings capable of pleasure, without reference to a "Summum Bonum" or ideal of a perfect state of existence at all? But without such reference is there any meaning in approval or disapproval at all? It is intelligible that without such reference the larger sum of pleasures should be desired as against the less; on supposition of benevolent impulses, it is intelligible that the larger sum should be desired by a man for others as well as for himself. But the desire is one thing, the approval of it—the judgment "in a calm hour" that the desire of the action moved by it is reasonable—is quite another thing. Without some ideal—however indeterminate—of a best state of existence, with the attainment of which the approved motive or action may be deemed compatible, the approval of it would seem impossible. Utilitarians have therefore to consider whether they can employ a criterion of action, as they do employ it, without some idea of ultimate good; and, since a greatest possible sum of pleasures is a phrase to which no idea really corresponds, what is the idea which really actuates them in the employment of their criterion?

When, having duly reflected on these points, we try (if the expression may be pardoned) to make sense of the Utilitarian theory—bearing in mind at once its implication of the conception of a "Summum Bonum," and the impossibility that of pleasures, so long as sentient beings continue to enjoy themselves, there should be any such greatest sum as can satisfy the conception—we cannot avoid the conclusion that the "Summum Bonum" which the Utilitarian contemplates is not a sum of pleasures, but a certain state of existence; a state in which all human beings, or all beings of whose consciousness he supposes himself able to take account, shall live as pleasantly as is possible for them, without one gaining pleasure at the expense of another. The reason why he approves an action is not that he judges it likely to make an addition to a sum of pleasures which never comes nearer completion, but that he judges it likely to contribute to this state of general enjoyable existence. If he says that the right object for a man is to increase the stock of human enjoyments, it is presumable that he is not really thinking of an addition to a sum of pleasant experiences, however large, which might be made and yet leave those who had had the experiences with no more of the good in possession than they had before. He does not mean that a thousand experiences of pleasure constitute more of a good than nine hundred experiences of the same intensity, or less of a good than six hundred of a double intensity. He is thinking of a good consisting in a certain sort of social life, of which he does not particularize the nature to himself further than by conceiving it as a pleasant life to all who share in it, and as one of which all have the enjoyment, if not equally, yet none at the cost of others. By increasing the stock of enjoyments he means enabling more persons to live pleasantly, or with less interruption from pain. The good which he has before him is not an aggregate of pleasures but a pleasant life—a life at all times and for all persons as pleasant, as little marred by pain, as possible; but good, *qua* a life in which the persons living are happy or enjoy themselves, not a *qua* a life into which so many enjoyments are crowded.

Now the objection to this conception of a chief good is not that, so far as it goes, it is otherwise than true. According to our view, since there is pleasure in all realization of capacity, the life in which human capacities should be fully realized would necessarily be a pleasant life. The objection is that, instead of having that definiteness which, because all know what pleasure is, it seemed at first to promise, it turns out on consideration to be so abstract and indefinite. It tells us nothing of that life, to the attainment of which our actions must contribute if they are to be what they should be, but merely that it would be as pleasant as possible for all persons, or for all beings of whose consciousness we can take account. The question is whether in thinking of an absolutely desirable life, as the end by reference to which the effects of our actions are to be valued, our view must be confined to the mere quality of its universal pleasantness, and whether in consequence productivity of pleasure is the ultimate ground on which actions are to be approved. The view for which we plead is that the quality of the absolutely desirable life, which renders it such in man's thoughts, is that it shall be the full realization of his capacities; that, although pleasure must be incidental to such realization, it is in no way distinctive of it, being equally incidental to any unimpeded activity, to the exercise of merely animal functions no less than to those that are properly human; that, although we know not in detail what the final realization of man's capacities would be, we know well enough, from the evidence they have so far given of themselves, what a fuller development of them would be; and that thus, in the injunction to make life as full a realization as possible of human capacities, we have a definiteness of direction, which the injunction to make life as pleasant as possible does not supply.

≈   ≈   ≈

(4) It is not because looked forward to as pleasant, that the form of conscious life in which our capacities shall be fully realized is an object of desire to us; it is because, in such self-conscious beings as we are, a desire for their realization goes along with the presence of the capacities, that the form of conscious life in which this desire shall be satisfied is looked forward to as pleasant. And it is because the object of this desire, when reflected on, from the nature of the case presents itself to us as absolutely final, not because we anticipate pleasure in its attainment as we do in that of any and every desired object, that "in a calm hour" we pronounce it supremely desirable.

Perfection a Rational Goal

(5) We have previously explained how it comes about that any true theory of the good will present an appearance of moving in a circle. The rational or self-conscious soul, we have seen, constitutes its own end; is an end at once to and in itself. Its end is the perfection of itself, the fulfillment of the law of its being. The consciousness of there being such an end expresses itself in the judgment that something absolutely should be, that there is something intrinsically and ultimately desirable.

     ❧   ❧   ❧

If we ask for a reason why we should pursue this end, there is none to be given but that it is rational to do so, that reason bids it, that the pursuit is the effort of the self-conscious or rational soul after its own perfection. It is reasonable to desire it because it is reasonably to be desired. Those who like to do so may make merry over the tautology. Those who understand how it arises—from the fact, namely, that reason gives its own end, that the self-conscious spirit of man presents its own perfection to itself as the intrinsically desirable—will not be moved by the mirth. They will not try to escape the charge of tautology by taking the desirableness of ultimate good to consist in anything else than in the thought of it as that which would satisfy reason—satisfy the demand of the self-conscious soul for its own perfection. They will not appeal to pleasure, as being that which in fact we all desire, in order to determine our notion of what reason bids us desire. They will be aware that this notion cannot be determined by reference to anything but what reason has itself done; by anything but reflection on the excellences of character and conduct to which the rational effort after perfection of life has given rise. They will appeal to the virtues to tell them what is virtuous, to goodness to tell them what is truly good, to the work of reason in human life to tell them what is reasonably to be desired; knowing well what they are about in so doing, and that it is the only appropriate procedure, because only in the full attainment of its end could reason learn fully what that end is, and only in what it has so far attained of the end can it learn what its further attainment would be.

(6) Now, according to the view already stated in this treatise, the rational soul in seeking an ultimate good necessarily seeks it as a state of its own being. An ultimate, intrinsic, absolute good has no meaning for us, except that which it derives from the effort of the rational soul in us to become all that it is conscious of a capacity for becoming. As the rational

soul is essentially the principle of self-consciousness, so the idea of ultimate good on the part of every one capable of it is necessarily the idea of a perfect self-conscious life for himself. The desirableness of that life is its desirableness as his own life. But to any one actuated by it the idea of a perfection, of a state in which he shall be satisfied, for himself will involve the idea of a perfection of all other beings, so far as he finds the thought of their being perfect necessary to his own satisfaction. Moral development, as has been previously explained more at large, is a progress in which the individual's conception of the kind of life that would be implied in his perfection gradually becomes fuller and more determinate; fuller and more determinate both in regard to the range of persons whose participation in the perfect life is thought of as necessary to its attainment by any one, and in regard to the qualities on the part of the individual which it is thought must be exercised in it. In the most complete determination within our reach, the conception still does not suffice to enable any one to say positively what the perfection of his life would be; but the determination has reached that stage in which the educated citizen of Christendom is able to think of the perfect life as essentially conditioned by the exercise of virtues, resting on a self-sacrificing will, in which it is open to all men to participate, and as fully attainable by one man, only in so far as through those virtues it is attained by all. In thinking of ultimate good he thinks of it indeed necessarily as perfection for himself; as a life in which he shall be fully satisfied through having become all that the spirit within him enables him to become. But he cannot think of himself as satisfied in any life other than a social life, exhibiting the exercise of self-denying will, and in which "the multitude of the redeemed," which is all men, shall participate. He has other faculties indeed than those which are directly exhibited in the specifically moral virtues—faculties which find their expression not in his dealings with other men, but in the arts and sciences—and the development of these must be a necessary constituent in any life which he presents to himself as one in which he can find satisfaction. But "when he sits down in a calm hour" it will not be in isolation that the development of any of these faculties will assume the character for him of ultimate good. Intrinsic desirableness, sufficiency to satisfy the rational soul, will be seen to belong to their realization only in so far as it is a constituent in a whole of social life, of which the distinction, as a social life, shall be universality of disinterested goodness.

We should accept the view, then, that to think of ultimate good is to think of an intrinsically desirable form of conscious life; but we should seek further to define it. We should take it in the sense that to think of such good is to think of a state of self-conscious life as intrinsically desirable for oneself, and for that reason is to think of it as something else than plea-sure—the thought of an object as pleasure for oneself, and the thought of it as intrinsically desirable for oneself, being thoughts which exclude each other. The pleasure anticipated in the life is not that which renders it desir-able; but so far as desire is excited by the thought of it as desirable, and so far as that desire is reflected on, pleasure comes to be anticipated in the satisfaction of that desire. The thought of the intrinsically desirable life, then, is the thought of something else than pleasure, but the thought of what? The thought, we answer, of the full realization of the capacities of the human soul, of the fulfillment of man's vocation, as of that in which alone he can satisfy himself—a thought of which the content is never final and complete, which is always by its creative energy further determining its own content, but which for practical purposes, as the mover and guide of our highest moral effort, may be taken to be the thought of such a social life as that described in the previous paragraph.

Self-sacrifice

(7) The statement that the act of self-sacrifice has its value in itself is not to be understood as denying that it has its value in its consequences, but as implying that those consequences, to be of intrinsic value, must be of a kind with the act itself, as an exercise of a character having its domi-nant interest in some form of human perfection. The injunction that would be founded on the view of that perfection as the end would never be "Sac-rifice inclination" simply, but "Sacrifice inclination in so far as by so doing you may make men better"; but the bettering of men would mean their advance in a goodness the same in principle as that which appears in the sacrifice enjoined, and this sacrifice itself would be regarded as already an installment of the good to be more largely attained in its consequences. The direction to the individual, in doubt whether he should deny himself some attractive pursuit or some harmless indulgence, would be, not that he should make the sacrifice for the sake of making it, but that he should be ready to make it, if upon honest consideration it appear that men would be the better for his doing so.

(8) It is otherwise when the exercise of the recognized virtues and excellences, as resting upon a self-devoted will or will to be perfect, is con-sidered to be an end in itself—to be itself, if not in completeness yet in principle and essence, the ultimate good for man. The general nature of the claim of other men upon him is plain to every one who contemplates it with reference to such an end. It is a claim for service in the direction of making the attainment of those virtues and excellences, by some persons

and in some form, more possible. The question for the individual will still remain, how he in particular may best render this service, and it may be one of much difficulty. He may easily deceive himself in answering it, but he will not have the excuse for answering it in favor of his own inclination, which is afforded by reference to a "Summum Bonum" of which the most readily ascertainable constituent must always be his own pleasure.

As to the particular instance we have been considering, while intrinsic value will not be denied to excellence in music as having a place in the fulfillment of man's vocation, it is a question, so to speak, of spiritual proportion, whether the attainment of such excellence is of importance in any society of men under the given conditions of that society. For, like all excellence in art, it has its value as an element in a whole of spiritual life, to which the moral virtues are essential; which without them would be no realization of the capacities of the human soul. In some Italian principality of the last century, for instance, with its civil life crushed out and its moral energies debased, excellence in music could hardly be accounted of actual and present value at all. Its value would be potential, in so far as the artist's work might survive to become an element in a nobler life elsewhere or at a later time. Under such conditions much occupation with music might imply indifference to claims of the human soul which must be satisfied in order to the attainment of a life in which the value of music could be actualized. And under better social conditions there may be claims, arising from the particular position of an individual, which render the pursuit of excellence in music, though it would be the right pursuit for others qualified as he is, a wrong one for him. In the absence of such claims the main question will be of his particular talent. Has he talent to serve mankind—to contribute to the perfection of the human soul—more as a musician than in any other way? Only if he has will he be justified in making music his main pursuit. If he is not to make it his main pursuit, the question will remain, to what extent he may be justified in indulging his taste for it, either as a refreshment of faculties which are to be mainly used in other pursuits—to be so used, because in them he may best serve mankind in the sense explained—or as enabling him to share in that intrinsically valuable lifting up of the soul which music may afford.

A Divine Principle Realizing Itself in Persons

(9) Through certain *media*, and under certain consequent limitations, but with the constant characteristic of self-consciousness and self-objectification, the one divine mind gradually reproduces itself in the human soul. In virtue of this principle in him man has definite capabilities, the realization of which, since in it alone he can satisfy himself, forms his true

good. They are not realized, however, in any life that can be observed, in any life that has been, or is, or (as it would seem) that can be lived by man as we know him; and for this reason we cannot say with any adequacy what the capabilities are. Yet, because the essence of man's spiritual endowment is the consciousness of having it, the idea of his having such capabilities, and of a possible better state of himself consisting in their further realization, is a moving influence in him. It has been the parent of the institutions and usages, of the social judgments and aspirations, through which human life has been so far bettered; through which man has so far realized his capabilities and marked out the path that he must follow in their further realization. As his true good is or would be[1] their complete realization, so his goodness is proportionate to his habitual responsiveness to the idea of there being such a true good, in the various forms of recognized duty and beneficent work in which that idea has so far taken shape among men. In other words, it consists in the direction of the will to objects determined for it by this idea, as operative in the person willing; which direction of the will we may, upon the ground stated, fitly call its determination by reason.

Our next step should be to explain further how it is that the idea in man of a possible better state of himself, consisting in a further realization of his capabilities, has been the moralizing agent in human life; how it has yielded our moral standards, loyalty to which—itself the product of the same idea—is the condition of goodness in the individual. Before we attempt this explanation, however, it will be well to clear up an ambiguity which will probably be thought to lurk in the doctrine already advanced. We have spoken of a certain "divine principle" as the ground of human will and reason; as realizing itself in man; as having capabilities of which the full development would constitute the perfection of human life; of direction to objects contributory to this perfection as characteristic of a good will. But what, it will be asked, is to be understood in regard to the relation of this "divine principle" to the will and reason of individuals? Does it realize itself in persons, in you and me, or in some impersonal humanity?

      ❧   ❧   ❧

It is clearly of the very essence of the doctrine above advanced that the divine principle, which we suppose to be realizing itself in man, should be supposed to realize itself in persons, as such. But for reflection on our personality, on our consciousness of ourselves as objects to ourselves, we could never dream of there being such a self-realizing principle at all, whether as implied in the world or in ourselves. It is only because we are consciously objects to ourselves, that we can conceive a world as an object to a single mind, and thus as a connected whole. It is the irreducibility of this self-objectifying consciousness to anything else, the impossibility of accounting for it as an effect, that compels us to regard it as the presence in us of the mind for which the world exists. To admit therefore that the self-realization of the divine principle can take place otherwise than in a consciousness which is an object to itself, would be in contradiction of the very ground upon which we believe that a divine principle does so realize itself in man.

NOTE

1. We say that his true good *is* this complete realization when we think of the realization as already attained in the eternal mind. We say that it *would be* such realization when we think of the realization as forever problematic to man in the state of which we have experience.

[Thomas Hill Green, *Prolegomena to Ethics*, ed. A. C. Bradley (New York: Thomas Y. Crowell, 1969). (1) Pp. 391–92. (2) Pp. 394–95. (3) Pp. 398–404. (4) Pp. 407–408. (5) Pp. 410–11. (6) Pp. 414–15. (7) P. 422. (8) Pp. 425–26. (9) Pp. 189–91.]

12

Friedrich Nietzsche

1844–1900

Value and the Overman
(From *The Portable Nietzsche*
and *Human, All Too Human*)

Nietzsche held that the values of life cannot be estimated because of his belief that values had to be revalued in the direction of the Overman (*Der Übermensch*, or Superman). At times he is extremely negative toward the values of ordinary life. He announces flatly that God is dead. At the same time he is positively inclined toward our living creative lives as free spirits (*q.v.* D13 and *Freedom* vol., R2c4, secs. 4–6). His values are aristocratic. He wants us to push toward excellence in the direction of transformed life, based on the will to power. Is he correct that the *death of God* and turning from established values can lead to a new innocence and a richer life?

Also see Study Guide (4b12), p. 38.

(1) Our Valuations.—All actions may be referred back to valuations, and all valuations are either one's own or adopted, the latter being by far the more numerous. Why do we adopt them? Through fear, *i.e.* we think it more advisable to pretend that they are our own, and so well do we accustom ourselves to do so that it at last becomes second nature to us. A valuation of our own, which is the appreciation of a thing in accordance with the pleasure or displeasure it causes us and no one else, is something very rare indeed!—But must not our valuation of our neighbor—which is prompted by the motive that we adopt his valuation in most cases—proceed from ourselves and by our own decision? Of course, but then we come to these decisions during our childhood, and seldom change them. We often remain during our whole lifetime the dupes of our childish and accustomed judgments in our manner of judging our fellowmen (their

minds, rank, morality, character, and reprehensibility), and we find it necessary to subscribe to their valuations.

(2) Judgments, judgments of value, concerning life, for it or against it, can, in the end, never be true: they have value only as symptoms, they are worthy of consideration only as symptoms; in themselves such judgments are stupidities. One must by all means stretch out one's fingers and make the attempt to grasp this amazing finesse, *that the value of life cannot be estimated.* Not by the living, for they are an interested party, even a bone of contention, and not judges; not by the dead, for a different reason. For a philosopher to see a problem in the value of life is thus an objection to him, a question mark concerning his wisdom, an un-wisdom. Indeed? All these great wise men—they were not only decadents but not wise at all?

(3) One would require a position *outside* of life, and yet have to know it as well as one, as many, as all who have lived it, in order to be permitted even to touch the problem of the *value* of life: reasons enough to comprehend that this problem is for us an unapproachable problem. When we speak of values, we speak with the inspiration, with the way of looking at things, which is part of life: life itself forces us to posit values; life itself values through us when we posit values. From this it follows that even that antinatural morality which conceives of God as the counterconcept and condemnation of life is only a value judgment of life—but of what life? of what kind of life? I have already given the answer: of declining, weakened, weary, condemned life. Morality, as it has so far been understood—as it has in the end been formulated once more by Schopenhauer, *as negation of the will to life*—is the very *instinct of decadence*, which makes an imperative of itself. It says: *Perish!* It is a condemnation pronounced by the condemned.

Let us finally consider how naive it is altogether to say: *Man ought to be such and such!* Reality shows us an enchanting wealth of types, the abundance of a lavish play and change of forms—and some wretched loafer of a moralist comments: "No! Man ought to be different." He even knows what man should be like, this wretched bigot and prig: he paints himself on the wall and comments, *Ecce homo!* But even when the moralist addresses himself only to the single human being and says to him, "You ought to be such and such!" he does not cease to make himself ridiculous. The single human being is a piece of *fatum* from the front and from the rear, one law more, one necessity more for all that is yet to come and to be. To say to him, "Change yourself!" is to demand that everything be changed, even retroactively. And indeed there have been consistent moralists who wanted man to be different, that is, virtuous—they wanted him remade in their own image, as a prig: to that end, they *negated* the world! No small madness! No modest kind of immodesty!

God Is Dead

(4) *The background of our cheerfulness.* The greatest recent event—that "God is dead," that the belief in the Christian God has ceased to be believable—is even now beginning to cast its first shadows over Europe. For the few, at least, whose eyes, whose *suspicion* in their eyes, is strong and sensitive enough for this spectacle, some sun seems to have set just now. . . . In the main, however, this may be said: the event itself is much too great, too distant, too far from the comprehension of the many even for the tidings of it to be thought of as having *arrived* yet, not to speak of the notion that many people might know what has really happened here, and what must collapse now that this belief has been undermined—all that was built upon it, leaned on it, grew into it; for example, our whole European morality. . . .

The Saint's Answer to Zarathustra

(5) The saint answered: "I make songs and sing them; and when I make songs, I laugh, cry, and hum: thus I praise God. With singing, crying, laughing, and humming, I praise the god who is my god. But what do you bring us as a gift?"

When Zarathustra had heard these words he bade the saint farewell and said: "What could I have to give you? But let me go quickly lest I take something from you!" And thus they separated, the old one and the man, laughing as two boys laugh.

But when Zarathustra was alone he spoke thus to his heart: "Could it be possible? This old saint in the forest has not yet heard anything of this, that *God is dead!*"

The Overman

When Zarathustra came into the next town, which lies on the edge of the forest, he found many people gathered together in the marketplace; for it had been promised that there would be a tightrope walker. And Zarathustra spoke thus to the people:

"*I teach you the overman.* Man is something that shall be overcome. What have you done to overcome him?

"All beings so far have created something beyond themselves; and do you want to be the ebb of this great flood and even go back to the beasts rather than overcome man? What is the ape to man? A laughingstock or a painful embarrassment. And man shall be just that for the overman: a laughingstock or a painful embarrassment. You have made your way from worm to man, and much in you is still worm. Once you were apes, and even now, too, man is more ape than any ape.

"Whoever is the wisest among you is also a mere conflict and cross between plant and ghost. But do I bid you become ghosts or plants?

"Behold, I teach you the overman. The overman is the meaning of the earth. Let your will say: the overman *shall be* the meaning of the earth! I beseech you, my brothers, *remain faithful to the earth*, and do not believe those who speak to you of otherworldly hopes! Poison-mixers are they, whether they know it or not. Despisers of life are they, decaying and poisoned themselves, of whom the earth is weary: so let them go.

"Once the sin against God was the greatest sin; but God died, and these sinners died with him. To sin against the earth is now the most dreadful thing, and to esteem the entrails of the unknowable higher than the meaning of the earth.

"Once the soul looked contemptuously upon the body, and then this contempt was the highest: she wanted the body meager, ghastly, and starved. Thus she hoped to escape it and the earth. Oh, this soul herself was still meager, ghastly, and starved: and cruelty was the lust of this soul. But you, too, my brothers, tell me: what does your body proclaim of your soul? Is not your soul poverty and filth and wretched contentment?

"Verily, a polluted stream is man. One must be a sea to be able to receive a polluted stream without becoming unclean. Behold, I teach you the overman: he is this sea; in him your great contempt can go under.

"What is the greatest experience you can have? It is the hour of the great contempt. The hour in which your happiness, too, arouses your disgust, and even your reason and your virtue.

"The hour when you say, 'What matters my happiness? It is poverty and filth and wretched contentment. But my happiness ought to justify existence itself.'

"The hour when you say, 'What matters my reason? Does it crave knowledge as the lion his food? It is poverty and filth and wretched contentment.'

"The hour when you say, 'What matters my virtue? As yet it has not made me rage. How weary I am of my good and my evil! All that is poverty and filth and wretched contentment.'

"The hour when you say, 'What matters my justice? I do not see that I am flames and fuel. But the just are flames and fuel.'

"The hour when you say, 'What matters my pity? Is not pity the cross on which he is nailed who loves man? But my pity is no crucifixion.'

"Have you yet spoken thus? Have you yet cried thus? Oh, that I might have heard you cry thus!

"Not your sin but your thrift cries to heaven; your meanness even in your sin cries to heaven.

"Where is the lightning to lick you with its tongue? Where is the frenzy with which you should be inoculated?

"Behold, I teach you the overman: he is this lightning, he is this frenzy."

When Zarathustra had spoken thus, one of the people cried: "Now we have heard enough about the tightrope walker; now let us see him too!" And all the people laughed at Zarathustra. But the tightrope walker, believing that the word concerned him, began his performance.

Zarathustra, however, beheld the people and was amazed. Then he spoke thus:

"Man is a rope, tied between beast and overman—a rope over an abyss. A dangerous across, a dangerous on-the-way, a dangerous looking-back, a dangerous shuddering and stopping.

"What is great in man is that he is a bridge and not an end: what can be loved in man is that he is an *overture* and a *going under*.

"I love those who do not know how to live, except by going under, for they are those who cross over.

"I love the great despisers because they are the great reverers and arrows of longing for the other shore.

"I love those who do not first seek behind the stars for a reason to go under and be a sacrifice, but who sacrifice themselves for the earth, that the earth may some day become the overman's.

"I love him who lives to know, and who wants to know so that the overman may live some day. And thus, he wants to go under.

"I love him who works and invents to build a house for the overman and tho prepare earth, animal, and plant for him: for thus he wants to go under.

"I love him who loves his virtue, for virtue is the will to go under and an arrow of longing.

"I love him who does not hold back one drop of spirit for himself, but wants to be entirely the spirit of his virtue: thus he strides over the bridge as spirit.

"I love him who makes his virtue his addiction and his catastrophe: for his virtue's sake he wants to live on and to live no longer.

"I love him who does not want to have too many virtues. One virtue is more virtue than two, because it is more of a noose on which his catastrophe may hang.

"I love him whose soul squanders itself, who wants no thanks and returns none: for he always gives away and does not want to preserve himself.

"I love him who is abashed when the dice fall to make his fortune, and asks, 'Am I then a crooked gambler?' For he wants to perish.

"I love him who casts golden words before his deeds and always does even more than he promises: for he wants to go under.

"I love him who justifies future and redeems past generations: for he wants to perish of the present.

"I love him who chastens his god because he loves his god: for he must perish of the wrath of his god.

"I love him whose soul is deep, even in being wounded, and who can perish of a small experience: thus he goes gladly over the bridge.

"I love him whose soul is overfull so that he forgets himself, and all things are in him: thus all things spell his going under.

"I love him who has a free spirit and a free heart: thus his head is only the entrails of his heart, but his heart drives him to go under.

"I love all those who are as heavy drops, falling one by one out of the dark cloud that hangs over men: they herald the advent of lightning, and, as heralds, they perish.

"Behold, I am a herald of the lightning and a heavy drop from the cloud; but this lightning is called *overman*."

∽   ∽   ∽

And thus spoke Zarathustra to the people: "The time has come for man to set himself a goal. The time has come for man to plant the seed of his highest hope. His soil is still rich enough. But one day this soil will be poor and domesticated, and no tall tree will be able to grow in it. Alas, the time is coming when man will no longer shoot the arrow of his longing beyond man, and the string of his bow will have forgotten how to whirl!

"I say unto you: one must still have chaos in oneself to be able to give birth to a dancing star. I say unto you: you still have chaos in yourselves.

"Alas, the time is coming when man will no longer give birth to a star. Alas, the time of the most despicable man is coming, he that is no longer able to despise himself. Behold, I show you the *last man*.

" 'What is love? What is creation? What is longing? What is a star?' thus asks the last man, and he blinks.

"The earth has become small, and on it hops the last man, who makes everything small. His race is as ineradicable as the flea-beetle; the last man lives longest.

" 'We have invented happiness,' say the last men, and they blink. They have left the regions where it was hard to live, for one needs warmth. One still loves one's neighbor and rubs against him, for one needs warmth."

"On the three metamorphoses"

(6) Of three metamorphoses of the spirit I tell you: how the spirit becomes a camel; and the camel, a lion; and the lion, finally, a child.

There is much that is difficult for the spirit, the strong reverent spirit that would bear much: but the difficult and the most difficult are what its strength demands.

What is difficult? asks the spirit that would bear much, and kneels down like a camel wanting to be well loaded. What is most difficult, O heroes, asks the spirit that would bear much, that I may take it upon myself and exult in my strength? Is it not humbling oneself to wound one's haughtiness? Letting one's folly shine to mock one's wisdom?

➤ ➤ ➤

All these most difficult things the spirit that would bear much takes upon itself: like the camel that, burdened, speeds into the desert, thus the spirit speeds into its desert.

In the loneliest desert, however, the second metamorphosis occurs: here the spirit becomes a lion who would conquer his freedom and be master in his own desert. Here he seeks out his last master: he wants to fight him and his last god; for ultimate victory he wants to fight with the great dragon.

Who is the great dragon whom the spirit will no longer call lord and god? "Thou shalt" is the name of the great dragon. But the spirit of the lion says, "I will." "Thou shalt" lies in his way, sparkling like gold, an animal covered with scales; and on every scale shines a golden "thou shalt."

Values, thousands of years old, shine on these scales; and thus speaks the mightiest of all dragons: "All value of all things shines on me. All value has long been created, and I am all created value. Verily, there shall be no more 'I will.' " Thus speaks the dragon.

My brothers, why is there a need in the spirit for the lion? Why is not the beast of burden, which renounces and is reverent, enough?

To create new values—that even the lion cannot do; but the creation of freedom for oneself for new creation—that is within the power of the lion. The creation of freedom for oneself and a sacred "No" even to duty—for that, my brothers, the lion is needed. To assume the right to new values—that is the most terrifying assumption for a reverent spirit that would bear much. Verily, to him it is preying, and a matter for a beast of prey. He once loved "thou shalt" as most sacred: now he must find illusion and caprice even in the most sacred, that freedom from his love may become his prey: the lion is needed for such prey.

But say, my brothers, what can the child do that even the lion could not do? Why must the preying lion still become a child? The child is innocence and forgetting a new beginning, a game, a self-propelled wheel, a first movement, a sacred "Yes." For the game of creation, my brothers, a sacred "Yes" is needed: the spirit now wills his own will, and he who had been lost to the world now conquers his own world.

Of three metamorphoses of the spirit I have told you: how the spirit became a camel; and the camel, a lion; and the lion, finally, a child.

(7) The higher its type, the more rarely a thing succeeds. You higher men here, have you not all failed?

Be of good cheer, what does it matter? How much is still possible! Learn to laugh at yourselves as one must laugh!

Is it any wonder that you failed and only half succeeded, being half broken? Is not something thronging and pushing in you—man's *future*? Man's greatest distance and depth and what in him is lofty to the stars, his tremendous strength—are not all these frothing against each other in your pot? Is it any wonder that many a pot breaks? Learn to laugh at yourselves as one must laugh! You higher men, how much is still possible!

And verily, how much has already succeeded! How rich is the earth in little good perfect things, in what has turned out well!

Place little good perfect things around you, O higher men! Their golden ripeness heals the heart. What is perfect teaches hope.

(8) "*The world is perfect*"—thus says the instinct of the most spiritual, the Yes-saying instinct; "imperfection, whatever is beneath us, distance, the pathos of distance—even the chandala still belongs to this perfection."

The most spiritual men, as the *strongest*, find their happiness where others would find their destruction: in the labyrinth, in hardness against themselves and others, in experiments; their joy is self-conquest; asceticism becomes in them nature, need, and instinct. Difficult tasks are a privilege to them; to play with burdens which crush others, a recreation. Knowledge—a form of asceticism. They are the most venerable kind of man; that does not preclude their being the most cheerful and the kindliest. They rule not because they want to but because they *are*; they are not free to be second.

A right is a privilege. A man's state of being is his privilege. Let us not underestimate the privileges of the *mediocre*. As one climbs higher, life becomes ever harder; the coldness increases, responsibility increases.

A high culture is a pyramid: it can stand only on a broad base; its first presupposition is a strong and soundly consolidated mediocrity. Handicraft, trade, agriculture, *science*, the greatest part of art, the whole quintessence of *professional* activity, to sum it up, is compatible only with a mediocre amount of ability and ambition; that sort of thing would be out of place among exceptions; the instinct here required would contradict both aristocratism and anarchism. To be a public utility, a wheel, a function, for that one must be destined by nature: it is *not* society, it is the only kind of *happiness* of which the great majority are capable that makes intelligent machines of them. For the mediocre, to be mediocre is their happiness; mastery of one thing, specialization—a natural instinct.

It would be completely unworthy of a more profound spirit to consider mediocrity as such an objection. In fact, it is the very *first* necessity if there are to be exceptions: a high culture depends on it. When the exceptional human being treats the mediocre more tenderly than himself and his peers, this is not mere politeness of the heart—it is simply his *duty*.

(9) *Moderation.*—When thought and inquiry have become decisive—when, that is to say, free-spiritedness has become a quality of the character—action tends to moderation: for thought and inquiry weaken covetousness, draw much of the available energy to themselves for the promotion of spiritual objectives, and reveal the merely half-usefulness or the total uselessness and perilousness of all sudden changes.

(10) *The noblest virtue.*—In the first era of higher humanity bravery is accounted the noblest of the virtues, in the second justice, in the third moderation, in the fourth wisdom. In which era do we live? In which do you live?

What is needed first.—A man who refuses to become master over his wrath, his choler and revengefulness, and his lusts, and attempts to become a master in anything else, is as stupid as the farmer who stakes out his field beside a torrential stream without protecting himself against it.

Whether we are able to forgive.—How *can* one forgive them at all, if they know not what they do! One has nothing whatever *to* forgive.—But does a man ever *know completely* what he does? And if this must always remain at least *questionable*, then men never do have anything to forgive one another and pardoning is to the most rational man a thing impossible. Finally: *if* the ill-doers really did know what they did—we would have a right to *forgive* them only if we had a right to accuse and to punish them. But this we do not have.

⋙   ⋙   ⋙

The ineptest educator.—In the case of one man all his real virtues have been cultivated in the soil of his spirit of contradiction, in the case of another in his inability to say no, that is in his spirit of assent; a third has developed all his morality out of his lonely pride, a fourth his out of his strong drive to sociability. Suppose, now, that in each of these four cases the seeds of virtue had, through the ineptitude of teachers and the vagaries of chance, not been sown in that region of his nature where the topsoil was richest and most plentiful, then they would be without morality and weak and joyless men. And who would have been the ineptest of all educators and the evil fatality of these four men? The moral fanatic, who believes that the good can grow only out of the good and upon the basis of the good.

(11) *Laughing and smiling.*—The more joyful and secure the spirit becomes, the more man unlearns loud laughter; on the other hand, a spiritual smile is continually welling up in him—a sign of his astonishment at the countless hidden pleasures existence contains.

(12) *Remorse.*—Never yield to remorse, but at once tell yourself: remorse would simply mean adding to the first act of stupidity a second.— If we have done harm we should give thought to how we can do good.—If we are punished for our actions, let us endure our punishment with the feeling that we are thereby already doing good: we are deterring others from falling victim to the same folly. Every ill-doer who has been punished is entitled to feel he is a benefactor of mankind.

⋙   ⋙   ⋙

When it is time to vow loyalty to oneself.—Sometimes we stray on to a spiritual course that contradicts our talents; for a time we struggle heroically against wind and tide, at bottom against ourself: we grow weary, gasping; what we achieve brings us no real joy, we feel we have paid too highly for it. Indeed, we *despair* of our fruitfulness and of our future, perhaps in the midst of victory. At long last we *turn round*—and now the wind is blowing into our sails and driving us into *our own* channel. What happiness! How *sure of victory* we feel! Only now do we know what we are and what we want, now we vow to be loyal to ourselves and *have a right* to do so—because we know what it means.

⊷ ⊷ ⊷

The three good things.—Greatness, repose, sunlight—these three things embrace everything a thinker desires and demands of himself: his hopes and duties, his claims in the intellectual and moral spheres, even in the way he lives day by day and the quality of the landscape where he dwells. They answer firstly to *elevating* thoughts, then to *quietening*, thirdly to *enlightening*—fourthly, however, to thoughts which participate in all three qualities, in which everything earthly comes to transfiguration: it is the kingdom where there reigns the great *trinity of joy*.

⊷ ⊷ ⊷

The heroic.—The heroic consists in doing a great thing (or in *not* doing a thing in a great fashion) without feeling oneself to be in competition *with* others *before* others. The hero always bears the wilderness and the sacred, inviolable borderline within him wherever he may go.

⊷ ⊷ ⊷

Possessing much spirit.—To possess much spirit keeps one *young*: but in exchange one must endure being thought *older* than one is. For men read the characters inscribed by the spirit as signs of *experience of life*, that is to say of having experienced many, and many bad things, of suffering, error, and remorse. Thus, one is thought not only older but *worse* than one is when one possesses much spirit and shows it.

⊷ ⊷ ⊷

The golden watchword.—Many chains have been laid upon man so that he should no longer behave like an animal: and he has in truth become gentler, more spiritual, more joyful, more reflective than any animal is. Now, however, he suffers from having worn his chains for so long, from being deprived for so long of clear air and free movement:—these chains, however, I shall never cease from repeating, are those heavy and pregnant errors contained in the conceptions of morality, religion, and metaphysics. Only when this *sickness from one's chains* has also been overcome will the first great goal have truly been attained: the separation of man from the animals.—We stand now in the midst of our work of removing these chains, and we need to proceed with the greatest caution. Only the *ennobled man may be given freedom of spirit*; to him alone does *alleviation of life* draw near and salve his wounds; only he may say that he lives for the sake of joy and for the sake of no further goal; and in any other mouth his motto would be perilous: *Peace all around me and goodwill to all things closest to me.*—With this motto for individuals he recalls an ancient great and moving saying intended for *all* which has remained hanging over all mankind as a sign and motto by which anyone shall perish who inscribes it on his banner too soon—by which Christianity perished. The time has, it seems, still *not yet come* when *all* men are to share the experience of those shepherds who saw the heavens brighten above them and heard the words: "On earth peace, good will toward men."—It is still *the age of the individual.*

(13) What is good? Everything that heightens the feeling of power in man, the will to power, power itself.

What is bad? Everything that is born of weakness.

What is happiness? The feeling that power is *growing*, that resistance is overcome.

Not contentedness but more power; not peace but war; not virtue but fitness (Renaissance virtue, *virtù*, virtue that is moraline-free[1]).

The weak and the failures shall perish: first principle of *our* love of man. And they shall even be given every possible assistance.

What is more harmful than any vice? Active pity for all the failures and all the weak: Christianity.

≈   ≈   ≈

Christianity should not be beautified and embellished: it has waged deadly war against this higher type of man; it has placed all the basic instincts of this type under the ban; and out of these instincts it has distilled evil and the Evil One: the strong man as the typically reprehensible man, the "reprobate." Christianity has sided with all that is weak and base, with all failures; it has made an ideal of whatever *contradicts* the instinct of the strong life to preserve itself; it has corrupted the reason even of those strongest in spirit by teaching men to consider the supreme values of the spirit as something sinful, as something that leads into error—as temptations. The most pitiful example: the corruption of Pascal, who believed in the corruption of his reason through original sin when it had in fact been corrupted only by his Christianity.

❱❱❱ ❱❱❱ ❱❱❱

I call an animal, a species, or an individual corrupt when it loses its instincts, when it chooses, when it prefers, what is disadvantageous for it. A history of "lofty sentiments," of the "ideals of mankind"—and it is possible that I shall have to write it—would almost explain too *why* man is so corrupt. Life itself is to my mind the instinct for growth, for durability, for an accumulation of forces, for *power*: where the will to power is lacking there is decline. It is my contention that all the supreme values of mankind *lack* this will—that the values which are symptomatic of decline, *nihilistic* values, are lording it under the holiest names.

❱❱❱ ❱❱❱ ❱❱❱

Let us not underestimate this: *we ourselves*, we free spirits, are nothing less than a "revaluation of all values," an *incarnate* declaration of war and triumph over all the ancient conceptions of "true" and "untrue." The most valuable insights are discovered last; but the most valuable insights are the *methods*. *All* the methods, *all* the presuppositions of our current scientific outlook, were opposed for thousands of years with the most profound contempt. For their sake, men were excluded from the company of "decent" people and considered "enemies of God," despisers of the truth, and "possessed."

(14) Wherever responsibilities are sought, it is usually the instinct of wanting to judge and punish which is at work. Becoming has been deprived of its innocence when any being-such-and-such is traced back to will, to purposes, to acts of responsibility: the doctrine of the will has been invented essentially for the purpose of punishment, that is, because one wanted to impute guilt. The entire old psychology, the psychology of will, was conditioned by the fact that its originators, the priests at the head of ancient communities, wanted to create for themselves the right to punish—or wanted to create this right for God. Men were considered

"free" so that they might be judged and punished—so that they might become *guilty*: consequently, every act had to be considered as willed, and the origin of every act had to be considered as lying within the consciousness (and thus the most fundamental counterfeit *in psychologicis* was made the principle of psychology itself).

Today, as we have entered into the reverse movement and we immoralists are trying with all our strength to take the concept of guilt and the concept of punishment out of the world again, and to cleanse psychology, history, nature, and social institutions and sanctions of them, there is in our eyes no more radical opposition than that of the theologians, who continue with the concept of a "moral world-order" to infect the innocence of becoming by means of "punishment" and "guilt." Christianity is a metaphysics of the hangman.

What alone can be *our* doctrine? That no one *gives* man his qualities—neither God, nor society, nor his parents and ancestors, nor he himself. (The nonsense of the last idea was taught as "intelligible freedom" by Kant—perhaps by Plato already.) No one is responsible for man's being there at all, for his being such-and-such, or for his being in these circumstances or in this environment. The fatality of his essence is not to be disentangled from the fatality of all that has been and will be. Man is not the effect of some special purpose, of a will, and end; nor is he the object of an attempt to attain an "ideal of humanity" or an "ideal of happiness" or an "ideal of morality." It is absurd to wish to devolve one's essence on some end or other. We have invented the concept of "end": in reality there is no end.

One is necessary, one is a piece of fatefulness, one belongs to the whole, one is in the whole; there is nothing which could judge, measure, compare, or sentence our being, for that would mean judging, measuring, comparing, or sentencing the whole. But there is nothing besides the whole. That nobody is held responsible any longer, that the mode of being may not be traced back to a *causa prima*, that the world does not form a unity either as a sensorium or as "spirit"—that alone is the great liberation; with this alone is the innocence of becoming restored. The concept of "God" was until now the greatest objection to existence. We deny God, we deny the responsibility in God: only thereby do we redeem the world.

NOTE

1. One who abstains from tobacco and coffee. [Ed.]

[Friedrich Nietzsche. (1) *The Dawn of Day*, tr. J. M. Kennedy (New York: Russell and Russell, 1964), pp. 100–101. (2) *Twilight of the Idols*, tr. W. Kaufmann, *The Portable Nietzsche* (New York: The Viking Press, 1968), p. 474. (3) *Twilight of the Idols*, pp. 490–91. (4) *The Gay Science, The Portable Nietzsche*, p. 447. (5) *Thus Spoke Zarathustra, The Portable Nietzsche*, pp. 124–29. (6) *Ibid.*, pp. 137–39. (7) *Ibid.*, pp. 404–405. (8) *The Antichrist, The Portable Nietzsche*, pp. 645–47. (9) *Human, All Too Human*, tr. R. J. Hollingdale (Cambridge: Cambridge University Press, 1986), p. 169. (10) *Ibid.*, pp. 326–27. (11) *Ibid.*, p. 351. (12) *Ibid.*, pp. 390–94. (13) *The Antichrist*, pp. 570–79. (14) *Twilight of the Idols*, pp. 499–501.]

13

Jean-Paul Sartre

1905–1980

Existentialism and Humanism

Holding that existence precedes essence (sec. 1), and, that there is no God (sec. 3), it is necessary for humans to invent themselves. It follows that values are subjective (sec. 5). He amends this later by saying they are intersubjective. Inventing our values (sec. 7), we make our choices in anguish (sec. 2), abandonment (sec. 3), and despair (sec. 4). Running throughout is the claim of our absolute freedom to choose. We are "condemned" to freedom. From this standpoint the selection supplements Sartre's discussion in the *Freedom* volume. There he argued that in freedom we invent possibilities out of nothing. Here we invent our values in the same way. The category of non-being, discussed in Sartre's *Freedom* essay as infusing human nature (*q.v.* (2a5) secs. 1–4) is assumed here. Freedom is the foundation of values (sec. 6), and authenticity (also sec. 6) which, when honored by avoiding "bad faith," allows any value system to be admissible.

Also see Study Guide (4b13), p. 38.

Existence precedes essence

(1) . . . there are two kinds of existentialists. There are, on the one hand, the Christians, amongst whom I shall name Jaspers and Gabriel Marcel, both professed Catholics; and on the other the existential atheists, amongst whom we must place Heidegger as well as the French existentialists and myself. What they have in common is simply the fact that they believe that *existence* comes before *essence*—or, if you will, that we must begin from the subjective.

Atheistic existentialism, of which I am a representative, declares that if God does not exist there is at least one being whose existence comes before its essence, a being which exists before it can be defined by any conception of it. That being is man or, as Heidegger has it, the human reality. What do we mean by saying that existence precedes essence? We mean that man first of all exists, encounters himself, surges up in the world—and defines himself afterwards. If man as the existentialist sees him is not definable, it is because to begin with he is nothing. He will not be anything until later, and then he will be what he makes of himself. Thus, there is no human nature, because there is no God to have a conception of it. Man simply is. Not that he is simply what he conceives himself to be, but he is what he wills, and as he conceives himself after already existing—as he wills to be after that leap towards existence. Man is nothing else but that which he makes of himself. That is the first principle of existentialism. And this is what people call its "subjectivity," using the word as a reproach against us. But what do we mean to say by this, but that man is of a greater dignity than a stone or a table? For we mean to say that man primarily exists—that man is, before all else, something which propels itself towards a future and is aware that it is doing so. Man is, indeed, a project which possesses a subjective life, instead of being a kind of moss, or a fungus or a cauliflower. Before that projection of the self nothing exists; not even in the heaven of intelligence: man will only attain existence when he is what he purposes to be. Not, however, what he may wish to be. For what we usually understand by wishing or willing is a conscious decision taken—much more often than not—after we have made ourselves what we are. I may wish to join a party, to write a book, or to marry—but in such a case what is usually called my will is probably a manifestation of a prior and more spontaneous decision. If, however, it is true that existence is prior to essence, man is responsible for what he is. Thus, the first effect of existentialism is that it puts every man in possession of himself as he is, and places the entire responsibility for his existence squarely upon his own shoulders. And, when we say that man is responsible for himself, we do not mean that he is responsible only for his own individuality, but that he is responsible for all men. The word "subjectivism" is to be understood in two senses, and our adversaries play upon only one of them. Subjectivism means, on the one hand, the freedom of the individual subject and, on the other, that man cannot pass beyond human subjectivity. It is the latter which is the deeper meaning of existentialism. When we say that man chooses himself, we do mean that every one of us must choose himself, but by that we also mean that in choosing for himself he chooses for all men. For in effect, of all the actions a man may take in order to create himself as he wills to be, there is not one which is not creative, at the same time, of an image of man such as he believes he ought to be. To choose between this or that is at the same time to affirm the value of that which is chosen; for we are unable ever to choose the worse. What we choose is always the better; and nothing can be better for us unless it is better for all. If, moreover, existence precedes essence and we will to exist at the same time as we fashion our image, that image is valid for all and for the entire epoch in which we find ourselves. Our responsibility is thus much greater than we had supposed, for it concerns mankind as a whole. If I am a worker, for instance, I may choose to join a Christian rather than a Communist trade union. And if, by that membership, I choose to signify that resignation is, after all, the attitude that best becomes a man, that man's kingdom is not upon this earth, I do not commit myself alone to that view. Resignation is my will for everyone, and my action is, in consequence, a commitment on behalf of all mankind. Or if, to take a more personal case, I decide to marry and to have children, even though this decision proceeds simply from my situation, from my passion or my desire, I am thereby committing not only myself, but humanity as a whole, to the practice of monogamy. I am thus responsible for myself and for all men, and I am creating a certain image of man as I would have him to be. In fashioning myself I fashion man.

Anguish

(2) This may enable us to understand what is meant by such terms—perhaps a little grandiloquent—as anguish, abandonment, and despair. As you will soon see, it is very simple. First, what do we mean by anguish? The existentialist frankly states that man is in anguish. His meaning is as follows—When a man commits himself to anything, fully realising that he is not only choosing what he will be, but is thereby at the same time a legislator deciding for the whole of mankind—in such a moment a man cannot escape from the sense of complete and profound responsibility. There are many, indeed, who show no such anxiety. But we affirm that they are merely disguising their anguish or are in flight from it. Certainly, many people think that in what they are doing they commit no one but themselves to anything: and if you ask them, "What would happen if everyone did so?" they shrug their shoulders and reply, "Everyone does not do so." But in truth, one ought always to ask oneself what would happen if everyone did as one is doing; nor can one escape from that disturbing

thought except by a kind of self-deception. The man who lies in self-excuse, by saying "Everyone will not do it" must be ill at ease in his conscience, for the act of lying implies the universal value which it denies. By its very disguise his anguish reveals itself.

$$\iff \quad \iff \quad \iff$$

Everything happens to every man as though the whole human race had its eyes fixed upon what he is doing and regulated its conduct accordingly. So every man ought to say, "Am I really a man who has the right to act in such a manner that humanity regulates itself by what I do?" If a man does not say that, he is dissembling his anguish. Clearly, the anguish with which we are concerned here is not one that could lead to quietism or inaction. It is anguish pure and simple, of the kind well known to all those who have borne responsibilities.

Abandonment

(3) And when we speak of "abandonment"—a favorite word of Heidegger—we only mean to say that God does not exist, and that it is necessary to draw the consequences of his absence right to the end. The existentialist is strongly opposed to a certain type of secular moralism which seeks to suppress God at the least possible expense. Towards 1880, when the French professors endeavored to formulate a secular morality, they said something like this:—God is a useless and costly hypothesis, so we will do without it. However, if we are to have morality, a society and a law-abiding world, it is essential that certain values should be taken seriously; they must have an *a priori* existence ascribed to them. It must be considered obligatory *a priori* to be honest, not to lie, not to beat one's wife, to bring up children and so forth; so we are going to do a little work on this subject, which will enable us to show that these values exist all the same, inscribed in an intelligible heaven although, of course, there is no God. In other words—and this is, I believe, the purport of all that we in France call radicalism—nothing will be changed if God does not exist; we shall rediscover the same norms of honesty, progress, and humanity, and we shall have disposed of God as an out-of-date hypothesis which will die away quietly of itself. The existentialist, on the contrary, finds it extremely embarrassing that God does not exist, for there disappears with Him all possibility of finding values in an intelligible heaven. There can no longer be any good *a priori*, since there is no infinite and perfect consciousness to think it. It is nowhere written that "the good" exists, that one must be

honest or must not lie, since we are now upon the plane where there are only men. Dostoievsky once wrote "If God did not exist, everything would be permitted"; and that, for existentialism, is the starting point. Everything is indeed permitted if God does not exist, and man is in consequence forlorn, for he cannot find anything to depend upon either within or outside himself. He discovers forthwith, that he is without excuse. For if indeed existence precedes essence, one will never be able to explain one's action by reference to a given and specific human nature; in other words, there is no determinism—man is free, man *is* freedom. Nor, on the other hand, if God does not exist, are we provided with any values or commands that could legitimize our behavior. Thus we have neither behind us, nor before us in a luminous realm of values, any means of justification or excuse. We are left alone, without excuse. That is what I mean when I say that man is condemned to be free. Condemned, because he did not create himself, yet is nevertheless at liberty, and from the moment that he is thrown into this world he is responsible for everything he does. The existentialist does not believe in the power of passion. He will never regard a grand passion as a destructive torrent upon which a man is swept into certain actions as by fate, and which, therefore, is an excuse for them. He thinks that man is responsible for his passion. Neither will an existentialist think that a man can find help through some sign being vouchsafed upon earth for his orientation: for he thinks that the man himself interprets the sign as he chooses. He thinks that every man, without any support or help whatever, is condemned at every instant to invent man.

❧   ❧   ❧

As an example by which you may the better understand this state of abandonment, I will refer to the case of a pupil of mine, who sought me out in the following circumstances. His father was quarrelling with his mother and was also inclined to be a "collaborator"; his elder brother had been killed in the German offensive of 1940 and this young man, with a sentiment somewhat primitive but generous, burned to avenge him. His mother was living alone with him, deeply afflicted by the semi-treason of his father and by the death of her eldest son, and her one consolation was in this young man. But he, at this moment, had the choice between going to England to join the Free French Forces or of staying near his mother and helping her to live. He fully realized that this woman lived only for him and that his disappearance—or perhaps his death—would plunge her into despair. He also realized that, concretely and in fact, every action he performed on his mother's behalf would be sure of effect in the sense of aiding her to live, whereas anything he did in order to go and fight would be an ambiguous action which might vanish like water into sand and serve no purpose. For instance, to set out for England he would have to wait indefinitely in a Spanish camp on the way through Spain; or, on arriving in England or in Algiers, he might be put into an office to fill up forms. Consequently, he found himself confronted by two very different modes of action; the one concrete, immediate, but directed towards only one individual; and the other an action addressed to an end infinitely greater, a national collectivity, but for that very reason ambiguous—and it might be frustrated on the way. At the same time, he was hesitating between two kinds of morality; on the one side the morality of sympathy, of personal devotion and, on the other side, a morality of wider scope but of more debatable validity. He had to choose between those two. What could help him to choose? Could the Christian doctrine? No. Christian doctrine says: Act with charity, love your neighbor, deny yourself for others, choose the way which is hardest, and so forth. But which is the harder road? To whom does one owe the more brotherly love, the patriot or the mother? Which is the more useful aim, the general one of fighting in and for the whole community, or the precise aim of helping one particular person to live? Who can give an answer to that *a priori*? No one. Nor is it given in any ethical scripture. The Kantian ethic says, Never regard another as a means, but always as an end. Very well; if I remain with my mother, I shall be regarding her as the end and not as a means: but by the same token I am in danger of treating as means those who are fighting on my behalf; and the converse is also true, that if I go to the aid of the combatants I shall be treating them as the end at the risk of treating my mother as a means.

If values are uncertain, if they are still too abstract to determine the particular, concrete case under consideration, nothing remains but to trust in our instincts. That is what this young man tried to do; and when I saw him he said, "In the end, it is feeling that counts; the direction in which it is really pushing me is the one I ought to choose. If I feel that I love my mother enough to sacrifice everything else for her—my will to be avenged, all my longings for action and adventure—then I stay with her. If, on the contrary, I feel that my love for her is not enough, I go." But how does one estimate the strength of a feeling? The value of his feeling for his mother was determined precisely by the fact that he was standing by her. I may say that I love a certain friend enough to sacrifice such or such a sum of money for him, but I cannot prove that unless I have done it. I may say, "I love my mother enough to remain with her," if actually I have remained with her. I can only estimate the strength of this affection if I have performed an action by which it is defined and ratified. But if I then appeal to this affection to justify my action, I find myself drawn into a vicious circle.

꿈   꿈   꿈

You may say that the youth did, at least, go to a professor to ask for advice. But if you seek counsel—from a priest, for example—you have selected that priest; and at bottom you already knew, more or less, what he would advise. In other words, to choose an adviser is nevertheless to commit oneself by that choice. If you are a Christian, you will say, Consult a priest; but there are collaborationists, priests who are resisters and priests who wait for the tide to turn: which will you choose? Had this young man chosen a priest of the resistance, or one of the collaboration, he would have decided beforehand the kind of advice he was to receive. Similarly, in coming to me, he knew what advice I should give him, and I had but one reply to make. You are free, therefore choose—that is to say, invent. No rule of general morality can show you what you ought to do: no signs are vouchsafed in this world.

Despair

(4) As for "despair," the meaning of this expression is extremely simple. It merely means that we limit ourselves to a reliance upon that which is within our wills, or within the sum of the probabilities which render our action feasible. Whenever one wills anything, there are always these elements of probability. If I am counting upon a visit from a friend, who may be coming by train or by tram, I presuppose that the train will arrive at the appointed time, or that the tram will not be derailed. I remain in the realm of possibilities; but one does not rely upon any possibilities beyond those that are strictly concerned in one's action. Beyond the point at which the possibilities under consideration cease to affect my action, I ought to disinterest myself. For there is no God and no prevenient design, which can adapt the world and all its possibilities to my will. When Descartes said, "Conquer yourself rather than the world," what he meant was, at bottom, the same—that we should act without hope.

Subjectivity

(5) Our point of departure is, indeed, the subjectivity of the individual, and that for strictly philosophic reasons. It is not because we are bourgeois, but because we seek to base our teaching upon the truth, and not upon a collection of fine theories, full of hope but lacking real foundations. And at the point of departure there cannot be any other truth than this, *I think, therefore I am*, which is the absolute truth of consciousness as it attains to itself. Every theory which begins with man, outside of this moment of self-attainment, is a theory which thereby suppresses the truth, for outside of

the Cartesian *cogito*, all objects are no more than probable, and any doctrine of probabilities which is not attached to a truth will crumble into nothing. In order to define the probable one must possess the true. Before there can be any truth whatever, then, there must be an absolute truth, and there is such a truth which is simple, easily attained and within the reach of everybody; it consists in one's immediate sense of one's self.

In the second place, this theory alone is compatible, with the dignity of man, it is the only one which does not make man into an object. All kinds of materialism lead one to treat every man including oneself as an object—that is, as a set of predetermined reactions, in no way different from the patterns of qualities and phenomena which constitute a table, or a chair or a stone. Our aim is precisely to establish the human kingdom as a pattern of values in distinction from the material world. But the subjectivity which we thus postulate as the standard of truth is no narrowly individual subjectivism, for as we have demonstrated, it is not only one's own self that one discovers in the *cogito*, but those of others too. Contrary to the philosophy of Descartes, contrary to that of Kant, when we say "I think" we are attaining to ourselves in the presence of the other, and we are just as certain of the other as we are of ourselves. Thus the man who discovers himself directly in the *cogito* also discovers all the others, and discovers them as the condition of his own existence. He recognizes that he cannot be anything (in the sense in which one says one is spiritual, or that one is wicked or jealous) unless others recognise him as such. I cannot obtain any truth whatsoever about myself, except through the mediation of another. The other is indispensable to my existence, and equally so to any knowledge I can have of myself. Under these conditions, the intimate discovery of myself is at the same time the revelation of the other as a freedom which confronts mine, and which cannot think or will without doing so either for or against me. Thus, at once, we find ourselves in a world which is, let us say, that of "intersubjectivity." It is in this world that man has to decide what he is and what others are.

Furthermore, although it is impossible to find in each and every man a universal essence that can be called human nature, there is nevertheless a human universality of *condition*. It is not by chance that the thinkers of today are so much more ready to speak of the condition than of the nature of man. By his condition they understand, with more or less clarity, all the *limitations* which *a priori* define man's fundamental situation in the universe. His historical situations are variable: man may be born a slave in a pagan society, or may be a feudal baron, or a proletarian. But what never vary are the necessities of being in the world, of having to labor and to die there. These limitations are neither subjective nor objective, or rather there is both a subjective and an objective aspect of them. Objective, because we meet with them everywhere and they are everywhere recognizable: and subjective because they are *lived* and are nothing if man does not live them—if, that is to say, he does not freely determine himself and his existence in relation to them. And, diverse though man's purposes may be, at least none of them is wholly foreign to me, since every human purpose presents itself as an attempt either to surpass these limitations, or to widen them, or else to deny or to accommodate oneself to them. Consequently every purpose, however individual it may be, is of universal value. Every purpose, even that of a Chinese, an Indian or a Negro, can be understood by a European. To say it can be understood, means that the European of 1945 may be striving out of a certain situation towards the same limitations in the same way, and that he may reconceive in himself the purpose of the Chinese, of the Indian or the African. In every purpose there is universality, in this sense that every purpose is comprehensible to every man. Not that this or that purpose defines man forever, but that it may be entertained again and again. There is always some way of understanding an idiot, a child, a primitive man, or a foreigner if one has sufficient information. In this sense we may say that there is a human universality, but it is not something given; it is being perpetually made. I make this universality in choosing myself; I also make it by understanding the purpose of any other man, of whatever epoch. This absoluteness of the act of choice does not alter the relativity of each epoch.

What is at the very heart and center of existentialism, is the absolute character of the free commitment, by which every man realizes himself in realizing a type of humanity—a commitment always understandable, to no matter whom in no matter what epoch—and its bearing upon the relativity of the cultural pattern which may result from such absolute commitment. One must observe equally the relativity of Cartesianism and the absolute character of the Cartesian commitment. In this sense you may say, if you like, that every one of us makes the absolute by breathing, by eating, by sleeping, or by behaving in any fashion whatsoever. There is no difference between free being—being as self-committal, as existence choosing its essence—and absolute being. And there is no difference whatever between being as an absolute, temporarily localized—that is, localized in history—and universally intelligible being.

Authenticity

(6) Since we have defined the situation of man as one of free choice, without excuse and without help, any man who takes refuge behind the excuse of his passions, or by inventing some deterministic doctrine, is a self-deceiver. One may object: "But why should he not choose to deceive

himself?" I reply that it is not for me to judge him morally, but I define his self-deception as an error. Here one cannot avoid pronouncing a judgment of truth. The self-deception is evidently a falsehood, because it is a dissimulation of man's complete liberty of commitment. Upon this same level, I say that it is also a self-deception if I choose to declare that certain values are incumbent upon me; I am in contradiction with myself if I will these values and at the same time say that they impose themselves upon me. If anyone says to me, "And what if I wish to deceive myself?" I answer, "There is no reason why you should not, but I declare that you are doing so, and that the attitude of strict consistency alone is that of good faith. Furthermore, I can pronounce a moral judgment. For I declare that freedom, in respect of concrete circumstances, can have no other end and aim but itself; and when once a man has seen that values depend upon himself, in that state of forsakenness he can will only one thing, and that is freedom as the foundation of all values. That does not mean that he wills it in the abstract: it simply means that the actions of men of good faith have, as their ultimate significance, the quest of freedom itself as such. A man who belongs to some communist or revolutionary society wills certain concrete ends, which imply the will to freedom, but that freedom is willed in community. We will freedom for freedom's sake, and in and through particular circumstances. And in thus willing freedom, we discover that it depends entirely upon the freedom of others and that the freedom of others depends upon our own. Obviously, freedom as the definition of a man does not depend upon others, but as soon as there is a commitment, I am obliged to will the liberty of others at the same time as mine. I cannot make liberty my aim unless I make that of others equally my aim. Consequently, when I recognize, as entirely authentic, that man is a being whose existence precedes his essence, and that he is a free being who cannot, in any circumstances, but will his freedom, at the same time I realize that I cannot not will the freedom of others. Thus, in the name of that will to freedom which is implied in freedom itself, I can form judgments upon those who seek to hide from themselves the wholly voluntary nature of their existence and its complete freedom. Those who hide from this total freedom, in a guise of solemnity or with deterministic excuses, I shall call cowards. Others, who try to show that their existence is necessary, when it is merely an accident of the appearance of the human race on earth—I shall call scum. But neither cowards nor scum can be identified except upon the plane of strict authenticity. Thus, although the content of morality is variable, a certain form of this morality is universal. Kant declared that freedom is a will both to itself and to the freedom of others.

Agreed: but he thinks that the formal and the universal suffice for the constitution of a morality. We think, on the contrary, that principles that are
too abstract break down when we come to defining action. To take once
again the case of that student; by what authority, in the name of what
golden rule of morality, do you think he could have decided, in perfect
peace of mind, either to abandon his mother or to remain with her? There
are no means of judging. The content is always concrete, and therefore
unpredictable; it has always to be invented. The one thing that counts, is to
know whether the invention is made in the name of freedom.

Inventing values

Sartre has just responded to two of "three not very serious objections," the first that subjectivism implies anarchy, the second that
existentialists cannot judge others, since there is no reason for pre-
ferring one purpose to another." He denied the first, granted the
second in one sense while retaining the right to make a logical "bad
faith" judgment. He now turns to the third objection.

(7) The third objection, stated by saying, "You take with one hand what
you give with the other," means, at bottom, "your values are not serious, since
you choose them yourselves." To that I can only say that I am very sorry that
it should be so; but if I have excluded God the Father, there must be somebody
to invent values. We have to take things as they are. And moreover, to say that
we invent values means neither more nor less than this; that there is no sense
in life *a priori*. Life is nothing until it is lived; but it is yours to make sense of,
and the value of it is nothing else but the sense that you choose. Therefore, you
can see that there is a possibility of creating a human community. I have been
reproached for suggesting that existentialism is a form of humanism: people
have said to me, "But you have written in your *Nauseé* that the humanists are
wrong, you have even ridiculed a certain type of humanism, why do you now
go back upon that?" In reality, the word humanism has two very different
meanings. One may understand by humanism a theory which upholds man as
the end-in-itself and as the supreme value.

≈   ≈   ≈

Existentialism dispenses with any judgment of this sort: an existentialist will never take man as the end, since man is still to be determined.
And we have no right to believe that humanity is something to which we
could set up a cult, after the manner of Auguste Comte. The cult of

humanity ends in Comtian humanism, shut-in upon itself, and—this must be said—in Fascism. We do not want a humanism like that.

But there is another sense of the word, of which the fundamental meaning is this: Man is all the time outside of himself: it is in projecting and losing himself beyond himself that he makes man to exist; and, on the other hand, it is by pursuing transcendent aims that he himself is able to exist. Since man is thus self-surpassing, and can grasp objects only in relation to his self-surpassing, he is himself the heart and center of his transcendence. There is no other universe except the human universe, the universe of human subjectivity. This relation of transcendence as constitutive of man (not in the sense that God is transcendent, but in the sense of self-surpassing) with subjectivity (in such a sense that man is not shut up in himself but forever present in a human universe)—it is this that we call existential humanism. This is humanism, because we remind man that there is no legislator but himself; that he himself, thus abandoned, must decide for himself; also because we show that it is not by turning back upon himself, but always by seeking, beyond himself, an aim which is one of liberation or of some particular realization, that man can realize himself as truly human.

You can see from these few reflections that nothing could be more unjust than the objections people raise against us. Existentialism is nothing else but an attempt to draw the full conclusions from a consistently atheistic position. Its intention is not in the least that of plunging men into despair. And if by despair one means—as the Christians do—any attitude of unbelief, the despair of the existentialists is something different. Existentialism is not atheist in the sense that it would exhaust itself in demonstrations of the nonexistence of God. It declares, rather, that even if God existed that would make no difference from its point of view. Not that we believe God does exist, but we think that the real problem is not that of His existence; what man needs is to find himself again and to understand that nothing can save him from himself, not even a valid proof of the existence of God. In this sense existentialism is optimistic, it is a doctrine of action, and it is only by self-deception, by confusing their own despair with ours that Christians can describe us as without hope.

[Jean-Paul Sartre, *Existentialism and Humanism*, tr. P. Mairet (London: Methuen and Co. Ltd., 1948). (1) Pp. 26–30. (2) Pp. 30–32. (3) Pp. 32–38. (4) P. 39. (5) Pp. 44–47. (6) Pp. 50–53. (7) Pp. 54–56.]

14

Dan Enright
1918–1992

The Fifties, by David Halberstam

In this brief selection Enright, television producer of the show, *Twenty-One*, gives us his final and chief values. They stand in contrast to most of the preceding choices. Enright produced the shows with fixed answers, and Charles Van Doren was one of the contestants.
Also see Study Guide (4b14), pp. 38–39.

(1) Fixing the show did not particularly bother Enright; the quiz shows had never been about intelligence or integrity as far as he was concerned; they were about drama and entertainment. "You cannot ask random questions of people and have a show," one game-show producer later said. "You simply have failure, failure, failure, and that does not make entertainment." That made it a predatory world, and Enright excelled in it. He was not, Dan Enright reflected years later, a very nice man in those days. He was totally compelled by work, wildly ambitious, and utterly self-involved. "I was determined to be successful no matter what it cost," he said, "and I was greedy, greedy, not for money, but for authority, power, prestige, and respect." The end, he believed at the time, always justified the means. People were to be used; if you did not use them, he believed, they in turn would use you. Soon—with considerable fixing—*Twenty-One* became a huge success; at a relatively young age, Enright had already exceeded his own expectations, and he was wealthy and powerful. People coveted his attention and gave him respect. Thus he was able to rationalize everything he was doing.

From then on, *Twenty-One* became the prototype of the completely crooked show. Enright cast it as he might a musical comedy. He wanted not just winners and losers but heroes and villains.

[Dan Enright, from David Halberstam, *The Fifties* (New York: Villard Books, 1993). (1) P. 649.]

15

Robert M. Pirsig
(Phaedrus)
1938–

Zen and the Art of Motorcycle Maintenance and *Lila*

In two best-selling books Pirsig, a philosophy and literature student at the University of Chicago, worked out a theory of value whose structure surfaced from time to time as the novelistic action of each book developed. The first book, *Zen and the Art of Motorcycle Maintenance*, is subtitled *An Inquiry into Value*, and the second book, *Lila*, is subtitled *An Inquiry into Morals*. In this theory "quality" becomes the final value of life, functioning somewhat like the idea of the good in Plato's theory of value. Pirsig as narrator also carries an alter ego, a composition teacher on the track of the theory of quality. The alter ego, named Phaedrus, is implanted in the narrator in a somewhat mysterious operation, following a mental breakdown. The narrator has moments of prescience becoming increasingly aware of his alter ego's life and thought. Pirsig gives this implanted personality the name Phaedrus, from one of the figures in Plato's *Philebus*. In what follows we sometimes hear from Pirsig and sometimes from Phaedrus.

This alternation continues in the second book, which features Lila, who suffers a period of insanity, as had the narrator, Pirsig, in the first volume. Even so, Lila's life (and surely, too, that of the narrator/Pirsig) is held to be one of dynamic quality. The line between sanity and insanity is touched upon in (4) below, a passage from the first of the two books: "to go outside the *mythos* is to be insane."

Knowing Phaedrus' mind, Pirsig often speaks for him. The voices we hear in the two books are those of Pirsig, Phaedrus, and Lila. In what follows we concentrate on passages dealing with quality.

Also see Study Guide (4b15), p. 39.

Quality a Cleavage Term

(1) The wave of crystallization rolled ahead. He was seeing two worlds, simultaneously. On the intellectual side, the square side, he saw now that Quality was a cleavage term. What every intellectual analyst looks for. You take your analytic knife, put the point directly on the term Quality and just tap, not hard, gently, and the whole world splits, cleaves, right in two—hip and square, classic and romantic, technological and humanistic—and the split is clean. There's no mess. No slop. No little items that could be one way or the other. Not just a skilled break but a very lucky break. Sometimes the best analysts, working with the most obvious lines of cleavage, can tap and get nothing but a pile of trash. And yet here was Quality; a tiny, almost unnoticeable fault line; a line of illogic in our concept of the universe; and you tapped it, and the whole universe came apart, so neatly it was almost unbelievable. He wished Kant were alive. Kant would have appreciated it. That master diamond cutter. He would see. Hold Quality undefined. That was the secret.

Phaedrus wrote, with some beginning awareness that he was involved in a strange kind of intellectual suicide, "Squareness may be succinctly and yet thoroughly defined as an inability to see quality before it's been intellectually defined, that is, before it gets all chopped up into words. . . . We have proved that quality, though undefined, exists. Its existence can be seen empirically in the classroom, and can be demonstrated logically by showing that a world without it cannot exist as we know it. What remains to be seen, the thing to be analyzed, is not quality, but those peculiar habits of thought called 'squareness' that sometimes prevent us from seeing it."

Thus did he seek to turn the attack. The subject for analysis, the patient on the table, was no longer Quality, but analysis itself. Quality was healthy and in good shape. Analysis, however, seemed to have something wrong with it that prevented it from seeing the obvious.

✐   ✐   ✐

Phaedrus' refusal to define Quality . . . was an attempt to break the grip of the classical sand-sifting mode of understanding and find a point of common understanding between the classic and romantic worlds. Quality, the cleavage term between hip and square, seemed to be it. Both worlds used the term. Both knew what it was. It was just that the romantic left it alone and appreciated it for what it was and the classic tried to turn it into a set of intellectual building blocks for other purposes. Now, with the definition blocked, the classic mind was forced to view Quality as the romantic did, undistorted by thought structures.

I'm making a big thing out of all this, these classical-romantic differences, but Phaedrus didn't. He wasn't really interested in any kind of fusion of differences between these two worlds. He was after something else—his ghost. In the pursuit of this ghost he went on to wider meanings of Quality which drew him further and further to his end. I differ from him in that I've no intention of going on to that end. He just passed through this territory and opened it up. I intend to stay and cultivate it and see if I can get something to grow.

I think that the referent of a term that can split a world into hip and square, classic and romantic, technological and humanistic, is an entity that can unite a world already split along these lines into one. A real understanding of Quality doesn't just serve the System, or even beat it or even escape it. A real understanding of Quality *captures* the System, tames it, and puts it to work for one's own personal use, while leaving one completely free to fulfill his inner destiny.

(2) The more he examined this argument the more formidable it appeared. This looked like the one that might do in his whole thesis.

What made it so ominous was that it seemed to answer a question that had arisen often in class and which he always had to answer somewhat casuistically. This was the question, If everyone knows what quality is, why is there such a disagreement about it?

His casuist answer had been that although pure *Quality* was the same for everyone, the *objects* that people said Quality *inhered* in varied from person to person. As long as he left Quality undefined there was no way to argue with this but he knew and he knew the students knew that it had the smell of falseness about it. It didn't really answer the question.

Now there was an alternative explanation: people disagreed about Quality because some just used their immediate emotions whereas others applied their overall knowledge. He knew that in any popularity contest among English teachers, this latter argument which bolstered their authority would win overwhelming endorsement.

But this argument was completely devastating. Instead of one single, uniform Quality now there appeared to be *two* qualities; a romantic one, just seeing, which the students had; and a classic one, overall understanding, which the teachers had. A hip one and a square one. Squareness was not the absence of Quality; it was classic Quality. Hipness was not just presence of Quality; it was mere romantic Quality. The hip-square cleavage he'd discovered was still there, but Quality didn't now seem to fall entirely on one side of the cleavage, as he'd previously supposed. Instead,

Quality itself cleaved into two kinds, one on each side of the cleavage line. His simple, neat, beautiful, undefined Quality was starting to get complex.

He didn't like the way this was going. The cleavage term that was going to unify the classic and romantic ways of looking at things had itself been cleaved into two parts and could no longer unify anything. It had been caught in an analytic meat grinder. The knife of subjectivity-and-objectivity had cut Quality in two and killed it as a working concept. If he was going to save it, he couldn't let that knife get it.

And really, the Quality he was talking about *wasn't* classic Quality *or* romantic Quality. It was beyond both of them. And by God, it wasn't subjective or objective either, it was beyond both of *those* categories. Actually this whole dilemma of subjectivity-objectivity, of mind-matter, with relationship to Quality was unfair. That mind-matter relationship has been an intellectual hang-up for centuries. They were just putting that hang-up on top of Quality to drag Quality down. How could *he* say whether Quality was mind or matter when there was no logical clarity as to what was mind and what was matter in the first place?

And so: he rejected the left horn. Quality is not objective, he said. It doesn't reside in the material world.

Then: he rejected the right horn. Quality is not subjective, he said. It doesn't reside merely in the mind.

And finally: Phaedrus, following a path that to his knowledge had never been taken before in the history of Western thought, went straight between the horns of the subjectivity-objectivity dilemma and said Quality is neither a part of mind, nor is it a part of matter. It is a *third* entity which is independent of the two.

He was heard along the corridors and up and down the stairs of Montana Hall singing softly to himself, almost under his breath, "Holy, holy, holy . . . blessed Trinity."

And there is a faint, faint fragment of memory, possibly wrong, possibly just something I'm imagining, that says he just let the whole thought structure sit like that for weeks, without carrying it any further.

≈   ≈   ≈

The world now, according to Phaedrus, was composed of three things: mind, matter, and Quality. The fact that he had established no relationship between them didn't bother him at first. If the relationship between mind and matter had been fought over for centuries and wasn't yet resolved, why should he, in a matter of a few weeks, come up with something conclusive about Quality? So he let it go. He put it up on a kind of mental shelf where he put all kinds of questions he had no immediate answers for. He knew the metaphysical trinity of subject, object, and Quality would sooner or later have to be interrelated but he was in no hurry about it. It was just so satisfying to be beyond the danger of those horns that he relaxed and enjoyed it as long as he could.

Eventually, however, he examined it more closely. Although there's no logical objection to a metaphysical trinity, a three-headed reality, such trinities are not common or popular. The metaphysician normally seeks either a monism, such as God, which explains the nature of the world as a manifestation of one single thing, or he seeks a dualism, such as mind-matter, which explains it as two things, or he leaves it as a pluralism, which explains it as a manifestation of an indefinite number of things. But three is an awkward number. Right away you want to know, Why three? What's the relationship among them? And as the need for relaxation diminished Phaedrus became curious about this relationship too.

He noted that although normally you associate Quality with objects, feelings of Quality sometimes occur without any object at all. This is what led him at first to think that maybe Quality is all subjective. But subjective pleasure wasn't what he meant by Quality either. Quality *decreases* subjectivity. Quality takes you out of yourself, makes you aware of the world around you. Quality is *opposed* to subjectivity.

I don't know how much thought passed before he arrived at this, but eventually he saw that Quality couldn't be independently related with either the subject or the object but could be found *only in the relationship of the two with each other.* It is the point at which subject and object meet.

That sounded warm.

Quality is not a *thing.* It is an *event.*

Warmer.

It is the event at which the subject becomes aware of the object.

And because without objects there can be no subject—because the objects create the subject's awareness of himself—Quality is the event at which awareness of both subjects and objects is made possible.

Hot.

Now he knew it was coming.

This means Quality is not just the *result* of a collision between subject and object. The very existence of subject and object themselves is *deduced* from the Quality event. The Quality event is the *cause* of the subjects and objects, which are then mistakenly presumed to be the cause of the Quality!

Now he had that whole damned evil dilemma by the throat. The dilemma all the time had this unseen vile presumption in it, for which there was no logical justification, that Quality was the *effect* of subjects and objects. It was *not*! He brought out his knife.

"The sun of quality," he wrote, "does not revolve around the subjects and objects of our existence. It does not just passively illuminate them. It is not subordinate to them in any way. It has *created* them. They are subordinate to *it*!"

And at that point, when he wrote that, he knew he had reached some kind of culmination of thought he had been unconsciously striving for over a long period of time.

Quality and Care

(3) There has been a haze, a backup problem in this Chautauqua so far; I talked about caring the first day and then realized I couldn't say anything meaningful about caring until its inverse side, Quality, is understood. I think it's important now to tie care to Quality by pointing out that care and Quality are internal and external aspects of the same thing. A person who sees Quality and feels it as he works is a person who cares. A person who cares about what he sees and does is a person who's bound to have some characteristics of Quality.

Thus, if the problem of technological hopelessness is caused by absence of care, both by technologists and antitechnologists; and if care and Quality are external and internal aspects of the same thing, then it follows logically that what really causes technological hopelessness is absence of the perception of Quality in technology by both technologists and antitechnologists. Phaedrus' mad pursuit of the rational, analytic, and therefore *technological* meaning of the word "Quality" was really a pursuit of the answer to the whole problem of technological hopelessness. So it seems to me, anyway.

So I backed up and shifted to the classic-romantic split that I think underlies the whole humanist-technological problem. But that too required a backup into the meaning of Quality.

But to understand the meaning of Quality in classic terms required a backup into metaphysics and its relationship to everyday life. To do that required still another backup into the huge area that relates both metaphysics and everyday life—namely, formal reason. So I proceeded with formal reason up into metaphysics and then into Quality and then from Quality back down into metaphysics and science.

Now we go still further down from science into technology, and I do believe that at last we are where I wanted to be in the first place.

But now we have with us some concepts that greatly alter the whole understanding of things. Quality is the Buddha. Quality is scientific reality. Quality is the goal of Art. It remains to work these concepts into a practical, down-to-earth context, and for this there is nothing more practical or down-to-earth than what I have been talking about all along—the repair of an old motorcycle.

Mythos over Logos

(4) The mythos-over-logos argument points to the fact that each child is born as ignorant as any caveman. What keeps the world from reverting to the Neanderthal with each generation is the continuing, ongoing mythos, transformed into logos but still mythos, the huge body of common knowledge that unites our minds as cells are united in the body of man. To feel that one is not so united, that one can accept or discard this mythos as one pleases, is not to understand what the mythos is.

There is only one kind of person, Phaedrus said, who accepts or rejects the mythos in which he lives. And the definition of that person, when he has rejected the mythos, Phaedrus said, is "insane." To go outside the mythos is to become insane. . . .

My God, that just came to me now. I never knew that before.

He knew! He must have known what was about to happen. It's starting to open up.

You have all these fragments, like pieces of a puzzle, and you can place them together into large groups, but the groups don't go together no matter how you try, and then suddenly you get one fragment and it fits two different groups and then suddenly the two great groups are one. The relation of the mythos to insanity. That's a key fragment. I doubt whether anyone ever said that before. Insanity is the *terra incognita* surrounding the mythos. And he knew! He knew the Quality he talked about lay outside the mythos.

Now it comes! Because Quality is the *generator* of the mythos. That's it. That's what he meant when he said, "Quality is the continuing stimulus which causes us to create the world in which we live. All of it. Every last bit of it." Religion isn't invented by man. Men are invented by religion. Men invent *responses* to Quality, and among these responses is an understanding of what they themselves are. You know something and then the Quality stimulus hits and then you try to define the Quality stimulus, but to define it all you've got to work with is what you know. So your definition is made up of what you know. It's an analogue to what you already know. It *has* to be. It can't be anything else. And the mythos grows this way. By analogies to what is known before.

The mythos is a building of analogues upon analogues upon analogues. These fill the boxcars of the train of consciousness. The mythos is the whole train of collective consciousness of all communicating mankind. Every last bit of it. The Quality is the track that directs the train. What is outside the train, to either side—that is the *terra incognita* of the insane. He knew that to understand Quality he would have to leave the mythos. That's why he felt that slippage. He knew something was about to happen.

Quality, integrity, reason

(5) A person who knows how to fix motorcycles—with Quality—is less likely to run short of friends than one who doesn't. And they aren't going to see him as some kind of *object* either. Quality destroys objectivity every time.

Or if he takes whatever dull job he's stuck with—and they are all, sooner or later, dull—and, just to keep himself amused, starts to look for options of Quality, and secretly pursues these options, just for their own sake, thus making an art out of what he is doing, he's likely to discover that he becomes a much more interesting person and much less of an object to the people around him because his Quality decisions change *him* too. And not only the job and him, but others too because the Quality tends to fan out like waves. The Quality job he didn't think anyone was going to see *is* seen, and the person who sees it feels a little better because of it, and is likely to pass that feeling on to others, and in that way the Quality tends to keep on going.

My personal feeling is that this is how any further improvement of the world will be done: by individuals making Quality decisions and that's all. God, I don't want to have any more enthusiasm for big programs full of social planning for big masses of people that leave individual Quality out. These can be left alone for a while. There's a place for them but they've got to be built on a foundation of Quality within the individuals involved. We've had that individual Quality in the past, exploited it as a natural resource without knowing it, and now it's just about depleted. Everyone's just about out of gumption. And I think it's about time to return to the rebuilding of *this* American resource—individual worth. There are political reactionaries who've been saying something close to this for years. I'm not one of them, but to the extent they're talking about real individual worth and not just an excuse for giving more money to the rich, they're right. We *do* need a return to individual integrity, self-reliance, and old-fashioned gumption. We really do. I hope that in this Chautauqua some directions have been pointed to.

Phaedrus went a different path from the idea of individual, personal

Quality decisions. I think it was a wrong one, but perhaps if I were in his circumstances I would go his way too. He felt that the solution started with a new philosophy, or he saw it as even broader than that—a new spiritual *rationality*—in which the ugliness and the loneliness and the spiritual blankness of dualistic technological reason would become illogical. Reason was no longer to be "value free." Reason was to be subordinate, logically, to Quality, and he was sure he would find the cause of its not being so back among the ancient Greeks, whose mythos had endowed our culture with the tendency underlying all the evil of our technology, the tendency *to do what is "reasonable" even when it isn't any good.* That was the root of the whole thing. Right there. I said a long time ago that he was in pursuit of the ghost of reason. This is what I meant. Reason and Quality had become separated and in conflict with each other and Quality had been forced under and reason made supreme somewhere back then.

The metaphysics of quality
    (6) The Metaphysics of Quality associates religious mysticism with Dynamic Quality but it would certainly be a mistake to think that the Metaphysics of Quality endorses the static beliefs of any particular religious sect. Phaedrus thought sectarian religion was a static social fallout from Dynamic Quality and that while some sects had fallen less than others, none of them told the whole truth.

    His favorite Christian mystic was Johannes Eckhart, who said, "Wouldst thou be perfect, do not yelp about God." Eckhart was pointing to a profound mystic truth, but you can guess what a hand of applause it got from the static authorities of the Church. "Ill-sounding, rash, and probably heretical," was the general verdict.

    From what Phaedrus had been able to observe, mystics and priests tend to have a cat-and-dog-like coexistence within almost every religious organization. Both groups need each other but neither group likes the other at all.

❧   ❧   ❧

    In all religions bishops tend to gild Dynamic Quality with all sorts of static interpretations because their cultures require it. But these interpretations become like golden vines that cling to a tree, shut out its sunlight, and eventually strangle it.

❧   ❧   ❧

He thought some more about Lila's insanity and how it was related to religious mysticism and how both were integrated into reason by the Metaphysics of Quality. He thought about how once this integration occurs and Dynamic Quality is identified with religious mysticism it produces an avalanche of information as to what Dynamic Quality is. A lot of this religious mysticism is just low-grade "yelping about God" of course, but if you search for the sources of it and don't take the yelps too literally a lot of interesting things turn up.

Long ago when he first explored the idea of Quality he'd reasoned that if Quality were the primordial source of all our understanding then it followed that the place to get the best view of it would be at the beginning of history when it would have been less cluttered by the present deluge of static intellectual patterns of knowledge. He'd traced Quality back into its origins in Greek philosophy and thought he'd gone as far as he could go. Then he found he was able to go back to a time *before* the Greek philosophers, to the rhetoricians.

Philosophers usually present their ideas as sprung from "nature" or sometimes from "God," but Phaedrus thought neither of these was completely accurate. The logical order of things which the philosophers study is derived from the "mythos." The mythos is the social culture and the rhetoric which the culture must invent before philosophy becomes possible. Most of this old religious talk is nonsense, of course, but nonsense or not, it is the *parent* of our modern scientific talk. This "mythos over logos" thesis agreed with the Metaphysics of Quality's assertion that intellectual static patterns of quality are built up out of social static patterns of quality.

Digging back into ancient Greek history, to the time when this mythos-to-logos transition was taking place, Phaedrus noted that the ancient rhetoricians of Greece, the Sophists, had taught what they called *aretê*, which was a synonym for Quality. Victorians had translated *aretê* as "virtue" but Victorian "virtue" connoted sexual abstinence, prissiness, and a holier-than-thou snobbery. This was a long way from what the ancient Greeks meant. The early Greek literature, particularly the poetry of Homer, showed that *aretê* had been a central and vital term.

With Homer Phaedrus was certain he'd gone back as far as anyone could go, but one day he came across some information that startled him. It said that by following linguistic analysis you could go even further back into the mythos than Homer. Ancient Greek was not an original language. It was descended from a much earlier one, now called the Proto-Indo-European language. This language has left no fragments but has been derived by scholars from similarities between such languages as Sanskrit, Greek, and

English which have indicated that these languages were fallouts from a common prehistoric tongue. After thousands of years of separation from Greek and English the Hindi word for "mother" is still "Ma." *Yoga* both looks like and is translated as "yoke." The reason an Indian *rajah*'s title sounds like "regent" is because both terms are fallouts from Proto-Indo-European. Today a Proto-Indo-European dictionary contains more than a thousand entries with derivations extending into more than one hundred languages.

Just for curiosity's sake Phaedrus decided to see if *aretê* was in it. He looked under the "a" words and was disappointed to find it was not. Then he noted a statement that said that the Greeks were not the most faithful to the Proto-Indo-European spelling. Among other sins, the Greeks added the prefix "a" to many of the Proto-Indo-European roots. He checked this out by looking for *aretê* under "r." This time a door opened.

The Proto-Indo-European root of *arete* was the morpheme *rt*. There, beside *aretê*, was a treasure room of other derived "rt" words: "arithmetic," "aristocrat," "art," "rhetoric," "worth," "rite," "ritual," "wright," "right (handed)," and "right (correct)." All of these words except arithmetic seemed to have a vague thesaurus-like similarity to Quality. Phaedrus studied them carefully, letting them soak in, trying to guess what sort of concept, what sort of way of seeing the world, could give rise to such a collection.

When the morpheme appeared in *aristocrat* and *arithmetic* the reference was to "firstness." *Rt* meant first. When it appeared in *art* and *wright* it seemed to mean "created" and "of beauty." "Ritual" suggested repetitive order. And the word *right* has two meanings: "right-handed" and "moral and esthetic correctness." When all these meanings were strung together a fuller picture of the *rt* morpheme emerged. *Rt* referred to the "first, created, beautiful repetitive order of moral and esthetic correctness."

〜 〜 〜

There was just one thing wrong with this Proto-Indo-European discovery, something Phaedrus had tried to sweep under the carpet at first, but which kept creeping out again. The meanings, grouped together, suggested something different from his interpretation of *aretê*. They suggested "importance" but it was an importance that was formal and social and procedural and manufactured, almost an antonym to the Quality he was talking about. *Rt* meant "quality" all right but the quality it meant was static, not Dynamic. He had wanted it to come out the other way, but it looked as though it wasn't going to do it. Ritual. That was the last thing he wanted *aretê* to turn out to be. Bad news. It looked as though the Victorian translation of *aretê* as "virtue" might be better after all since "virtue" implies ritualistic conformity to social protocol.

It was in this gloomy mood, while he was thinking about all the interpretations of the *rt* morpheme, that yet another "find" came. He had thought that surely this time he had reached the end of the Quality-*aretê*-*rt* trail. But then from the sediment of old memories his mind dredged up a word he hadn't thought about or heard of for a long time: *Ṛta*. It was a Sanskrit word, and Phaedrus remembered what it meant: *Ṛta* was the "cosmic order of things." Then he remembered he had read that the Sanskrit language was considered the most faithful to the Proto-Indo-European root, probably because the linguistic patterns had been so carefully preserved by the Hindu priests.

Ṛta came surrounded by a memory of bright chalky tan walls in a classroom filled with sun. At the head of the classroom, Mr. Mukerjee, a perspiring *dhoti*-clad brahmin was drilling dozens of ancient Sanskrit words into the assembled students' heads—*advaita, māyā, avidyā, brahmān, ātman, prajñā, sāmkhya, visiṣṭādvaita, Ṛg-Veda, upaniṣad, darśana, dhyāna, nyāya*—on and on. He introduced them day after day, each in turn with a little smile that promised hundreds more to come.

At Phaedrus' worn wooden desk near the wall in back of the classroom, he had sat sweaty and annoyed by buzzing flies. The heat and light and flies came and went freely through openings in a far wall which had no window-glass because in India you don't need it. His notebook was damp where his hand had rested. His pen wouldn't write on the damp spot, so he had to write around it. When he turned the page he found the damp had gotten through to the next page too.

In that heat it was agony to remember what all those words were supposed to mean—*ajīva, mokṣa, kāma, ahiṃsa, suṣupti, bhakti, saṃsāra*. They passed by his mind like clouds and disappeared. Through the openings in the wall he could see real clouds—giant monsoon clouds towering thousands of feet up—and white-humped Sindhi cows grazing below.

He thought he'd forgotten all those words years ago, but now here was *ṛta*, back again. *Ṛta*, from the oldest portion of the *Ṛg Veda*, which was the oldest known writing of the Indo-Aryan language. The sun god, *Sūrya*, began his chariot ride across the heavens from the abode of *ṛta*. *Varuṇa*, the god for whom the city in which Phaedrus was studying was named, was the chief support of *ṛta*.

Varuṇa was omniscient and was described as ever witnessing the truth and falsehood of men—as being "the third whenever two plot in secret." He was essentially a god of righteousness and a guardian of all that is worthy and good. The texts had said that the distinctive feature of *Varuṇa* was his unswerving adherence to high principles. Later he was overshadowed by *Indra* who was a thunder god and destroyer of the enemies of the Indo-Aryans. But all the gods were conceived as "guardians of *ṛta*," willing the right and making sure it was carried out.

One of Phaedrus' old school texts, written by M. Hiriyanna, contained a good summary: "*Ṛta*, which etymologically stands for 'course' originally meant 'cosmic order,' the maintenance of which was the purpose of all the gods; and later it also came to mean 'right,' so that the gods were conceived as preserving the world not merely from physical disorder but also from moral chaos. The one idea is implicit in the other: and there is order in the universe because its control is in righteous hands. . . ."

The physical order of the universe is also the moral order of the universe. *Ṛta* is both. This was exactly what the Metaphysics of Quality was claiming. It was not a new idea. It was the oldest idea known to man.

This identification of *ṛta* and *aretê* was enormously valuable, Phaedrus thought, because it provided a huge historical panorama in which the fundamental conflict between static and Dynamic Quality had been worked out. It answered the question of why *aretê* meant ritual. *Ṛta* also meant ritual. But, unlike the Greeks, the Hindus in their many thousands of years of cultural evolution had paid enormous attention to the conflict between ritual and freedom. Their resolution of this conflict in the Buddhist and Vedantist philosophies is one of the profound achievements of the human mind.

The original meaning of *ṛta*, during what is called the *Brāhmaṇa* period of Indian history, underwent a change to extremely ritualistic static patterns more rigid and detailed than anything heard of in Western religion.

∾   ∾   ∾

But what made the Hindu experience so profound was that this decay of Dynamic Quality into static quality was not the end of the story. Following the period of the *Brāhmaṇas* came the *Upaniṣadic* period and the flowering of Indian philosophy. Dynamic Quality reemerged within the static patterns of Indian thought.

"*Ṛta*," Hiriyanna had written, "almost ceased to be used in Sanskrit; but . . . under the name of *dharma*, the same idea occupies a very important place in the later Indian views of life also."

The more usual meaning of *dharma* is, "religious merit which, operating in some unseen way as it is supposed, secures good to a person in the future, either here or elsewhere. Thus the performance of certain sacrifices is believed to lead the agent to heaven after the present life, and of certain others to secure for him wealth, children, and the like in this very life."

But he also wrote, "It is sometimes used as a purely moral concept and stands for right or virtuous conduct which leads to some form of good as a result."

Dharma, like *ṛta*, means "what holds together." It is the basis of all order. It equals righteousness. It is the ethical code. It is the stable condition which gives man perfect satisfaction.

Dharma is duty. It is not external duty which is arbitrarily imposed by others. It is not any artificial set of conventions which can be amended or repealed by legislation. Neither is it internal duty which is arbitrarily decided by one's own conscience. *Dharma* is beyond all questions of what is internal and what is external. *Dharma* is Quality itself, the principle of "rightness" which gives structure and purpose to the evolution of all life and to the evolving understanding of the universe which life has created.

Within the Hindu tradition *dharma* is relative and dependent on the conditions of society. It always has a social implication. It is the bond which holds society together. This is fitting to the ancient origins of the term. But within modern Buddhist thought *dharma* becomes the phenomenal world—the object of perception, thought, or understanding. A chair, for example, is not composed of atoms of substance, it is composed of *dharmas*.

This statement is absolute jabberwocky to a conventional subject-object metaphysics. How can a chair be composed of individual little moral orders? But if one applies the Metaphysics of Quality and sees that a chair is an inorganic static pattern and sees that all static patterns are composed of value and that value is synonymous with morality then it all begins to make sense.

                ☙   ☙   ☙

For example, you would guess from the literature on Zen and its insistence on discovering the "unwritten *dharma*" that it would be intensely anti-ritualistic, since ritual is the "written dharma." But that isn't the case. The Zen monk's daily life is nothing but one ritual after another, hour after hour, day after day, all his life. They don't tell him to shatter those static patterns to discover the unwritten *dharma*. They want him to get those patterns perfect!

The explanation for this contradiction is the belief that you do not free yourself from static patterns by fighting them with other contrary static patterns. That is sometimes called "bad karma chasing its tail." You free yourself from static patterns by putting them to sleep. That is, you master them with such proficiency that they become an unconscious part of your nature. You get so used to them you completely forget them and they are gone. There in the center of the most monotonous boredom of static ritualistic patterns the Dynamic freedom is found.

Phaedrus saw nothing wrong with this ritualistic religion as long as the rituals are seen as merely a static portrayal of Dynamic Quality, a sign-post which allows socially pattern-dominated people to see Dynamic Quality. The danger has always been that the rituals, the static patterns, are mistaken for what they merely represent and are allowed to destroy the Dynamic Quality they were originally intended to preserve.

[Robert M. Pirsig. (1) *Zen and the Art of Motorcycle Maintenance* (New York: William Morrow, 1974; Bantam, 1975; Bantam New Age, 1981), pp. 218–19 and 222–23. (2) *Ibid.*, pp. 236–37; 238–40. (3) *Ibid.*, pp. 275–76. (4) *Ibid.*, pp. 350–51. (5) *Ibid.*, pp. 857–58. (6) *Lila* (New York: Bantam Books, 1991), pp. 376–85.]

Appendix A
Nonclassical Value Structures

If you feel uncomfortable with the pyramidal value profile, that is a sign you must look elsewhere. John Dewey (*q.v.* D4 and Value 3) held all values to be part of a "means-end continuum." In a sense they are all instrumental, or mixed instrumental-final and subject to change. You may also wish to follow Perry (*q.v.* D3 and Value 4), Korn (*q.v.* D5 and Value 5), Scheler (*q.v.* D2 and Value 6), or Von Wright (*q.v.* D2 and Value 8) in separating out types of value to be explored (social, religious, ethical, aesthetic).

Although the Detailed Outline centered on the Greek division of instrumental values, instrumental-final, and final values, a somewhat different approach developed in my classes. Students began to relate their values to their time commitments. The approach was not unlike psychologist Kurt Lewin's interest in personal "life space" and his talk of the boundaries of the self (New York: McGraw-Hill, 1935, 1936). My students began to think of the self as having an ovoid shape. They named it "the pickle of life," and divided up the pickle according to their interests as represented by their time commitments: the greater the commitment the larger the area. The next step was to determine the values rising from each area. The values most often repeated would be given the more important rankings. A variety of values with different levels of importance would come from these commitments. Picture the instrumental-final, and final, values of the classical pyramid rising not from instrumental values, but from the pickle of life.

A woman student in one of these classes found her values by considering the roles she played each day. Identifying five roles—student, family member, girlfriend, friend, and citizen, she distilled the relevant values from each role. As a student she valued responsibility, diligence, quality in her work, as well as curiosity, and creativity. These values led to knowledge, self-confidence, self-realization, and satisfaction. As a family member, respect, trust, patience, health, appreciation of the inner beauty of each family member. These values led to generosity, a sense of personal security, and a deep sense of love. As a girlfriend, loyalty, relaxation, pleasure, trust, thoughtfulness, and self-love, leading again to love, self-esteem and security. As a friend, acceptance, honesty or truthfulness, sense of humor, helpfulness leading to peace of mind, and relaxation. As a citizen, courage, pride, freedom, tolerance, and respect, leading to the goals of equal opportunity, equality before the law, and justice for all. The repetition of value terms suggested convergence toward her final values.

Another student divided values into two lists: ideal values, and practical values. The first list consisted of values the student wished to follow; the other list consisted of the values actually in use in his ordinary life. A third student worked out a structure of supporting values and on top a roulette wheel of basic values, each of which would become the final value depending on the situation: in times of illness, health; in a situation of poverty, wealth; in ignorance, knowledge; in intimate relations, sensitivity. (Aristotle considers this possibility in R5, sec. 2.) All of these might still be compatible with a final value of happiness.

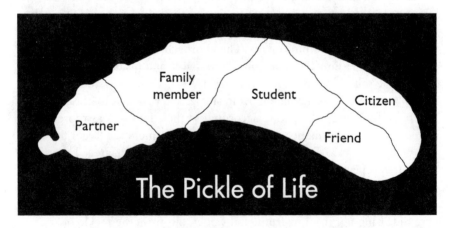

A fourth student was impressed by the constant change in the position of her values. It was for her, as though they were suspended in a huge jar, moving in a kind of liquid, stirred by a current of change. From time to time certain values would rise to the top, getting stuck in the neck of the jar. The values stuck in the neck of the jar were her final values of the moment.

The point is to experiment until you find the appropriate manner of representing your own individual position.

Appendix B

The titles of the volumes constituting the 8-volume set of Study Guides and Readings in the projected eight-volume set, in addition to *Freedom* are *Value, Self, Truth, Beauty, Right and Wrong, Social Philosophy*, and *God and Immortality*. These are the unavoidable questions of philosophy from which introductory problems courses in philosophy are constructed. Individual students and classes are provided maximum flexibility in following out their adventures into philosophy. While the books of Readings can be used by themselves, or in any combination, they can also be used with a *Dictionary* of philosophy, including the *Dictionary of Philosophy and Religion: Eastern and Western Thought* as companion volume, providing the student with a wealth of additional information on philosophy. The instructor can thus combine study of one or more problems through the Readings, while utilizing the *Dictionary* to provide mini-study guides for problems considered less fully. The following resources for the eight problems are also available on the Fundamental Issues in Philosophy web page (www. albany.edu/~wlr/fip.html).

Freedom:
> —the entire Freedom entry. 31 entry listings on philosophers who have held each of the four definitions with references (*q.v.*'s) to their own entries in the *Dictionary*, and relevant paragraphs of those entries. Such entry listings provide a summary of the important ideas on the given topic.
> —Free Will (5 entry listings)
> —Determinism (16 entry listings)

Value:
    —Value (8 entry listings)
    —Final Value (18 entry listings)
    —Value Theory (11 entry listings)

Self:
    —Person (14 entry listings)
    —Self (10 entry listings)
    —Soul (7 entry listings)

Truth:
    —Truth (38 entry listings, 5 definitions)
    —Epistemology (10 entry listings)
    —Knowledge (16 entry listings)
    —Skepticism (30 entry listings)
    —Wisdom (7 entry listings)

Beauty:
    —Aesthetics (37 entry listings)
    —Art (8 entry listings)
    —Poetry (3 *q.v.* references)

Right and Wrong:
    —Good (12 entry listings)
    —Right (6 entry listings)
    —Ethics (44 entry listings)
    —Evil (16 entry listings)
    —Utilitarianism (13 entry listings)
    —Axiology (4 entry listings)

Social Philosophy:
    —Social Contract Theory (14 entry listings)
    —Natural Rights (6 entry listings)
    —Natural Law (12 entry listings)
    —Sovereignty (6 entry listings)
    —and entry listings for Hobbes, Locke, Marx, Plato, Rousseau, Jefferson, T. Paine, Rawls, Nozick

God and Immortality:
- —God (75 entry listings, divided among nature of God, arguments for God, and God as a projection of human awareness)
- —Religion (27 entry listings, plus entries on basic faiths of the world)
- —Immortality (11 entry listings)
- —Reincarnation, and Metempsychosis (numerous *q.v.* references)
- —Faith (16 entry listings)
- —Myth (15 entry listings)
- —Reason (15 entry listings)

The material listed above can be consulted on, or downloaded from, the Fundamental Issues in Philosophy web page. In addition, the web page provides an open forum for philosophical discussion through its Bulletin Board, Chat Room, sample outlines on the eight problems, alternate argument forms, and Grammatology.

Index

261